BUDDHIST ESSAYS

BUDDHIST ESSAYS

BY

PAUL DAHLKE

TRANSLATED FROM THE GERMAN

BY

BHIKKHU SILACARA

GYAN

Published by

GYAN

Gyan Publishing House
5, Ansari Road
Daryaganj, New Delhi-110002
Phone: 011-47034999, 9811692060
E-mail: books@gyanbooks.com

Distribution Network
gyanbooks.com
India, USA, Canada, UK, Australia, France

ISBN : 978-81-212-2454-3 (HB)
First Published, 1908

2nd Impression 2021

Printed at: Gyan Press, Delhi.

Buddhist Essays
Author: Paul Dahlke

BUDDHIST ESSAYS

BY

PAUL DAHLKE

TRANSLATED FROM THE GERMAN

BY

BHIKKHU SĪLĀCĀRA

MACMILLAN AND CO., LIMITED
ST. MARTIN'S STREET, LONDON
1908

FOREWORD

THE following essays contain nothing new or original concerning Buddhism, but they may perhaps serve to render easier the understanding of some so-called obscure points in the teaching of the Buddha. What claim—if any—this work may have to superiority over many others upon the same subject, rests in this—that it is the outcome, not only of the study of books, but also of personal intercourse with native scholars both in Ceylon and Burma.

The quotations, where no other sources are given, are for the greater part taken from the Middle Collection of the Second Book of the Pāli Canon — the Majjhima Nikāya — which, in K. E. Neumann's beautiful translation, is by far the richest mine of Buddhism that has been made accessible to us during the last decade.

So far as has appeared necessary to a full understanding of the text, references in the original tongue have been added, but as the book is designed for the lay reader alone, no particular effort has been made to meet the demands of an exacting scholarship.

One reproach, however, may possibly be brought against it—that it abounds in repetitions—but the cause of this is to be found in the specific character of the Buddha's thought, which is no mere picture, but a genuine product of nature existing, as it were, in three dimensions. And just as, in order adequately to portray such an object, one requires to take a series of photographs, each member of which series must slightly overlap its neighbour and not merely come into juxtaposition with it, so that a little of number one of the series may appear in number two also, and so on through the entire succession of views—in like manner is it with any adequate representation of the Buddha's teaching. To produce a faithful picture, repetition is unavoidable. Moreover, I am of the opinion that if old Empedokles obtained assent to his "Twice and thrice the beautiful," we also have some title to the same with our "Twice and thrice the necessary."

DR. DAHLKE.

CONTENTS

I

THE LIFE OF THE BUDDHA

BUDDHISM, that wonderful teaching which declares life to be sorrow and yet is free from pessimism; which apparently inculcates the profoundest egoism and yet is charged with the loftiest morality; which denies the "I," the soul, and yet teaches absolute responsibility for our own deeds through rebirth; which is without God or faith or prayer and yet offers the most certain salvation,—this wonderful teaching was founded by Gautama, of the aristocratic Sakya clan—the "proud Sakyas." His father's name was Suddhodana; his mother's, Māyā. His birthplace was the town of Kapilavastu, situated on a southern spur of the Himalayas, in modern Nepal. He was born about 560 B.C., according to some about 500 B.C. His personal name was Siddhartha. Brought up in the greatest luxury, married early, and the father of a son, in his thirtieth year he arrived at a perception of the true nature of life. He saw and felt that all life was sorrow, and, pained and disgusted, "black-haired, in the bloom of youth," he left his father's palace as a mendicant, in order that by religious exercises and mortifications he might find salvation from the universal sorrow. The horrors of disease, old age, and death all at once burst upon his sight. It was with him as with some traveller by night who believes himself in the midst of a beautiful landscape. Suddenly the moon comes out and he perceives himself surrounded by a graveyard, and in front of him rises a gallows. Thus did his previous life seem to the Buddha. From such a state of things relief must be found at any price. It was no lofty design but simply dislike and disgust that drove him forth.

The whole of India, at any rate, the whole of religious India,—and perhaps there is no real distinction between these two expressions,—in Gautama's day lay under the domination of that frightful dictum: "Asceticism purifies." In the midst of otherwise unexampled freedom of speculation this was a fixed point, and, like some butterfly impaled upon a needle, round it whirled the fluttering wings of all religious life: no salvation without mortification!

Gautama also took the self-same road that so many before him had trodden. He entered upon it with the eagerness of youth and the energy of despair. After six long years of excessive but all unavailing mortifications and ascetic practices, he attained, under the Bodhi-tree at Uruvelā, to true knowledge. He became the Buddha—that is, the Enlightened, the Awakened One. There is nothing of the supernatural concealed behind the expression *Buddha*. It means nothing more than perfect penetration into the universally operative natural law of mutability. *Buddha* signifies one who has done what all can do,—followed up and worked out to its ultimate this particular idea of mutability. This Gautama attained to; otherwise expressed, he perceived the cause of sorrow, and at the same time the possibility of its annihilation. Upon this was founded his doctrine, which later became a religion. This single-eyed, concentrated effort to achieve freedom from pain is the starting-point of Buddhism, and the attainment of the condition of freedom from pain is its goal. With the exactness of a pendulum, Buddhist thought swings between these two points —sorrow and freedom from sorrow. Outside these nothing exists for the Buddhist, just as for a competitor in the arena there exist only two things, the beginning and the end of the race.

For seven days, so tradition tells us, Gautama, now the Buddha, sat at the foot of the Bodhi-tree at Uruvelā enjoying the bliss of deliverance. It was the peace that followed upon the storm of six years of asceticism.

At last, when he came to himself again, he reflected: "What shall I do, now that I have acquired this sacred knowledge, this clearness of comprehension? This race of mankind, that only lives for pleasure, will not understand me; and if I make known this my teaching, born of sorrow, my only reward will be vexation and disillusionment."

The desire came to him to be contented in himself, but Brahma Sahampati—so the legend says—appeared before him, begging him not to leave the world forlorn. Then the Buddha, recognising that among the great mass of creatures there might well be a few capable of sounding the depths of his doctrine, decided to go forth and preach.

So he set out on the road to Benares, to reveal the truth to the five monks there who had been his companions during his six years' asceticism. On the way thither he meets the naked ascetic Upaka, who asks him: "Thy countenance is so peaceful and serene! who is he as whose pupil thou hast renounced the world?"

But Gautama, impelled by his genius, answers: "I have no teacher. There is none like me. I am the Perfect One, the Buddha. I have attained to peace. I have won Nibbāna. I go now to the town of Benares to found the kingdom of righteousness. There will I beat life's drum in this world of darkness."

"So thou art the all-conquering?" Upaka inquires.

"Evil have I conquered," the Buddha answers, "therefore am I the conqueror of all."

At Benares he entered the deer-park of Isipatana, and there found the five bhikkhus—ascetics, beggar-monks—whom he sought. When these latter saw him in the distance they said one to another, "Yonder comes that Gautama who has given up asceticism and now leads a life of pleasure. Let us refuse to receive him."

However, when the Buddha came up to them their plan failed them. One of them took his bowl and robe from him; the other prepared him a seat; a third brought water for his feet, and so forth. And now the Buddha speaks to them: "Listen, monks, the deathless (amataṁ) is found." But they pay no heed, for they have lost confidence in him. Twice more he is obliged to repeat his declaration. "Did I ever speak thus to you before?" he asks with insistence. Then finally they yield, and the Buddha sets forth his law of cause and consequence, of sorrow, and of the Middle

Path; Gautama the Buddha begins his career as a teacher of the world.

Now follows the narrative of the conversion of various persons, mostly people of high social and intellectual standing, and of entire schools of philosophy, and therewith the thread of the Buddha's course of life is broken off, at least so far as it is given in the Mahāvagga, a part of the first book of the Pāli canon. Only in the Sutta Piṭaka, in the Mahā-Parinibbāna Sutta, after a long interruption, does the continuation follow. What is there given is the story of the Buddha's last days on earth. Between the narrative of the Mahāvagga and this latter there intervenes a space of some forty-five years.

In the town of Rājagriha, one of his favourite resorts, we again meet with the Exalted One. Accompanied by his favourite disciple, Ânanda, and a crowd of monks, he sets out thence upon one of his usual wanderings from place to place, everywhere delivering religious discourses. The one self-same theme is perpetually recalled: "Great truly is the fruit, rich verily is the reward of persevering reflection, if supported by right conduct. Great truly is the fruit, rich verily the reward of insight, if supported by persevering reflection. The mind, supported by insight, is freed from the great evils: from sensuality, from personality, from delusion, from ignorance."

Wandering on, and preaching as he wandered, he came to the rich town of Vesālī, where he accepted the hospitality of the courtesan Ambapālī. Thence he betook himself to the neighbouring town of Beluva and dismissed his monks, in order that here he might spend by himself the three months of the rainy season (Vassa), as was his custom every year. But now he was overtaken by serious sickness, and he thought within himself: "It would not be right to depart from existence without first having spoken to my disciples. By an effort of will I will subdue this sickness, and remain in life until the time comes." And the sickness departed from him.

When the rainy season is over, he has his disciples called together and warns the Brothers, informing them that in three months his life will come to its close. He then resumes his wanderings. At Pāvā he is entertained in a mango grove by the smith Cunda, and soon thereafter is again attacked by serious and painful illness. He bears it patiently, but on the way from Pāvā to Kusināra he breaks down. Refreshing himself with a mouthful of water, he travels farther on, and finally arrives at the Sāla grove of Kusināra, the last stage of his pilgrimage. He has his couch prepared for him between two Sāla-trees, and—so it is said—the trees let fall a shower of blossom over him, notwithstanding that it is not the time of the year for blossom. Then the Buddha says to Ânanda: "See! Those Sāla-trees are full of blossom out of their season; they let a rain of blossoms descend upon the body of the Tathāgata[1] as a token of respect for the successor of the Buddhas of old. But it is not thus, Ânanda, that the Tathāgata rightly is honoured, reverenced, venerated; but he who truly follows the Law, he it is who rightly honours,

[1] Tathāgata means "The Perfect One." Along with Bhagavat (The Blessed One), it is the title most frequently bestowed upon the Buddha.

reverences, and venerates the Successor of the Buddhas of old."

Yet once more he calls his monks together; yet once more he asks them whether in any one of them there yet lurks any kind of doubt regarding any point whatsoever in his teaching, "that ye may not later regret not having asked me whilst I yet tarried among you." All are silent, and he begins his final exhortation to them, the last words that left his lips being, "Behold now, Brethren, I exhort you: decay is inherent in all component things! Work out your salvation with diligence." Thus upon the last accents of his dying tongue was stamped the impress of the leading idea of all his life and teaching.

The date of his death is placed somewhere about 480 B.C.

Of his eighty years of life, fifty were spent in unwearied teaching activity, devoted to a single idea, and with just cause he could say to Subhadda, his last disciple, as, with death immediately in front of him, he once more cast his glance backwards:

> "Scarce thirty youthful years were mine, Subhadda,
> When I forsook my home to seek the highest.
> And one-and-fifty years have past, Subhadda,
> While I have still fared forth, a strenuous pilgrim,
> Though the wide realms of righteousness and truth.
> For there, and there alone, is freedom found."

It is very little that we know of the life of this extraordinary man. The more delicate lines of the picture especially are painfully blurred, and there is a lack of colour. The Suttas, the sermons, which the Buddha himself delivered, do not sufficiently supply this want. Of his personality we learn little else from them but that at such and such a time the Exalted One tarried at such and such a place; sometimes in Sāvatthī at Anāthapiṇḍika's garden or in the bamboo grove at Rājagriha, and so forth. Everywhere and always the Buddhist style is the same. That lack of warmth, that passionlessness, which, for the rest, cling to the system, here make themselves particularly prominent in the most perturbing manner. The Buddha never speaks with the heat of Christ or Paul, to say nothing of the dark, death-like glow of the old prophets. In a legend of the Buddha it is said: "The dignity of his appearance proclaims him as the embroidered flag, the temple." This dignity, carried even to heaviness, is characteristic of his religious discourses also. With a sublime uniformity the sermon flows along, every expression studiously moderate in tone. Under the burden of the endless schematic repetitions every flight of fancy becomes impossible.[1] With difficulty, when some one or another of the brethren falls into heretical views, does a stray gleam of emotion shine through. "Perverted of understanding, witless one, thou seekest to correct us, and diggest thine own grave, and heapest up guilt for thyself. For long, foolish one, will this work harm and sorrow to thee." Afterwards, however, the sermon glides back again into its wonted peaceful channel.

Rarely also does the discourse unfold itself in the shape of connected, living speech and reply. Rarely is direct question followed by direct answer. More often the questioner is thrown back upon himself

[1] These repetitions, found in the Suttas, are placed there solely for mnemonic purposes.

with a counter-question. When by this means he has found in himself the basis needed for the adequate production of proofs, then the Buddha begins his stereotyped system of questions, upon which follows an equally stereotyped system of answers.

It is but seldom told of the Buddha that he either smiled or wept. Such phrases as: "Then was he seized with indignation and troubled of mind, and his eyes filled with tears," are wholly absent from the Buddhist canon. It is only legend that says that the Buddha smiled. As, for example, upon his return to Kapilavastu, his native town, when his father-in-law met him with reproaches, the Buddha is said to have smiled. "This was the first time," it is expressly said, "that he smiled since he attained to Buddhahood."

A plunge into purely human feeling is no affair of the Buddha. Emotion is ignorance. Seldom do we see affectionate feeling like bright clouds, spread over this brazen clearness which stretches high above all that is human as the dome of heaven over the earth. Still, it is possible that here it is not the man but only the rigid encasement of Buddhist diction that is to blame. The personality of Gautama the Buddha is too great, too many-sided, that anything human should remain alien to it.

For example, how moving and delicate is that episode narrated in the Mahā-Parinibbāna Sutta! Ânanda, the favourite disciple, stands weeping behind the door, overcome with grief at the approaching departure of his Master. The Buddha calls him to him and comforts him as a mother might comfort her child. "Be of good cheer, Ânanda," he says. "Do not weep. Have I not told you oftentimes that this is the regular course of things; that we must part from all that is precious and dear to us? How should it be possible that anything that has arisen should not also pass away?"

At another time he comes upon a sick monk lying helpless and forsaken in his cell. Then he exhorts his monks: "You have neither father nor mother; wherefore be father and mother to one another. As you would tend and wait upon me, so also tend and wait upon the sick."

When monks come to him from a distance he does not consider it beneath his dignity to ask them: "How is it with you, O monk? Have you lacked for food? Have you had a tiresome journey?"

He also knows well how to wield the lash of raillery. One day the Exalted One sat under a shady tree, enjoying meditation. While so engaged there came along the road the distinguished dandy, Daṇḍapāṇi, who greeted the Exalted One, and, leaning on his walking-stick, looked down on him and asked: "What does the ascetic profess and preach?" "That nothing in the world can put him out of countenance; that perceptions do not adhere to the Holy One who no longer puts questions, has put an end to all depression, craves neither existence nor non-existence. This I profess, brother; this I preach." Which in plain Anglo-Saxon meant, "I have not the least regard for you."

The nature of the relations that existed between himself and his monks is reflected in the following episode, taken from the Sutta of the "Holy Goal."

"Now many monks betook themselves to the venerable Ânanda and said to him: 'It is long, brother Ânanda, since we heard an edifying discourse from the lips of the Exalted One. Good were it, brother Ânanda, if we might get to hear an edifying discourse from the lips of the Exalted One.'

"'Well, venerable ones, betake yourselves to the hermitage of the Brahmin Rammako. Perhaps you will get to hear an edifying discourse from the lips of the Exalted One.'

"'That we will do, brother,' replied the monks to the venerable Ânanda.

"Now, after the Exalted One had gone from house to house in Sāvatthī, and had returned from his begging-round, having finished his meal, he turned to the venerable Ânanda and said: 'Come, Ânanda, let us go to the East Grove, to the Terrace of the Mother of Migāra, and stay there until the evening.'

"'Very good, Master!' answered the venerable Ânanda to the Exalted One. And now the Exalted One betook himself to the East Grove, to the Terrace of the Mother of Migāra, for the day. And when, towards evening, the Exalted One had come to the end of his period of meditation, he turned to the venerable Ânanda: 'Come, Ânanda,' he said, 'let us go to the *Old Bath* and refresh our limbs.'

"'Very good, Master,' replied the venerable Ânanda to the Exalted One.

"And the Exalted One now went with Ânanda to the 'Old Bath' to refresh his limbs. Then the venerable Ânanda addressed the Exalted One thus: 'The hermitage of the Brahmin Rammako, O Master, is not very far from here; it is pleasantly situated, in peaceful solitude. Good were it, O Master, if the Exalted One, moved by compassion, should betake himself thither.' The Exalted

One by silence gave his assent. And the Exalted One betook himself to the hermitage of the Brahmin Rammako.

"At this time, however, many monks were gathered together there, engaged in edifying conversation. Then the Exalted One stood before the door of the hermitage and awaited the end of their discourse. When now the Exalted One saw that the talk was at an end, he cleared his throat and rapped at the knocker. The monks within opened the door to the Exalted One. And the Exalted One entered the Brahmin Rammako's hermitage and seated himself upon the seat that was offered him. Then the Exalted One turned to the monks," and so on.

Up to the very last the Buddha himself closely adhered to the rules he had laid down for his monks. Even when he is eighty years old we still see him, when the rainy season is ended, wandering about from place to place, living upon public charity. Not seldom we meet in the Suttas with this or the like introductory phrase: "Now the Exalted One rose early in the morning, took his cloak and begging bowl, and went out," and so on; which means that, like each of his monks, he himself went the begging-round in the morning hours. When the begging-round and morning meal were over, the remainder of the day was spent in meditation under a tree in the forest.

"At one time," it is said in a Sutta of the Aṅguttara Nikāya,[1] "the Exalted One stayed at Âḷavī, on the cattle-path, in the Siṁsapā forest, upon a couch

[1] Nikāya means collection, division. This and all later-mentioned Nikāyas are parts of the Sutta Piṭaka, the second of the three books that make up the Pāli canon.

of leaves. Now a dweller in Âḷavī, one Hatthako, as he went through the forest, noticed the Exalted One sitting upon his couch of leaves, on the cattle-path, in the Siṁsapā forest, absorbed in meditation. Whereupon he went up to the place where was the Exalted One, greeted the Exalted One with respect, and sat down at his side. Sitting there, he addressed the Exalted One thus:

"'Master, does the Exalted One live happily?'

"'It is so, young man; I live happily. Of those who live happily in the world, I also am one.'

"'Cold, Master, is the winter night; the time of frost is coming; rough is the ground trodden by the hoofs of the cattle; thin is the couch of leaves; light the monk's yellow robe; sharp the cutting winter wind.'

"With sublime uniformity the Buddha replies:

"'It is so, young man. I live happily. Of those that live happily in the world, I also am one.'"

In another scene the Buddha comes before us, in his controversies with those of other faiths. Somewhat schematically, the figure of the weary, sweat-covered opponent is contrasted with that of the Buddha himself, who sits there quietly, free from every outward sign of agitation, "his skin of the colour of bright gold." He himself frankly declared: "That in disputation with any one whatsoever, I could be thrown into confusion or embarrassment,—there is no possibility of such a thing; and because I know of no such possibility, on that account it is that I remain quiet and confident." An old man, he declared to Sāriputta, his principal disciple, with that pride which is only permissible in genius:

"And when ye shall carry me hither upon a bed,

Sāriputta, the intellectual vigour of the Perfect One will remain unabated."

Almost we feel across the intervening centuries the influence that must have radiated from the over-powering personality of this wonderful man, when he says in another place:

"I know well, when I have preached the doctrine to a crowd of many hundreds of people, that each one thinks of me: 'This ascetic Gautama has preached the doctrine just for me.' Yet it is not to be understood that this is so, since the Perfect One preaches the doctrine to the enlightening of others as well. But when such an exposition has come to an end, then I set up the individual mind of each one who seeks peace, bring it to quietude, unify it, gather it together. And this I constantly do all the time, all the time."

Certainly, in the perpetually repeated answer of his monks, "From the Exalted One comes all our wisdom," we have no merely formal phrase, but in it have revealed to us their recognition of a mental capacity, towering high above that of them all. None the less, the Buddha does not consider it beneath his dignity to place himself among the company of his monks and submit himself to their criticism, just like any other of the company.

"At that time," says the Saṁyuttaka Nikāya, "at the celebration of Uposatha,[1] on an evening of the full moon, at the annual final assembly of the disciples, before the time of wandering began, the Exalted One sat surrounded by the company of his disciples in the open air.

[1] Celebrated twice a month, at which there was a public confession of faults.

"Then the Exalted One looked round over the silent company and said to the monks:

"'Well, ye disciples, I summon you to say whether you have any fault to find with me, whether in word or in deed.'"

When a Brahmin asked him, "Does the honoured Gautama allow sleeping by day?" he was not ashamed to reply, simply and unequivocally: "In the last month of summer, after the meal, when one has returned from the begging-round, I confess to lying down upon the right side, upon the cloak, folded in four, and, with collected senses, falling asleep."

With what noble humanity he appears before us when he speaks of his efforts to achieve the Buddhahood he so much craved! With what an undeniable emotion of sympathy and veneration do we here catch his words! Never before did founder of religion speak like this. One who thus speaks needs not allure with hopes of heavenly joys. One who speaks like this of himself attracts by that power with which the truth attracts all who enter her domain.

"I also, ye monks, once before my full awakening, as yet not wholly awakened, still striving after awakening,—myself subject to birth, I sought after what also is subject to birth; myself subject to old age, I sought after what also is subject to old age; myself subject to sickness, I sought after what also is subject to sickness; myself subject to death, I sought after what also is subject to death; myself subject to pain, I sought after what also is subject to pain; myself subject to impurity, I sought after what also is subject to impurity.

"Then, ye monks, the thought came to me: 'What, then, am I doing? Myself subject to birth, old age, sickness, death, pain, impurity,—seeking what also is subject to birth, old age, sickness, death, pain, and impurity! How if now, myself subject to birth, seeing the misery of this law of nature,—how if I seek the birthless, incomparable surety, the extinction of illusion! Myself subject to old age, seeing the misery of this law of nature, —how if I seek the ageless, incomparable surety, the extinction of illusion! Myself subject to sickness, seeing the misery of this law of nature,—how if I seek the diseaseless, incomparable surety, the extinction of illusion! Myself subject to death, seeing the misery of this law of nature,—how if I seek the deathless, incomparable surety, the extinction of illusion! Myself subject to impurity, seeing the misery of this law of nature,—how if I seek the stainless, incomparable surety, the extinction of illusion!'

"And, ye monks, after some time, while still in my first bloom, shining, dark-haired, in the enjoyment of happy youth, in the first years of manhood, against the wish of weeping and wailing parents, with shorn hair and beard, clothed in ragged raiment, I went forth from home to homelessness."

Can man say anything of more importance to man?

And how much we feel him to be even as ourselves when he confesses:

"Already before full awakening, as one not wholly awake, but still striving for awakening, I had recognised, with perfect wisdom and according to the truth, the law: 'Unsatisfying are desires;

full of torment, full of despair, and still more, of misery,' and yet, outside of desire, outside of evil, I knew of no felicity."

How our hearts feel and faint with his, as we see him engaged in combat with this unruly body! As he himself tells us:

"Then I said to myself: 'How now if upon those nights of evil omen, on full moon and new moon, and upon the waxing and the waning quarters of the moon,—how if I seek out the grave-hills in the groves and forests, under the trees, and tarry there in those places of horror and affright, that then I may know how it is, that fear and terror.' And in the course of time, upon those very nights of evil omen, full and new moon, and the first and last quarters of the moon, I sought out the grave-hills in the groves and forests, under the trees, and tarried there in those places of horror and affright. And as I sat there a deer came past, or a wood-hen pecked at a bough, or the wind shook the leafage. But I thought: 'Here now certainly that fear and terror will begin,' and I said to myself: 'Why do I sit still, waiting for the coming of fear? As soon as that fear and terror make their appearance,—how if I immediately go and meet that fear and terror?' And that fear and terror came over me as I went to and fro. But I neither stood still, nor sat down, nor lay down, until going to and fro I had faced that fear and terror. And that fear and terror came as I stood still. But I neither went to and fro, nor sat down, nor lay down, until standing still I had faced that fear and terror. And that fear and terror came nigh me as I sat. But I did not then lie down, nor stand up, nor did I go to and fro, until sitting still I had faced that fear and terror. And that fear and terror came on me as I lay down. But I neither raised myself up, nor stood up, nor went to and fro, until lying down I had faced that fear and terror.'"

How genuine, how serious, how child-like is this conflict. How it draws all our sympathies towards him! The very unexampled, almost supernatural nature of these his extreme self-mortifications, by the natural truth, the poignant simplicity with which he sets them forth, draws us all the closer to him. Breathless we feel with him, are convinced along with him: "This is the highest; further can no man go!" How sad, and yet how comforting it sounds, when he says to his disciples: "It is lack of understanding and insight into the Four Holy Truths that is to blame, O Brothers, that we—both you and I—so long have travelled the dreary road of Saṁsāra."[1]

Perhaps never while the world has lasted has there been a personality who has wielded such a tremendous influence over the thinking of humanity as has Gautama, the bearer of the Buddha-thought. This statement becomes indubitable fact for every one who rids himself of the baseless obscurantism which by the word "world" understands only the centre of Greco-Roman Christian culture, and the radiations in time and space that proceed from that centre. Again, this statement becomes an undeniable fact for every one who has learnt to understand by culture something else besides the mere art of living comfortably and making money quickly;—

[1] Saṁsāra means the universal wandering; the world of birth and death; the endless round of rebirths.

who has learnt to understand that progress does not proceed upon outward lines, but that true development consists of that inwardness which seeks and tries to comprehend that of which the world either knows nothing, or else treats with indifference, perhaps even with contempt. Whoso recognises this, will also recognise that already, almost two and a half millenniums ago, the supreme summit of spiritual development was reached, and that at that distant time, in the quiet hermit groves along the Ganges, already had been thought the highest man can think. He will recognise that with time it is only the shell that has changed, never the kernel, the manner of expression, never the thing expressed, and that in the endless millenniums yet to come it will never be otherwise. For higher thought there is not than that Buddha-thought which wipes out the world, and with it its bearer.

These were those times in the which a life devoted to the search for the highest, for a felicity beyond all that the world could give, was not considered madness, but as something worthy of all honour. These were the times, the unique times, in which it seemed natural not only to preach the good and the true, but also to live it. If such consistent uniformity can be ascribed to any men at all, then most surely is Gautama the Buddha among such men.

II

A BRIEF SURVEY OF THE LEADING DOCTRINES OF BUDDHISM

"Above all, the immediate object of religious teaching is the satisfaction of the intellect, but in such a way that the will is led along the true path—that of morality and renunciation."—Schopenhauer's *Letters*.

As the body is supported upon two feet, so the Buddha's system is based upon these two axioms: First, All life is sorrow; and, second, Always keep to the path of the true mean. These two, in their direct results and in their mutual interactions, comprehend the entire body of what is called Buddhism. Both theses are summed up by the Buddha himself in the Four Holy Truths. The first three of these Truths contain the philosophy of the teaching; the last, the morality of the teaching as seen through the spectacles of this philosophy.

The Four Holy Truths run as follows:—"This is the Holy Truth of Sorrow: Birth is Sorrow; Old Age is Sorrow; Disease is Sorrow; Death is Sorrow. To be united to the unloved is Sorrow. To be divided from the loved is Sorrow. Not to receive what one craves is Sorrow. In brief, the five Bases of the Elements of Being are Sorrow.

"This is the Holy Truth of the Arising of Sorrow. It is the craving which leads from rebirth to rebirth, accompanied by lust and passion; which snatches delight, now here and now there; it is the craving for the gratification of the passions, the craving for continued existence, the lust for present delight.

"This is the Holy Truth of the Annihilation of Sorrow; even the remainderless, total annihilation of this very craving; the forsaking it, the breaking loose, freeing, deliverance from it.

"This is the Holy Truth of the Path that leads to the Annihilation of Sorrow. It is the Holy Eight-staged Path, which consists of Right Comprehension, Right Resolve, Right Speech, Right Action, Right Livelihood, Right Effort, Right Mindfulness, Right Meditation."

This Holy Eight-staged Path, however, is only the thesis of the Middle Path in another shape.

The Four Holy Truths, not only intellectually but also formally, comprehend Buddhism in its entirety, from beginning to end. Beginning with the fact of suffering, they lead on to the Annihilation of this suffering; beginning with Saṁsāra, this world of suffering, they lead on to Nibbāna.

Because the Buddha starts with the fact of suffering, because the world, for him, begins with suffering, therefore is it that with the destruction of suffering we obtain the natural end of all, the answer to the problem set us for solution.

Hence at the very outset it becomes abundantly clear that Buddhism is only adapted to such as find life to be suffering. Those only who build upon this foundation can reach the end. Nothing is to be gained by preaching Buddhism except where life is felt and understood to be suffering. Wherever this is not the case, the conclusions drawn by the Buddha will seem merely absurd where they do not appear as frightful.

Now the Buddha declares that life in every form and in every expression is sorrow, but why is all life sorrow? Because all life is transient and unenduring. Everything transient and changing, however, is painful because it stands in natural contrast to freedom from pain, to blessedness regarded as something changeless.

But why is everything unenduring?

Because everything has arisen from some cause or reason, it follows that it must come to an end just as soon as this cause ceases to act. And this is the reason why not only where life is felt to be sorrow, but wherever there is anything that arises and passes away, wherever there is transiency, there also the Buddha's law obtains. Not merely the experiencing of life as sorrow, but the cognising of it as such, constitutes the capacity for Buddhism.

But how is it possible to extricate oneself from this sorrow when firm standing-ground is nowhere provided us? Through correct cognition, true knowledge. How reached? By following, step by step, the Eight-staged Path.

And what is this knowledge? It is this,—that my own *I*, this my personality—because like all else wholly and entirely arisen from a cause—is also wholly and entirely transient, and hence in this *I* is contained no ingredient that is eternal, no "soul." This proposition embraces the potentiality of supreme sorrow as well as of supreme bliss; the keenest sorrow, because by this my own *I* is torn from me and transformed into a "body of sorrow"; the keenest bliss, because at the very moment when such cognition takes place the way to deliverance opens out before me. Sorrow is not punishment,—the result of sin: sorrow is ignorance.

Because this *I*, this my personality, like everything else in the world, is conditioned, has arisen from a cause, and thus is wholly transient,—therefore it cannot truly be my *I*, to which latter alone can be ascribed the demand for a "soul," an eternal principle. Hence this *I* is only an apparent *I*; as the Buddha says, "It is not mine."

"As, for example, disciples, if a man carried away, or burnt, or did anything else he pleased with the grasses and twigs and leaves lying about here in this Jeta thicket, would you seriously think thus: 'This man is carrying away, or burning, or doing as he pleases with us'? What does not belong to you,—that, surrender! that which you surrender will for ever conduce to your well-being and health."

Therein lies blessedness, deliverance. The *I* can be renounced, wiped out; it disappears with the cause which has led to its formation, which would be impossible with a genuine, soul-endowed *I*.

Now what follows from the proposition that all that has arisen is conditioned by a cause?

This: That this cause itself must have a cause to which it must stand in the relation of effect, and so on backwards *ad infinitum*. All which simply means in other words: Life is eternal, has no beginning.

The consciousness of this, added to the facts of birth and death, have, in the thought of India, led to the doctrine of the transmigration of the soul. One existence follows another in an unbroken chain, and the "soul" is the thread that binds them together. Now Buddhism teaches that a soul, an enduring element, is not to be found in this body, and therefore it has no "transmigration of the soul," but in its place a "round of rebirths."

But how is this possible if nothing eternal remains over at death to furnish the link between one existence and the next?

The function of the "soul" is here to a certain extent assumed by Karma. The development of the idea is as follows.

This personality[1] is an apparent *I*, as we have seen, since it presents us with the illusive picture of something actual and eternal,—a "soul," where there is really nothing but a *Becoming*, void of any enduring core. Every illusion, however, must have something real behind it, by reason of which it comes to exist. Hence this, my apparent *I*, this Bhava, must be based upon something real. This something real, this substratum, is the five Khandhas,[2] namely, corporeality (*rūpa*), sensation, perception, differentiation (*sankhāra*), and consciousness (*viññāna*). All five inclusive, as representing the *I*, are also called *nāma-rūpa* (name and form), *nāma* representing the four latter, with *viññāna* at their head.

One sees these as realities, though such a statement is only permitted him for whom in truth nothing exists but sorrow. In themselves, each of them is a nothing; only in their union do they constitute

[1] Condition of being, of becoming.

[2] Pāli, Khandha; literally, aggregate. The verb from the same root means "to cause to coagulate."

personality, Bhava. Five fictitious realities thus blend together to form a real fiction! Life is at once illusion and reality, being and non-being.

But what is produced by the blending together of the Khandhas?

Karma, called in Pāli, Kamma. All five are held together—that is to say, constitute life—so long as Kamma is in force. They fall apart as soon as Kamma is exhausted. It is to be noted that nothing is destroyed by death; nothing is overthrown but the appearance, the illusion of this Bhava. The successive existences are nothing but the self-loosing and fresh self-binding again of the Khandhas.

But what then is Kamma?

It is that potency in virtue of which action gives rise to reaction. It is that which out of the action of this life creates as due reaction the life that follows. The will of this life, the present life impulse, is like a latent energy, which, as Kamma, creates the bridge that leads to the next existence, and at the same time creates this next existence itself. The will to live, the lust of living, is the force which keeps going the endless play of action and reaction, the arising of one life out of another. Just to the extent and for the time that life is the equivalent of will, so to that degree, and during that time exactly, does Kamma arise. To the extent that this life is the equivalent of will, to that extent is concealed in it the life that succeeds it. As that which unites action and reaction on one hand belongs to action, and upon the other to reaction, so, as being that which binds this life to the next, Kamma belongs to the one as well as to the other. "There is Kamma," simply means that with this life is already given the next and the next again, and so on through the endless series of existences. "Life" is synonymous with the beginninglessness and endlessness of life, and Kamma is merely the concise formula for the fact that this unfathomable endlessness, this play of life, is in progress.

If the connection between this and the next existence is of this kind, will not this next existence be a matter of small concern to me? No "soul" unites one existence to another; no consciousness passes from one to the other; for consciousness is individual, arising afresh with each Bhava, with each Bhava again passing away. What possible interest can I have in a succeeding existence of this sort?

A very close interest. In it I meet with the reward or punishment for the deeds of this existence.

But how is that possible when there is no *I* present? If there is no *I* present, there is also no doer present. If there is no doer present, how can there be any consequence of deed, any punishment, any reward? Hence, how is it possible to think aught else but that all struggle is vanity, all morality a jest?

To be sure, there is no *I*-doer, but there is a deed. For its effectuation no true *I* is necessary; it clings to the apparent *I*, which ever and again rebuilds itself anew out of the will to live. How this latter, however, "clings" we shall see later.

Every deed incontestably brings its consequences along with it, as the body casts a shadow, as the stone thrown into the water gives rise to its ripples. And as every reaction is conditioned by the specific nature of the action, so the mode and manner in which the consequences of deed find expression are determined by the deed itself. In other words, reward follows good deeds; punishment, evil deeds. The next existence accordingly will correspond in its make-up to the deeds of this existence. Even if there is no *I* present, yet the tiniest particle of my action is never lost. Every act-atom, so to speak, assists in the construction of the next existence.

Well and good! But what does all this matter to me if my consciousness does not pass over with me? I know nothing at all of the pain of other existences. It stands immeasurably farther off from me than, for example, the suffering of my neighbour, with whose pain, moreover, I stand in some sort of relation through the medium of my senses.

For a correct understanding of this we must again recall the definition of the conception of "sorrow," supplied by the Buddha himself. "Sorrow" must be experienced, but, much more, it must be understood. Certainly, if sorrow to any man only means sorrow that is experienced, such a man may well regard any succeeding existence with utter unconcern. The cycle of rebirths becomes of moment—nay, becomes the terror of all terrors—only when sorrow becomes an object of cognition, becomes a part of knowledge. The complete cognition of sorrow, however, is only possible where there is complete cognition of transiency. Complete cognition of transiency is synonymous with insight into the law of cause and effect, and this latter with insight into the working of Kamma. Whoso, however, understands the working of Kamma understands that the next existence is already contained in this; nay, that this existence is itself the next. He darkly suspects the illusory nature of "before and after," of time; in the illusion of time he feels the presence of another illusion—that of the *I*; and when the mind's eye, in reflection, turns inwards upon itself, the first flight is taken toward Nibbāna. But of this, more farther on.

To return: he understands that in this existence already, the next lies concealed. He perceives himself to be identical with it, and so learns to be afraid of its sorrow, as one who has endured great pain dreads a renewal of the same. The pain no longer exists, nor yet the consciousness of the pain; it is only reawakened with the new pain, and yet he is afraid of it, and does his utmost to prevent its return. Pain lives in the memory, in the mind; so also lives in the mind the dread of the pain of the next existence.

Whoso has recognised and understood the true connection between this and the next existence knows: With every good deed I only advantage myself; with every evil deed I only injure myself, and these return to me after no matter how many existences in the shape of reward or punishment.

So far, so good! But even if deed undeniably brings along with it its due consequence, how do I know that the consequence of my deed will necessarily always befall *me*?

I know it by my penetration into the law of cause and effect; by my comprehension of the idea: There is no *I*. For if there is no *I* present which could commit the deed, no doer whose product the deed is, then am I myself the deed. I am deed, corporealised If, however, I myself am the deed, then I myself am also the consequence of the deed; just as the reaction represents precisely the same energy as the action. Punishment and reward do not need first to seek me in order to find me. I myself am both punishment incorporate, reward incorporate. It is after this mode and manner that the deed and its consequences "cling" to the doer.

With this, that most universal of natural laws (the law of cause and effect), as by the stroke of a magician's wand, is transformed into the supreme judge of the world; and the creature, lacking of an immortal soul, free from the oversight of any god, apparently absolved of all responsibility, is forced into the mould of an iron, moral law whose justice is so exalted that to our minds it is scarcely ever distinguishable from cruelty. Under the brutal constraint of egoism I am moral to the best ability of this phenomenal *I*; for every immoral activity but drives the goad into my own flesh. Egoism is indeed the most coldly calculating foundation for morality which this world offers, but it is also the soundest, the most solid.

For man eternally lives through the will to live, notwithstanding that there is neither "soul" nor aught else eternal in him. He eternally lives through the consequences of his deeds that unchangeably come into existence; he "experiences" his deeds. Expressed after the fashion of India: He lives by reason of his Kamma.

To thoroughly understand the meaning of the words, "He lives by reason of his Kamma," we must cast a glance at the doctrine of *Becoming*. It belongs to the very heart and core of the system;

to that which found expression from the lips of the Buddha himself.

All—because conditioned by causes—is unenduring, is in a state of continual *Becoming*, perpetual arising and passing away. Whether the vibration-period of these waves is as brief in duration as the flash of a thought in consciousness, or whether it extends over countless world-periods, the enlightened mind, through all the disguising wrappings of forms, perceives that all is comprehended in the vibration of *Becoming*. It was this that the Buddha meant when, in the famous "Fire Sermon," he cried to his disciples: "All things burn." As the burning light constitutes a body of flame, which apparently is constant, but in reality is never the same for two consecutive moments, so with all that has arisen. And this my personality, this phenomenal *I*, is like the seeming body of the flame, a thing that exists flickeringly, in a state of continual arising and passing away, in which nothing is constant but change. It consists, like the flame, of separate *Becoming*-moments. The inexperienced, "the uninstructed in the doctrine of the Noble One," know only of a passing away, what men call death. The experienced know that our whole life is an imperceptible, oft-repeated arising and passing away, and that both kinds of passing away, that commonplace, and this sublime, are in no respect different save as regards duration. The commonplace *Becoming* which comes to an end in death, by reason of the rate of its vibration, comes within the scope and reach of our senses. The other and subtler *Becoming* lies below our threshold of sensation.

In the same way that Kamma joins this existence to the next, so within the limits of this existence it takes the numberless flashing, individual life-sparks and welds them together into this personality, which pictures itself to me as a being, as an "I." Each of these life-sparks, ceaselessly arising through "coincident action," is actually itself a complete existence, differing from this ordinary sensible existence only by its extreme brevity.

And just as Kamma not only supplies the link with the next existence, but at the same time itself constitutes this next existence, so also it not only supplies the link with the next *Becoming*-moment, but is itself this latter. Where there is no link with the next, there is no "next." Now only do we perceive the full significance of the words: "We live by our Kamma."

But now, since all life is sorrow, and it is Kamma that keeps going this life-process,—that is, this sorrow *ad infinitum*,—the burning question is: "How shall we find deliverance from this Kamma?" or, what is the same thing, "How shall we find deliverance from this sorrow?"

As already indicated, this *I* is only an apparent *I*; a something that in its totality has arisen and is arising, and which, therefore, can be removed with the removal of the cause that led to its arising. On the same grounds,—because it is a *Becoming*, a transient thing,—this apparent *I* becomes sorrow, *is* sorrow, corporealised. Sorrow does not attach to me; I do not produce sorrow, but I *am* sorrow, in the same way precisely that I do not perform the deed, but *am* myself the deed. Consequently the abrogation of sorrow can only set in with the abrogation of personality; these two conceptions are identical, and herein lies the ultimate reason why sorrow must not only be experienced but must also be understood. Only in sorrow cognised as such is the *I*, and with it the sorrow, abrogated, cancelled out. Sorrow that is simply experienced does not work deliverance.

The abrogation of sorrow can only take place through the abrogation of personality. Personality, however, revives again and again so long as there is any Kamma. Kamma is the efficient cause of this continual reconstruction of personality. Kamma—that is, the consequences that follow upon action—on its own side can only cease when the action itself ceases. The deed, however, can only cease when the cause of the deed ceases, namely, the delight of the senses in objects, the attachment to such objects; hence, in the attachment of the senses we have found the source of all sorrow.

But what is the reason that all attachment of the senses to objects produces sorrow? Because it continually produces new life; and where new life arises, there also it passes away; and wherever there is arising and passing away—change—there is transiency, there is sorrow.

But how can life arise from the activity of our senses?

The entire world as object stands in contradistinction to me as subject—as something known to me, the knower. Where there is nothing that knows, there also there can be nothing that is known; where there is no subject, there is also no object. The world as object is conditioned by me as subject. The world is conditioned by my five senses, with the mind as a sixth.[1] Upon the activity

[1] According to the Indian view, man has six senses.

of my six senses depends the world. It is the activity of my six senses which makes it that this world ever and again, in unbroken flow, comes to new being. The world, life, is merely the totality of the impressions which arise when my six senses are united to corresponding objects. The activity of our senses, their attachment to objects, is nothing but a process of generation; the arising of the impression is birth, its cessation is death. Thus it is our senses that create, in unbroken stream, this arising and passing away, this birth and death—that is, life as well as sorrow; and the Buddhist, with unaverted gaze, proceeds towards that endlessly fluctuating boundary line, which at every step forms itself anew, and within whose limits, as within some horizon, individuality ever and again posits itself afresh.

We might say that the teaching of the Buddha is the purest Kantian transcendental idealism applied to the ends of religion. This idea, the profoundest man yet has thought or is perhaps capable of thinking, has been perceived most clearly by the Buddha, by him has been worked out to the fullest extent and made to do the utmost service towards his ends. If this idea has not been developed in the jargon of current philosophy, it still stands before us—perhaps even on that very account—in crystal clearness, a proof that human thought already more than two thousand years ago reached its natural ultimate.

But more. If the activity of the six senses gives rise to the world—in other words, if there is no other world for the individual but this individual world, which it makes for itself with its own organs of sensation—it follows that this world, together with its sense activities, must come to an end. Where there is no longer any world, there is also no more sorrow. Sorrow as well as salvation have their root in myself, and the way to salvation—nay, salvation itself—is involved in the ceasing of my senses from continually weaving fresh life—that is, fresh sorrow. This happens at the moment when contact with objects is broken off.

But how can contact between the senses and their objects be broken off? Not by violence; not by killing them; that would leave their root behind in the soil. Contact can only be dissolved naturally, through the dissolution of my desire, my will. This, however, dissolves as soon as I recognise the painful transiency of life. The later recognition finds its culminating point in the fact that this my own *I*, as respects transiency, can in no way be differentiated from the rest of the world; this *I* is only a seeming *I*. With this, the will is in quite natural fashion brought to the ground. Every fresh sprouting of will is blighted by the newly acquired knowledge. The will is deprived, not only of the object but also of the subject; for in truth I can non-will for the first time only when I know there is no *I* present that can will.

Willing can only come to pass where there is *I*-consciousness—that is to say, willing is founded upon a misconception of the true nature of things, upon an ignorance. With this ignorance (Avijjā) all begins. Out of this, as out of some sort of counterpart of the primordial cell, the Buddha has his Buddha-world issue in twelve distinct stages; the twelve Nidānas, as they are called, whereof the final phase of development, the bloom of sorrow, takes shape as old age, disease, death, misery and distress, grief and despair. If this ignorance passes into true knowledge, into the knowledge of *I* as not-*I* (Anattā),[1] with it of necessity willing passes into non-willing. When there is no longer any will present, there is also no longer any deed. When deed fails, fails also the consequence of deed—that is, Kamma. Where there is no Kamma, there is no renewed existence; the cycle of rebirth is at an end.

Otherwise expressed. Where ignorance is transformed into knowledge, there of necessity willing turns to non-willing. Where there is no willing, there is no attachment of the senses to objects. Where there is no attachment, there is no arising and passing away. Where there is no change, there is no sorrow. Where there is no sorrow, there is no *I*. Where no *I*, no world. Sorrow, world, I,—all these are present as a product of ignorance, and with their dissolution in knowledge the cognition takes place: "This world is no more." And with this cognition takes place also this other: "All is done that was to do." The knowledge proves itself by itself; itself furnishes the proofs of its efficacy by dissolving in non-willing, its very possessor.

How then? The possessor of the knowledge still is there, and still *must* be there, in order to be able to demonstrate his freedom from sorrow. How then can he himself be dissolved and done away in knowledge?

To be quite exact, no knowledge can do away

[1] An-attā means not-self, void of soul, and is the most concise expression for the Buddha's doctrine of transiency. Everything without exception (this my *I* included) is anattā, because all without exception (my *I* included) is transient, is void of soul.

with this body, for the latter has been built up out of previous Kamma and can only crumble away with the exhaustion of this Kamma. But knowledge can prevent the building up of fresh existences. In this sense it does away with its possessor. If knowledge could do away with this phenomenal form, in which and through which it has been acquired, deliverance certainly could not be demonstrated, Nibbāna could not be glimpsed, and the entire system would be aimless and void of support, an empty play with no possibility of realisation.

But how can I know that this is my last birth, that with this present form sorrow shall have its end?

As the Buddha's system starts out with the idea of "sorrow," so it finds its natural issue in the idea of "sorrowlessness." As sorrow, in order that it may be of any utility, must not only be experienced but must also be comprehended, so also sorrowlessness, to be efficacious, must be understood as well as experienced. As sorrow experienced is pain, but sorrow understood is change and transiency, so sorrowlessness experienced is bliss, but sorrowlessness understood is that unshakable deliverance of the mind, that unalterable equanimity which bears in itself the proof that an *I* is no longer present. Where this serenity, this equanimity is present, so long as it is present, there is no longer any possibility of an *I*-thought; just as, where non-willing reigns there is no possibility of willing.

To be sure, we here have nothing but the fact of temporary freedom from sorrow, and not the fact of the ending of rebirth. But as the particular usefulness of sorrow understood lies in this, that it furnishes the assurance that the next existence is already contained in this, that the sorrow of the next existence is my sorrow, so the precise utility of sorrowlessness comprehended lies in this, that it provides me with the certain knowledge that Nibbāna, the ceasing of all *Becoming*, of all life, already *is*, in this my present existence. This serenity, this realised freedom from sorrow, is the next; it is what follows upon the last existence, and in so far as I recognise this, I know that this is my last birth.

And what now is the end, the conclusion of the whole matter? The end is nothing but this precise, unshakable certainty of ending; unshakable because founded not upon faith, but upon knowledge. As the beginning of all is the certainty of sorrow, so the end of all is the certainty of freedom from sorrow. As world-arising lies in me, is subjective, so the passing away of the world likewise rests in me and is subjective. Deliverance is nothing but the certainty of deliverance. This certainty is the final motion in the process of the transformation of ignorance into knowledge. Hence the Buddha says: "And therefore, ye monks, the gain of asceticism is neither alms, nor honour nor fame, neither the virtues of the Order, nor the bliss of self-absorption, nor clearness of knowledge. This immovable deliverance of the mind, ye monks, this truly is the end; this is asceticism; this is the central core; this is the goal." Who knows himself delivered, is delivered!

One question alone remains. How does this change from ignorance to knowledge take place? And the reply is: Through the teaching of the

Buddha or of such as have comprehended his doctrine, and by deep reflection.

This in its main features is the doctrine of the Buddha as set forth in the Pāli scriptures. It begins with the morality of the Eight-staged Path, with reflection as the first and lowest step accessible to all, and it ends in the dizzy heights of perfect knowledge. With the highest degree of art, and also with perfect naturalness, morality and knowledge are made to depend one upon the other. Each is conditioned by the other; each rises through the aid of the other, until both alike reach their natural consummation upon the heights, in the dissolution of their possessor.

On the long way upwards, however, not a step, not a link is missing. In the soundness of its basis, in the iron logic of its construction, this religion, even in the eyes of a non-adherent, must always appear as one of the most colossal and astonishing productions that have ever proceeded from the human mind. It is the completest conceivable victory of mankind over itself.

III

SOME CHARACTERISTICS OF BUDDHISM

BUDDHISM is one half philosophy, and the other half moral doctrine. It became a religion, on one hand, through the indissoluble union of both of these, and upon the other hand, through the success which attended it and made it the spiritual monarch of Asia. It is not a religion, however, in the sense that we are accustomed to attach to that word. The starting-point of all religion is a feeling after the infinite, after something lying beyond the reach of sense and understanding; a longing and fear based upon the unknown; in brief, the fear of God. If this definition is an exhaustive one, then Buddhism is certainly not a religion; nay, there never yet has been a philosophy that has kept itself so free from all admixture of religion as has Buddhism; for it is the only one of all existing philosophical or religious systems which resolutely overleaps every form of the unknown, and starts out with that fact of the present moment, the fact of sorrow. This is the stroke of genius in Buddhism. Its surpassing excellence is at once apparent. Here is needed no mystical, primeval night, nor any equally mystical god, who in threefold, mystic action brings the first life forth from the primal gloom. The whole mind-perplexing question as to the beginning of the beginning falls to the ground. And why? because it has been solved by the Buddha? Not at all! The Buddha also is powerless to solve it, but he has taught us to disdain any solution of it. As a Christian I am unable to elude the question of the creation of the world; it is bound up with the idea of God, and therefore with the ultimate—with eternal life in God. As a Buddhist, the question of the creation of the world for me has no meaning. Hence Buddhism is the only one among all the religions of the world which is able to keep itself free from the poison of hypotheses. If the idle inquirer here asks about the beginning of the beginning, with proud consistency he gets the answer: "In the beginning was sorrow!" Though the mental horizon be widened out so as to include infinitude, yet does the mental eye perceive sorrow and only sorrow. As, for a man swimming in mid-ocean, naught but the ocean exists, so, for the Buddhist, naught exists but sorrow. Whatsoever does not issue forth from the seed-grain, "All life is sorrow," does not belong to the genuine tree of Buddhist thought.

As the traveller by night sees the landscape around him by each flash of the lightning, and the picture so obtained long thereafter swims before his dazzled eyes, so the Buddha, by the flashing light of his genius, perceived life to be sorrow with such clearness, that the after picture nevermore faded from the retina of his mind.

Before this blinding flash all obscure hypotheses as to the beginning of the beginning utterly disappeared. He perceived nothing but sorrow; strove for nothing but freedom from this sorrow; that was his "sacred goal." There exists but one thing, and that one thing is everything: there exists sorrow. This is the fixed, immovable point of departure of Buddhist thought. "And what, ye monks, do the wise and I declare to be present in the world? A body, a sensation, a perception, a differentiation, a consciousness, which are all transient, painful, subject to change;—these the wise declare to be present in the world, and I also say they are present."

Thus Buddhism takes its departure from the present moment, with its incontestable fact of sorrow, and ends with the knowledge, with the consciousness, of the dissolution of sorrow. The Buddha created, as it were, a new thought-world, lighted by the sun of sorrow. He classified things after a new fashion. He did not deal with thought and being, mind and matter, energy and substance, a good and a bad principle, and such-like abstractions, but from his lips a startled world for the first time learnt of the classification of sorrow and freedom from sorrow. As our solar system requires the five organs of sense with their specific functions, so the Buddha's solar system requires as its organ the capacity for experiencing sorrow. This is the only requirement; nothing is necessary but a sensitivity to, and an understanding of, the sorrow of this life. How clear, how positive, how purely human!

The conception of life as sorrow, like a skein of scarlet, runs through all Indian philosophy. Unlike us of the West, it is not before death—true, precious, peace-bestowing death—that the Hindu stands affrighted, but before life, that in rebirth keeps on endlessly renewing itself. Saṁsāra, the cycle that runs its course through ceaseless rebirths, is the one spectre of horror that haunts the Indian mind. And this view is not merely the product of philosophic thought, but to an unusual degree it is the common property of the whole Indian people. To be able to understand its religion we must go back to the fundamental ideas of a people. Religion is nothing extraneous to, or above a people, but is something that arises from among them, a product of their inherent character. This inherent character also may partly permit of explanation, but we finally come to a point where further derivation from any source ceases, and we have to content ourselves with the simple fact. In this connection it is a fact that one people is more intensely attached to life than another. The indifference of the American races with regard to this so-called highest good is well known. The inhabitant of Eastern Asia also resorts to suicide with a—to us—incomprehensible light-heartedness, and the Malay is prepared, when all other ways are barred against him, to take revenge on his enemy by hanging himself before that enemy's door. The Indian peoples, to a marked degree, share in this peculiarity of character, and thus stand in clear contradiction to the Semitic races with their strong, persistent vitality, which reflects itself under the garb of religion, in their teaching of this consciousness after death being endowed with life in some heavenly place. No matter how ill it may go with the galley-slave of life, he sees the cause of this, not in the imperfection attaching to all life, but in his own private misfortune and special, individual conditions. And thus he is always hoping for betterment up to the last moment, and when at last nothing more can be expected, his hope leaps over to the life after death. All good for him is lodged in life, and only because even the most short-sighted cannot avoid the sight of the misery that is here, is this curtailed experience of one existence concluded to be an unfortunate specimen, and all the others are transferred *en masse* to a paradise endowed with every possible perfection. Thus does man allow himself to be deceived by life, like a good-natured audience, before which a jack-of-all-trades gives a mediocre performance, and when it is over, aware of its shortcomings, says: "This is only just an indication of what I can do. This and that went wrong, but next time—*then* you will see!" The good man, however, has really done all he is able to do, and every time that he gives his performance, makes the same old, set speech. Whoever seeks for the sorrow of life among the accidents of circumstance is like one suffering from a sore on his foot who looks in his boot for the cause of his pain.

Another, however, perceives in his individual sorrow the common sorrow that clings to all life. In particular phenomena he glimpses the universal law of nature, and soon pain and satiety seize upon him and he renounces. Thus for reasons inexplicable to us, the phenomena of life react upon one man in this way and upon another in that. The method of this reaction is like that of the crystal in a salt solution, it is the starting-point round which one thought-molecule after another groups itself until the complete development of the religious system is reached.

Once more: Nothing is needful to the Buddhist but sensitivity to, and understanding of the sorrow of life. In religions founded upon a revelation, belief in certain supernatural occurrences is indispensable for one to be able truly to call oneself an adherent of the religion. This capacity for belief, however, is an inborn feature of the character; it cannot be assumed; it is not to be acquired. Hence, if my understanding will not permit me to accept the dogmas of Christianity;—if the pains with which it threatens and the promises with which it seeks to allure, are to me empty words, then, in spite of the strictest obedience to the behests of morality, I am not a Christian. Entry for me is irrevocably barred by my understanding. It is as if I went looking for darkness with a light in my hand; no power on earth can help. On the other hand, it is not necessary to be able to believe in order to be a Buddhist. Here belief is dethroned and replaced by knowledge and by understanding; for something unteachable is substituted a something that can be taught. Wherefore hail, all ye that are unable to believe! To you, chiefest of all, are the Buddha's promises addressed! He will teach you to understand, and, understanding, the highest shall be made clear to you!

But even if I need not believe in anything supernatural, do I not need to believe in the Buddha, and in his doctrine?

Even that is unnecessary. More than once this very point is dealt with in the Suttas, and it is never required that any one should begin his journey with faith in the doctrine. It is only said, and that continually: "After he had listened to the doctrine he acquired confidence in the Perfect One (the Buddha)." This confidence may arise as if a chord vibrated in sympathetic unison in the recesses of one's heart, in the same way that one tuning-fork vibrates in answer when another pitched in the same key is struck. Or confidence may arise through seeing in others the results of the doctrine. Like a sick man undertaking a new course of treatment, so may one begin his career as a Buddhist. As a sick man, who sees others cured by a certain course of treatment, makes up his mind to follow the requirements of the same cure, even though as yet he is without faith in it, so the beginner in Buddhism makes up his mind to follow the demands of the Buddha, to walk the Holy Eight-staged Path, even though as yet he has but little faith in its efficacy. Faith begins with progress in morality and knowledge. Complete faith, however, it must be admitted, is only reached with complete knowledge, as one must first climb the highest peak of a mountain before he can obtain a full view of the surrounding country.

In Buddhism, faith is purely the product of knowledge; it is mathematical certainty pure and simple. The New Testament definition of faith does not apply to it, for that means the derivation of something certain from something uncertain, of the unquestionable from the questionable. Mental gymnastics of this sort are not to be found in Buddhism. As there are no ghosts in a house that is lit up from roof to cellar, so in Buddhism that is lit up in every remotest corner by the light of knowledge, there is no such thing as faith in the Christian sense of the word; no something which in contradiction to the universally valid laws of nature would deduce its reliability simply and solely from its inexplicability! In the Buddha's system that only has a place which falls into line with the iron law of cause and effect; here is no chasm over which the understanding has to take a *salto mortale*.

Without further argument it is clear that a system which does not require faith has also no need of God. For what sight is to things visible and hearing to things audible, that faith is with respect to the God-conception. One conditions the other; with the fall of the one, the other also falls. Buddhism is not atheistical in the sense of denying the existence of God; the Buddha never argued against the existence of a divine being. It lay, however, in the very nature of his system, in its entire construction, that he treated and was obliged to treat this question with utter indifference. He had cognised sorrow; sorrow must be destroyed. With the exactitude of a sum in arithmetic, this problem was solved; no more was desired or sought for. The introduction of the God-idea would have made the solution of this arithmetical sum an impossibility. The Buddha discovered a footpath to the highest summit of human achievement, freedom from pain, up which every man can climb who has the natural use of his limbs. But he never disputed or denied that upon wings also, or in a balloon, or in some other wonderful way, we might be able to attain to this highest. He contents himself with saying in effect: "This way I have found; whoso will entrust himself to me, him I can serve as guide."

"I understand the temporal; I understand the eternal; and whoso will confide in my art of swimming, long shall it conduce to his health and well-being."

As a merchant who is convinced of the excellence of his wares has no need of advertisement or commercial cunning, so the Buddha simply needs to lay down his law of sorrow, how sorrow arises, and how it passes away. This is the great law that all the Buddhas before him taught, and that all the Buddhas after him will teach. Anything else additional that may be taught is contained in this, the basic law of all, "as the elephant's track contains the track of every other living creature."

Thus everything is carried on with refreshing straightforwardness, as in an honourable business. The buyer knows the goods and knows the price that is asked. The article for sale is freedom from pain; the price to be paid is resolute renunciation, resolute non-willing. Naturally, only one who has a use for such an article, only one who keenly enough feels life to be sorrow, will be disposed to pay what, in our eyes, must seem such an exorbitant price.

We ought not to lose sight of the fact that any comparison between Buddhism and other religions is in many respects a comparison of incongruous quantities. For the Buddhist, the highest is something quite different from what it is for the adherent of another religion. His (the Buddhist's) goal is not heaven, union with any deity; it is freedom from pain. Only in Buddhism does the conception "freedom from pain" remain purely a negative thing, and not a positive in disguise — heavenly bliss. Buddhism is the only one among all the religions of the world that is based upon negation, issues in negation, yea, *is* negation. Hence it has value solely for such as seek the door that leads out of life; in fact, Buddhism is nothing else but the way to this door. Hence we need not wonder that the apparatus also with which it works is quite different from that used by other religions; we need not be surprised to find that faith and the God-idea are both lacking, and their place taken by comprehension.

As in respect to the beginning of the world, so also with regard to its end, Buddhism stands alone among the religions of the world in this respect that it does not bring all to an end with heaven, with a union with deity, but instead ends in the bald but perfectly clear idea of freedom from pain. Since, then, for the Buddhist, life in every form is sorrow, the highest goal for him is unalloyed freedom from sorrow, which logically is only conceivable apart from life. Life and freedom from sorrow mutually exclude one another. The longing for heaven is not only the most sublimated but also the most intense form of the craving for life. But it is through the craving for life that I am in life. If for me life truly is sorrow, the longing for heaven must immediately collapse. But the longing for heaven *is* heaven. Where there is no longing for heaven, there is likewise no heaven. Where there is no heaven, heaven needs not to be proved, explained, or represented—the most comforting, and at the same time the most dubious task the world is engaged upon. Whilst all other religions are always under the fatal necessity of expounding their heavens to their adherents in such a fashion that, in spite of the most careful reserve, some purely human colouring still shines through, everything, for the Buddhist, is comprehended in these words, which are the expression of unalloyed negation: "I suffer no more."

Yet Buddhism has its heaven and its gods, indeed—in consonance with a tendency towards the colossal—huge groups of gods, but (to speak again in the symbolic language above used) their track also is comprehended in the elephant's track of the teaching of sorrow. They also are subject to the great law of sorrow and transiency. In vain the deluded mind seeks sanctuary in the lap of Godhead; the refugee, together with his refuge, is plucked back again into the endless round of rebirth by the inexorable law of Kamma, as the vapourised water, however high it may have risen into the air, yet must ever return to the sea again in the form of rain.

What, then, of the joys of heaven?

Just like those of earth, they are nothing else but the reaction from previous miseries, and fresh miseries as their reaction in turn, will inevitably follow them. And though the tremendous length of the swing gives rise to the appearance of eternal being, eternal rest, the wise man here also darkly perceives the mere swing of a pendulum, perceives mutability and sorrow.

The gods in Buddhism are like those allegorical frescoes with which the interiors of public buildings are decorated, so that they may not look too bare. The gods stand in no closer relation to the Buddhist system than do the allegories to the buildings whose interiors their pictorial representation decorates.

"All well and good!" it may here be said, "but if the Buddhist does not believe in God nor in the Buddha, he yet believes in his Nibbāna. What union with God is to the Christian, that to him is entry into Nibbāna. Nibbāna, too, is invisible, and yet he does not doubt its existence. Hence there is faith here as elsewhere, and everything finally resolves itself into a question of verbal distinctions!"

Nothing is less true than this. The Nibbāna-idea is dealt with more fully elsewhere; here only we would say that as no longing or striving after Nibbāna is possible, so also no faith in Nibbāna is possible. Nibbāna is nothing but the conception of freedom from sorrow that proceeds from absolute negation. The Buddhist does not long for Nibbāna but for deliverance from sorrow. Understood thus, Nibbāna itself is present as darkness is present when the light is extinguished. He does not put his faith in Nibbāna, but he knows that sorrow is abolished. Hence his mind sees Nibbāna as his eye sees darkness—by not-seeing!

But to return. Buddhism really recognises nothing but the faith that arises from knowledge. It is under no necessity of working with the faith-ideas of the religions that are founded upon revelation. The thinking mind here is not compelled to wrestle with an insoluble problem. Nay more, it is not even under the necessity of denying the dogmas of the religions of revelation. So completely does the Buddha's world lie apart, that none of his reaches of thought intersect or contact even one of these vexed questions. They may be true, they may be false, but neither way have they the slightest influence upon the closed circle of causes and effects in the Buddhist system. And here another unusual excellence in this teaching comes to light.

Alone among world-religions it stands in no *a priori* contradiction to science and the development of science. Ultimately it is itself nothing but the application in the moral domain of the laws that obtain in the realm of natural science. Buddhism knows nothing of that attitude of arrogant aversion that belongs to other religions. It readily adopts the facts of science, as being only so many supports of its own doctrinal structure. It must, however, be said that that search for a knowledge which, in the inexhaustible fulness of its facts, overwhelms and prostrates its possessor is strictly forbidden. The attachment to curiosity is one of the four varieties of the craving for life which are hindrances to salvation. But salvation is the one goal, and is only possible of attainment through continual thinking thereupon. If I allow myself to become absorbed in studies, how can I arrive at salvation? Here also we must adhere to the Path of the True Mean. The phrase, "to devote his life to science," is here an immorality! The passion for knowledge—in the vulgar sense of that word—because it has the material for its basis, carries in itself imperfection and disappointment, and is thus powerless to lead to peace, to perfect serenity. There are in Buddhism no forbidden books, there is no forbidden knowledge, but the man of understanding will detect the taint of imperfection and sorrow in each newly acquired piece of knowledge. Though the mind, like the bee, seeks food in the flowers that lie on every hand, he who comprehends will, like the bee, work up sweet and bitter alike into the honey of salvation. Like life in its entirety, science also is nothing else but a mirror which reflects back the sorrow and transiency of the world. It can never be an end in itself. Only he who takes up science in this spirit, takes it up rightly. The world does not need learned men or geniuses; what it needs is thoughtful men, moral men. And yet science here can never become so much the antithesis of religion as it has become in Christendom, because the tenets of the Buddha contain nothing in themselves contradictory to the findings of science.

The importance of this point can scarcely be overestimated. The results of the separation between science and religion are becoming more and more prominent in the domain of Christian culture. The cleavage penetrates even to the deepest stratum of the social structure. The dissension dates from those early days when Christianity first rose superior to the Greco-Roman world. Never were social distinctions so enormously pronounced as during the times of the Roman Empire. Never was the world so near to being divided into two great classes with no intermediate and connecting stage as at that period of its history. To endeavour to bring the society of those times to one common viewpoint, to unite it in one common effort, was something like trying to make a cake out of salt and sugar alone. The flour, the connecting condition, was amissing. Hence it was inevitable that the new religion should supply the requirements of one class and become for it a bed of ease while becoming a bed of Procrustes for the other.

Like a gash in the bark of a young tree, this cleavage between science and religious faith has become deeper and more pronounced with the growth of the former. The time is long past when the ever-widening gulf might be stopped up with hecatombs of human sacrifices, if only because the rent has grown too great for there to be any longer any possibility of filling it up in this fashion. But the terrible result of this division has been, that, encouraged by certain favouring tendencies in the character of the people, it has called fanaticism into existence. As in chemistry the harmless alkali, when divided into its two constituent parts, gives us poisonous cyanide, so culture, which in its perfection arises from the organic union of faith and knowledge, by the separation of these two gives rise to the deadly poison of fanaticism. And as a cancer, in spite of its apparently merely local growth, is gradually eating up the whole organism and itself along with it, so fanaticism, despite its apparently purely local results, finally destroys the entire system and of course its own basis along with it.

Fanaticism was quite foreign to the ancient world. Like so many precious wares there was a mutual exchange of the divinities of the different countries that lay within the limits of the Roman Empire. As Rachel took her father's household gods into her new country, so the Syrian, the Jew, the Egyptian, took their country's god with them to Rome, and, crystal-clear, the huge mass took up the radiations that emanated from all these new centres of light, without bursting into flame, without even being appreciably warmed thereby. The other world-powers also, the Macedonian and the Persian, were never religious despotisms. Politics and religion, earthly and heavenly domination, in the ancient view of things, were always kept separate from one another. Only among the Jewish people, by a combination of peculiar traits of character and special circumstances, was a quickening of both produced. Hence it was always this little people that stuck in the organism of the giant kingdoms that succeeded one another, somewhat like a thorn in the paw of a lion. Hence, because it refused to allow itself to be incorporated into these organisms, and because, wholly encased in its faith, it maintained a fanatical opposition to everything outside its own borders, the chastisements to which it was in consequence subjected also partook of the character of fanaticism. Every restriction of its political life became synonymous with an act of violence against its religion. As a matter of fact, the religious war, the most frightful because the most irrational of all wars, was unknown among the world-powers of antiquity.

It may be affirmed that into the character of no race has the content of fanaticism so largely entered as it has into that of the Semitic stock, and if the cult of Jehovah has anywhere been surpassed in fanaticism, it has been by Islam. Christianity as an offshoot of Judaism has inherited a tendency to fanaticism, as the child inherits from the father his liability to any disease. The constant friction which soon arose with the highly-developed exact science of Greco-Roman culture easily provided the degree of heat necessary for the development of the seed. Because reasoning here was impotent, fire and sword were called in. And thus with Christianity, religious fanaticism overflowed the countries of Europe. And that most frightful of all the pictures presented us by world-history, the spectacle of one people overcoming another in war in order that they might force their religion upon them, this most dreadful comedy of the divine was first played under the auspices of the religions that sprang from the Semitic stem.

It is no exaggeration to say that Buddhism is the only one of all the religions in the world which has remained wholly free from every form of fanaticism. The cause of this is to be found in its entire lack of dogmas. Just as little as it can be a subject of contention whether the solution of a given mathematical problem is correct or not—for the correct solution itself furnishes the proof of its correctness—just as little can the outcome of the Buddhist course of thought be disputed. From each point, with mathematical exactitude, the whole can be deduced, and nowhere is left over that remainder, that unaccountable, inexplicable thing which, like nothing else in the world, possesses the secret property of causing human passions to burst out into flame.

Whoever in following up the thought of the Buddha stumbles upon anything that appears inexplicable, unable to take its place as part of the whole, may be sure that it has not been built up in line with the foundation: "All life is transient." In the Buddhist system there is nothing unexplained, mysterious, cosmic; which was what the Buddha meant when he said to one of his disciples: "With respect to the doctrine, the Tathāgata has nothing resembling the closed hand of a teacher who is concealing something."

Moreover, this unguarded publicity can only be displayed where it can be founded upon a sense of perfect, inner security. In Buddhist worship—if worship it may be called—there is nothing secret or hidden; indeed, in Southern Buddhism, which prevails in Ceylon and Burma, this publicity extends even to externals. With the exception of a few old, rock-cut temples, there are no enclosed halls of worship. Instead, prayer is offered upon the open platform of the pagoda. Entry is open to all, and at all times. Among all their ceremonies there are none in which the alien of another faith may not join without any previous initiation, if only he be inspired by the feeling of reverence. Buddhist "divine service" is the most charming in the world, and more especially in places where it exists alongside such religions as Hinduism and Muhammedanism with their bigoted exclusiveness, it stands out in all its loveliness and unaffected spontaneity. Whoever has visited the platform of Shwe Dagon (the Golden Pagoda of Rangoon) or the sacred mount of Mahintale in Ceylon will readily concur in this.

Buddhist countries, too, have always been noted for tolerance and accessibility. Ceylon in the early Middle Ages was famed throughout the whole of the then known world for the perfect impartiality with which it treated different religions. Tibet has become the most closely sealed country in the world, not by reason of its Buddhism, but because of its hierarchy, whose conduct is in complete opposition to the spirit of true Buddhism.

To the Buddhist, religion is each man's private affair which he must settle for himself. The Buddha was so far from exercising compulsion over his own flock, that, just before he passed away, he said: "The Tathāgata does not think that it is he who must lead the brotherhood or that the Order is dependent upon him."

Buddhism finally is nothing else but an inward transformation in the human being, having for its foundation quiet reflection. Nothing is effected by force or compulsion, nor even by persuasion. The only thing that may be done is to point out the true Law; all else must be left to the individual himself. The only thing the sun needs do is to show its light; it does not require to compel any to make use of it. In similar wise the Tathāgata sets flowing the fount of salvation. Whoso is thirsty let him drink. Every form of violence is here entirely out of place. What good is there that requires to be forced upon others? That highest good—God—is absent. There is nothing here of which to make a gift; more especially there is none of that ideal good which in experience is found much easier to offer to another than the contents of one's purse. The highest good here is no positive thing, but consists solely in the removal of an illusion. But the removal of an illusion only follows upon correct perception. Since, however, I not only *have* this illusion—of the *I* as a true *I*—but *am* it, correct perception depends entirely upon myself. Another, by causing the fountain of the doctrine to flow, may furnish the opportunity for correct perception, but correct perception itself is only possible through my own efforts.

Thus everything impels to that concentration which, looking away from fellow-man, and forgetful of heaven and hell, past and future, keeps its gaze exclusively fixed upon this *I*, upon this astounding, unexampled experience of sorrow, and its transformation into bliss.

In no religion is the *I* so entirely nothing, and yet so completely everything, as in this religion. Every reference of the spiritual centre of gravity to something external is a sheer fall into illusion; useless to others and inevitably damaging to myself. Hence the resolute rejection of every line of thought that lies outside this system of salvation. Hence also the combat against and contempt for that passion for hypotheses which flourished so extensively in ancient India, and produced the same outgrowths as appeared among the Sophist Schools of Hellas. It is to this futile passion for hypotheses that the Buddha alludes when he says to the Brahmin, Janussoni: "There are still, O Brahmin, many ascetics and Brahmins, who take night for day, and day for night. I, however, Brahmin, take night for night and day for day." And to his disciples he says: "Think not such thoughts as the world thinks, that 'the world is eternal,' or that 'the world is not eternal'; 'the world has an end,' or 'the world has not an end.' If you think at all, disciples, ye may think thus: 'This is sorrow.' You may think: 'This is the arising of sorrow.' You may think: 'This is the removing of sorrow.' You may think: 'This is the Way to the removing of sorrow.'" And he himself to a

Brahmin utters the proud words: "The Tathāgata has nothing to do with theories."

Buddhism has been compared with Christianity, and it has been said that the one, like the other, is a religion for the poor, the oppressed, the miserable, the enslaved. I think that anything more untrue could scarcely be said. Here some have allowed themselves to be misled by the fact that the Buddha broke the bonds in which Indian life had fettered itself;—that he threw wide open the door of his doctrine, threw it *so* wide open that the members of all castes could enter therein alongside one another. He himself said: "As in the ocean all the great rivers lose name and being, so in my doctrine all the castes merge." It is true that early Buddhism took up all that the others were obliged to reject, bound as these latter were in the bondage of caste-ideas, yet this was merely part of the mission of Gautama as the Buddha. He was indeed the saviour of the world, and as he stood high above the gods, so also he stood far above all divine institutions. Blamed by the other sects for his catholicity in this respect, he answered: "My law is a law of grace for all."

In a certain sense it may be said that Christianity is not for the world, but for the poor, for those who have been disinherited, shut out from all material and intellectual enjoyment of the world, but, if there is anything we can *not* say of Buddhism, it is this! We need only consider that the Indian people, for whom, more than for any other people, life is sorrow, have permitted Buddhism to be taken away from them again, while the peoples who to-day profess Buddhism are among the most jovial on the face of the earth. I am here thinking more especially of the Burmese. This of course does not exclude the poor and enslaved from making their own application of the teachings of Buddhism, but these teachings were not set forth solely for them.

It was freedom from the bondage of caste that attracted the poor to the doctrine, and only too often it may not have been an inward necessity but the consideration of an external advantage that supplied the ruling motive. The Buddha probably had good cause to cry to his monks: "O that my disciples were heirs of truth and not heirs of necessity!"

Still less applicable in Buddhism are the words: "Blessed are the poor in spirit!" It is significant of his whole system, that Gautama's first thought after he attained Buddhahood was: "Will my fellow-men understand me?" "Whether," it is said elsewhere, "whether I proclaim the truth briefly, or whether I proclaim it at length, those who can understand me are hard to find." Without further argument any one can see that this is no doctrine for the poor in the Christian sense of the word. Here again some have allowed themselves to be deceived by the style of the Buddha's language, by his method of teaching, which spreads itself out in a copious flow of words, abounding in somewhat tedious repetitions, the whole standing in sharp contrast to the teaching of the Brahmins with its obscure depths and enigmatic brevity. But the doctrine of the Buddha was not thus set forth because meant particularly and above all for the lower classes, but solely because he was the first to preach publicly a connected body of teaching. Further, he evolved new lines of thought from the old stock phrases, and it was necessary that these new lines of thought should be retained in the memory, for writing was not yet in use in his time; hence the ceaseless repetition of certain phrases.

The poor man who has never yet tasted the joys of this world will scarcely grow very enthusiastic over a "renouncing of every lust for life"; an ideal state must be placed before him, in a heaven that will make up to him twofold for what was denied him here below. The religion of the poor is a religion of promises; the Buddhist religion, however, is a religion of renunciation.

Here a veritable gulf yawns between Buddhism and Christianity, as indeed also between the Jewish carpenter's child and the son of the Indian prince, whom disgust of luxury drove forth; who saw around him naught but sorrow, since all ordinary happiness for him had long since taken its flight. This sorrow, however, is not to be confounded with the sorrow of the really poor, which gives birth to joys as delicate and beautiful as flowers that push up through snow. The sorrow of Gautama is that dark sorrow which lies dead like an extinct volcano, awaiting a cosmic revolution to call it forth again into renewed activity. To some such revolution Buddhism owes its origination; it was a reaction against asceticism, and the volcanic fertility of the freshly vivified soil gave birth to a flower of inexpressible purity: the Buddha's teaching of deliverance.

All the Buddhas speak after the same fashion when they address laymen. First of all they preach the meritoriousness of almsgiving, the obligations of ordinary morality, the sinfulness of lust, the blessedness of the renunciation of lust. Only then, when they perceive that their hearers are sufficiently prepared, sufficiently ready and receptive,—then only do they preach the great doctrine of all the Buddhas; that is, sorrow, the cause of sorrow, the annihilation of sorrow, and the Path that leads to the annihilation of sorrow. This is how all the Buddhas are accustomed to teach.

From all this it becomes evident, as the Buddha himself never once forgot, that his doctrine is not adapted for every one. Notwithstanding that he came as a saviour of the world, a certain strain of nobility and exclusiveness is peculiar to his teaching. "Others will only take an interest in what lies before their eyes; will seize it with both hands; will with difficulty let go. We, however, will not take an interest only in what lies before our eyes; will not seize it with both hands; will let go without difficulty," says a passage in one of the Suttas. It can be demonstrated that the well-meant but often very troublesome obtrusion of religious convictions—that most banal of all expressions of the feeling of human benevolence—has always been more of a rarity in Buddhism than in any other world-religion. This perhaps is due to the personality and upbringing of its founder. He was of a princely family, and in more ways than one, Gautama was a king among ascetics. Kings sympathised with him as with one of their own kin; we find kings among the earliest of his adherents. The sorrow he preaches is the sorrow that kings feel more than beggars, not, however, that it is confined to the former. Oh no! It dwells with the exalted as well as with the lowly, only the one, as it were, provides a better sounding-board for it than does the other. And "the sons of noble houses" were more willing to take the path of renunciation that led from home to homelessness. They possessed in a higher degree the faculty of perceiving sorrow in transiency, and from their lips sounds most appropriately the famous verse to which Sakka, the king of the gods, gave utterance at the Buddha's decease, and which most clearly exhibits the distinctive colouring of Buddhism :—

> " All that arises,—O, how unlasting !
> Increase and swift decay,—such is its life.
> All that has e'er arisen, all this must fall again.
> No more to rise or fall : that peace is best ! "

IV

PESSIMISM AND SORROW

"For long, ye disciples, have ye endured sorrow, endured pain, endured misfortune and fed the graveyards full—long enough truly, disciples, to become dissatisfied with every form of existence, long enough to turn away from all existence, long enough to seek deliverance from it all."—*Saṁyuttaka Nikāya.*

It is to a large extent due to Schopenhauer's distorted apprehension of the two leading religious systems of India, Vedanta[1] and Buddhism, that both—but especially the latter—have obtained the reputation of glorifying pessimism, in similar fashion to the Schopenhauerian system itself. Than this view, nothing could be more erroneous. Above all, to represent Buddhism as the religion of the ordinary, commonplace pain of the world is the crowning height of misunderstanding.

Pessimism can only exist where there is egoism. It is nothing else but wounded,—and despite all its wounds and bruises—unabated egoism. Pessimism, despite all its apparent denial, is yet at bottom nothing but a form of the affirmation of life, and beyond question its most unhappy and most paradoxical form. The only natural outcome of the affirmation of life is the conception of deity.

[1] Vedanta means "End of the Vedas." It signifies that religious tendency of Brahmanism, the main ideas of which are found in the Upanishads.

Now in the specific line of thought of the Vedanta, egoism has taken on such a form that in its perfect comprehension lies the highest divine bliss. The full comprehension is this: "All is *I*; this entire world, God, the highest Brahman, all is *I*." With the knowledge of this, my *I*, I become God. "Knowing Brahman he becomes Brahman." Vedanta is thus pure, unalloyed optimism. All sorrow, as present to perception, is pure delusion, and rests upon ignorance. What greater rapture can there be than to be God! There is no room for pessimism in this system.

Still further removed is pessimism from the teaching of the Buddha, since here the very *I* itself is dissolved in correct comprehension. The man of knowledge sees through this phenomenal form, the body, and perceives no *I*. Where, however, there is no *I*, there naturally can be no egoism either, no *I*-mania. In the Buddha's system, not only is pessimism done away with, but also the very possibility of pessimism, and of optimism as well. There remains only that unmoved serenity, that conscious indifference, which has its basis in a comprehension to which all things are of equal value.

It is not going very far wrong to say that pessimism first took shape and form with the advent of Christianity. Greco-Roman culture was optimistic with what we might call positive and immanent optimism. Life was something beautiful, made for enjoyment, and, as such, enjoyed without any misgiving. In the sense of Goethe, personality was the chief delight of these children of mother earth. In point of importance, the "afterwards" always yielded precedence to the "now."

The artist in living, of antiquity, got up from the banquet of life with a feeling of satisfied comfort akin to that of the rich man who has finished a sumptuous meal.

The Indian religions are optimistic with a kind of other-worldly, transcendental optimism, since there is perhaps no people on earth with a stronger leaning toward the transcendental than the Indian people. As already said, optimism is based upon this: that all the sorrow of this life of ours is a pure delusion which will disappear in correct apprehension as spectres vanish before the light of day. As behind a dark dream there waits the sunlit day, so behind this life's sorrow there always awaits that great, divine Brahman, all compact of delight.

Thus, in that Christianity declared this life to be sorrow, this world a vale of tears, it placed itself in total opposition to the thought of antiquity. The centre of gravity which heretofore had been placed in this present world was suddenly removed to that other, and thus, in a certain measure, things were turned topsy-turvy. The philosophers of antiquity taught happy living; Christianity taught happy dying. The thought that life was only a preparation for death would have seemed monstrous to the Greeks. As the Greek passion for life was a genuine passion, so the Christian sorrow of life was a real sorrow.

Here the divergence between Christianity and the Indian religions emerges from its wrappings. In the former, as said, the sorrow of life is a genuine sorrow; it is not, as in Indian thought, an illusion. Jehovah has no love for make-believe or surprises. That word of the Upanishads: "The Gods ever love the mysterious," does not apply to him. Life, in Christianity, is guilt; in the Indian religions, ignorance. Here, at their very root, East and West, Indian and Christo-Judaic thought part company. Here also is to be found the explanation of the totally different modes of comprehending sorrow on the one side and on the other.

In Christianity sorrow is a something that is real because it is something that comes from God. It is the rod with which a god chastises his children. He who is to be made better receives the rod. To be made better, however, means to come nearer to God. Consequently, sorrow is the means by which a god draws his children to himself. He shows his interest, his kindness, his love for them by punishing them, laying sorrow upon them, and thus sorrow becomes synonymous with divine favour. An astonished world hears for the first time from the lips of Christianity the unprecedented phrase: "Blessed are the sorrowful."

Quite otherwise is the fashion of presenting sorrow in the system of the Buddha. Sorrow as identical with life is here an ignorance, a lack of knowledge, which must be got rid of. In Buddhism sorrow is always something that must be repulsed, escaped from — a mode of comprehending it which all will agree is a most human and natural one. The system in its entirety owes its origin purely to this intense horror of sorrow, this intense effort to achieve freedom from sorrow. Upon no point did the Buddha lay such complete stress as upon this—that he only came into the world that he might put an end to sorrow. "One thing only, monks, now as always, declare I unto you—sorrow and the uprooting of sorrow." Sorrow, and sorrow alone, is all that the Buddhist recognises in this world of illusion ; of nothing else does he think but the removal of this sorrow. As the eagle upon the unclouded sun, so unfalteringly gazes the Buddhist upon the glowing mass of sorrow that pervades the entire world.

With one full chord, as it were, the Buddha begins his teaching with the Four Holy Truths of Sorrow. The Four Holy Truths of Sorrow are beginning, middle, and end. "As all creatures endowed with feet are found in the track of the elephant, so the Four Holy Truths of Sorrow include all that is good within themselves." And here I would like to say that the whole point of Buddhism is to be found in the particular definition of sorrow that it supplies.

What is sorrow in the Buddha's system? "Birth is sorrow ; old age is sorrow ; sickness is sorrow ; death is sorrow ; woe, misery, pain, grief, and despair are sorrow ; not to receive what one desires is sorrow—in brief, the Five Bases of the Elements of life are sorrow."

From this we see that the sorrow to which the Buddha refers can scarcely be the sorrow of the common acceptation of that word. The sorrow of the Buddha is nothing else but the perception of the transiency of all that has arisen. Sorrow is simply transiency, looked at from a particular point of view.

> Regard, ye wise, how all things go.
> To rise, to fall : that is their woe!

Everywhere, as far as sense or mind can reach, growth and decay prevail ; I perceive a beginning and an ending. Otherwise expressed : thinking is only possible in time; it is therefore impossible for thought to grasp what lies outside of time, the eternal—pure Being. Hence I can say that everywhere, wherever my senses penetrate—there, like some plague, transiency also creeps in. And thus divinity itself is disenthroned and brought to my own level as regards transiency, so long as I do not approach it with faith, but seek instead to seize it with my understanding. So our own corporeality, because *in toto* arisen and *in toto* passing away again, becomes a content of the concept of transiency. Life and transiency become synonymous ideas; whether the life be an earthly or a heavenly one makes no difference whatever; life and transiency are one and the same. To the reflective eye the entire universe resolves itself into a fermenting, changing mass, that ever arises and ever passes away again; in which the only real thing is precisely this eternal process of *Becoming*. This latter has the same reality as is possessed by the whirlpool in the water, the rainbow in the air.

The argument of the Buddha runs in the following oft-repeated track: "What do you think, monks? is the body eternal or transient?"

"Transient, Master."

"And that which is transient, is it painful or joyful?"

"Painful, Master."

"And that which is transient, painful, subject to change, can one really think of it: 'This belongs to me; this am I; this is my self'?"

"That is impossible, Master."

Any other proof that sorrow is one with transiency is nowhere supplied. Without further argument both are set down as being the same. Here we come upon the natural limitations of the system. Unquestionably, it is the peculiarity of a certain particular disposition of thought to be able to accept as self-evident the oneness of transiency and sorrow. This special trait it was to which the Buddha probably alluded when he said to his disciples: "Only a few men are seized by the things that really seize, in comparison with the great number who are not seized by the things that really seize." He only makes a sounding-board for the words of the Buddha who is seized by the idea of transiency as sorrow. For the fundamental proposition of the whole system "life is sorrow" is only demonstrable, is only fruitful, where these two, sorrow and transiency, are understood to be but one.

Now the ultimate ground for the identity of these two lies concealed in the Anattā-idea, in the perception that this *I* is not a true *I*. Since, however, the Anattā-idea again presupposes the inability to believe, to accept upon mere faith, from this side also we stumble upon a something unexplainable, upon a natural feature, or disposition of thought and sensation. If the capacity for belief, for faith, is lacking—that is, the capacity to assume as proved what still remains to be proved: namely, the existence of a soul, an eternal entity—then the body becomes something that has arisen *in toto*, and is therefore *in toto* transient, void of soul—that is, it becomes a not-self, it becomes Anattā. For the true self, the *I*—to be a true *I*—must somewhere within itself conceal an eternal principle, a soul. However, in this transition process of the *I* into the Not-*I*, transiency of necessity becomes somewhat painful.

"Thus, for example, one cherishes the belief: 'This is the world, this is the soul, this will I become after my death, unchangeable, persisting, eternal, untransmutable, always the same, yea, thus will I remain.' He hears from the Perfect One the teaching of truth, which leads to the cessation of all existence. Then it comes thus into his mind: 'Annihilated shall I be; O, to perish! Alas! I shall be nevermore!' He is sad, heart-broken; he laments, groans, beats his breast, and gives way to despair."

Transiency, however, inasmuch as it touches me myself, my noblest part, takes that one of all the countless shapes it can assume, which, so to speak, is the determining and decisive shape. And because in this outstanding form it is painful, this *is* its outstanding form. If, however, the fact, "transiency is one with sorrow," is recognised, with such recognition life also becomes one with sorrow, for both are one with transiency. If, however, life in itself is one with sorrow, then every expression of life also becomes sorrow, and thus all those natural events, birth, old age, death, are transported within the limits of the sorrow-idea. They are verily the hands upon the dial-plate of transiency. Birth, old age, disease, and death—these are the four great evils of the world, from which the Buddha longed to escape when he forsook his father's house and betook himself to the ascetic life. Corporeality and sorrow became identical. "Whoso, disciples, finds joy in the body, finds joy in sorrow; whoso finds joy in sorrow is undelivered from sorrow—so I say."

"The transient, the transient, one says, O Master!

what now, O Master, is this transient?" so a monk one day asks the Buddha.

"The body truly is transient; sensation, perception, the differentiations, consciousness, are transient."

"Sorrow, sorrow, one says, O Master! But what is this sorrow, O Master?"

"The body truly is sorrow; sensation, perception, the differentiations, consciousness, are sorrow."

"The Not-self, the Not-self, so one says, O Master! But what now, O Master, is this Not-self?"

"The body truly is the Not-self; sensation, perception, the differentiations, consciousness, are Not-self."

Transiency, sorrow, Not-self, corporeality, are synonymous ideas, but not in such a way that one can be substituted for the other, but after such a fashion that with any one of these the three remaining are given. A man may feel the sorrow of life, but he does not perceive its transiency, does not perceive Not-self, and so has nothing but the pain; his sorrow does not bear fruit. On the other hand, he may understand the transiency, the not-selfness of the body, but this understanding does not "grip" him; calls forth no reaction in him, does not go forth from him again as sorrow, and so nothing is effected. For only where transiency is felt to be sorrow, does the necessity arise of finding deliverance from transiency. The teaching of the Buddha, however, is nothing else but the guiding path to this deliverance. When corporeality exhibits itself as a blending together of transiency, sorrow, and not-*I*—only then do we get Buddhism. Transiency and not-*I* must be felt to be sorrow; sorrow must be understood to be transiency and not-*I*. The expression, "to feel transiency," and the expression, "to understand sorrow," are synonymous; both alike comprehend the whole. "To understand sorrow" means to assign to it its place between transiency and not-*I*, and that means to understand everything.

Sorrow merely felt is quite useless in the system of the Buddha; at the most, it can only pave the way to the understanding of sorrow. However, sorrow felt is not the necessary preliminary to sorrow understood. One may come to a perfect understanding of sorrow—that is, to deliverance, without ever having experienced sorrow. The sage Nagasena says of himself: "I was taken into the Order as a mere boy, without knowing anything of the highest goal. But I thought, 'These disciples of Buddha are wise; they will teach me.' And they did teach me. And now I both know and understand the basis as well as the reward of renunciation." This is the outstanding characteristic of sorrow in Buddhism: that it does not depend upon sensation but upon understanding. It is not the vulgar but the philosophical conception with which we have to do, and it is only this particular transposition, as it were, which makes it possible for us to fill up our field of mental vision to its full extent with the conception of sorrow. Only where transiency is looked upon as sorrow can life become *in toto* sorrow—can sorrow be understood, recognised. Only thus is it possible, wherever life is not recognised as sorrow, to lay the blame upon a lack of true perception, upon an ignorance. Only thus is it possible to set forth the law of the Buddha as being valid for all beings endowed with *I*-consciousness. All who do not recognise this, who do not recognise life to be sorrow, do so, not because life in reality is not sorrow, but only because their ignorance prevents them from perceiving the true nature of life.

Then the sorrow of the Buddhist is a real sorrow just like that of the Christian?

Not at all! Sorrow is real only so long as life is real—that is, so long as this corporeality is looked upon as a true, soul-endowed *I*. The reality of sorrow falls along with the reality of the *I*. When the *I* is perceived to be illusion, the sorrow also is perceived to be illusion. Like the idea, "here is an *I*," sorrow also is nothing but the result of an ignorance.

Here we seem to get the wonderful double fact that not to recognise life as sorrow is the consequence of an ignorance, and that sorrow itself is the consequence of an ignorance. To open any one's eyes to the perception of life as sorrow would henceforth appear to be merely leading them out of one ignorance into another!

In reality the case lies quite otherwise. Sorrow as the consequence of an ignorance means nothing else but this, that sorrow is salvation in disguise; salvation is nothing else but sorrow looked at from a certain standpoint. Thus, to show any one the sorrow of life, means to offer him salvation; to teach him to understand the sorrow of life, means to give him salvation. To perceive life as sorrow — to understand that life not merely *has* sorrow but *is* sorrow—means to comprehend both as illusions.

If sorrow is the consequence of an illusion, of an

ignorance, it must be removable with the removing of this ignorance, with its transmutation into knowledge. If, however, sorrow is not the product of the *I* (sorrow felt), but itself *is* the *I* (sorrow understood), then the removing of sorrow must be synonymous with the removing of this corporeality, this *I*. This *I*, however, can only be removed if it is no true *I* with an eternal at its core, but instead, an apparent *I* void of any eternal core. The knowledge of *I* as Not-*I*, the Anattā-idea, is therefore the great, the only knowledge,—the knowledge *par excellence*, the Buddha knowledge, because at one stroke abolishing both sorrow and life.

Freedom from pain, because the most desired, is here put at a high price; nothing less than my own *I* is the purchase money in this transaction.

There still remains one, I had almost said, more, human set of considerations, which likewise explains the oneness of mutability and sorrow. Wheresoever the six senses are in activity, there is arising and passing away. But it is not the worlds only that arise and pass away; what does it matter about the worlds if only it is well with me! There is a consideration of more weight than that: wishes arise, will awakens; the senses cling to the perceived, as warmth to a sunny place after the light has gone. In the depths of our hearts we all feel that bliss finally depends upon rest, upon changelessness; hence the senses wish to rest upon objects. That, however, is impossible; the union of the senses with objects is nothing but a perpetual change. The tendency of the senses to attachment is the longing after rest in the midst of restlessness, the latter being found unsatisfying and full of pain. The activity of the senses is nothing but a being born, and a being buried again of the desires—a painful process so long as there is the feeling of gratification in things, so long as the cessation of the union of sense and the object of sense is a parting, a tearing asunder. "Gratification is the root of sorrow," it is said, and again, "Will, pleasure, affirmation, gratification in these Five Bases of the Elements of Life; this is the arising of sorrow."

The same idea is presented under a different guise in another place. In the Milindapañha, the above-mentioned book of the questions put by the Greek king Milinda (Menander) to the sage Nāgasena, it is said: "The contact of the organs of sense with objects is the same as if two rams fought with one another; the eye may be compared to one ram, the form seen, to the other." As in every combat the passions flame up as flame bursts forth when flint and steel are struck together, so is it with the fire of lust, hatred, and error, when the senses come into contact with objects.

We thus have two explanations of the oneness of sorrow and transiency: one philosophical, according to which the law of not-*I* furnishes the necessary vehicle, and the other purely human, in which the will plays the part of effective medium. Wheresoever there is will, there is pain, there is sorrow. These two are as indivisible as light and heat in a flame. Alongside ignorance we have also a second birth-moment of sorrow—the will, and hence a second way to the removing of sorrow: the abolition of will—non-willing. Where there is no willing, there is no desire, no gratification, no attachment to objects. Where there is no attachment, there is no parting, no passing away, no sorrow. Will, however, can only be dissolved in knowledge, and ignorance thus becomes the source of sorrow felt, as well as of sorrow understood. With knowledge, the one as well as the other falls to the ground. It would be quite useless to reject this cognition which the Buddha wishes us to learn from him, and which is founded upon the transformation of the entire world into something transient, and therefore painful, under the pretext: "It is only with this cognition that sorrow arises. Where there is no cognition of transiency, there can be no sorrow either." Sorrow is here present because it adheres to willing. One who so resists only bars his own way to deliverance. He bears the burden of sorrow but does not receive the reward; for sorrow only felt is of no avail. Only sorrow comprehended can complete the process of its transformation into deliverance. As the beam of light, after it has been passed through certain media, takes on certain specific qualities, so sorrow only acquires the capacity of being transformed into deliverance when it has passed from sorrow felt into sorrow comprehended—that is, after it has become synonymous with transiency.

The question now is, would there be such a thing as transiency in nature, apart from the human race? Would nature, the universe, be full of sorrow, even if there were no human beings in existence? Not at all! Transiency, mutability, of themselves would not make sorrow—even as rest, changelessness, would not make blessedness—if there were present no spectator, no perceiver of mutability. The surface of the sea and the sunbeam unite with one another and part again without desire and without sorrow. It is only the *I* that makes sorrow. Only so far as perception extends, are sorrow and mutability synonymous terms. It is the specific function of all and every individuality to transform mutability into sorrow, as the ferment-fungus transforms the juice of the grape into alcohol. The individual does not manufacture sorrow out of this or that trait of character, as we might be inclined to imagine from the point of view of our ignorance, but it is itself a form of sorrow, and every actualisation of corporeality is sorrow actualising itself.

If sorrow and mutability were not only synonymous but identical, sorrow and mutability alike would exist, even if there were no perceiver present; sorrow would become a something existing of itself; —a sort of cosmic power, opposed to which there would of necessity exist a corresponding idea of blessedness. Sorrow by itself does not exist. Being transiency as reflected in the individual, it is and it is not; as the image reflected in a mirror at one and the same time is and is not; as this corporeality at the self-same moment is and again is not.

Sorrow, like everything else, is a relative conception, which comes into being with me and with me expires; it is conditioned by me, and depends upon me, as this world, as all perceived, depends upon me. As the world depends upon me and yet I myself *am* the "world," so sorrow depends upon me and I myself *am* sorrow. The idea, "all life is sorrow," is only thus far something specific among the crowd of perceptions, because it is precisely that one of the ideas of mutability transformed in the organism of the individuality which leads to deliverance—which *is* deliverance.

To perceive that the world depends upon me as I upon the world; that god depends upon me as I upon god—this the Vedantist also perceives, and yet falls into the snare of an eternal blessedness; this by no means produces deliverance. To apprehend, however, in all its completeness the idea of mutability, as the eye apprehends the entire world, to let it penetrate me through and through, like some beam of light, and in its passage to transmute it entirely into sorrow, put the stamp of sorrow upon it as the shapeless ingots of gold are stamped into pieces of current coin in the mint—this constitutes deliverance. For if deliverance is to be obtained, it must be sought after. But it will not be sought for in earnestness until all and everything, without exception, is perceived to be sorrow—something from which deliverance of necessity must be sought. However cruel may appear this transformation into sorrow, it is necessary and for the good of every individual, since sorrow felt, which is founded upon willing, is comprehended in sorrow known, which is founded upon ignorance. Sorrow known and comprehended covers sorrow felt and experienced, as the world of daylight covers and contains the world of night. Sorrow felt is only removable by its transmutation into sorrow understood. As the transformation of the night-world into the day-world can only take place by reason of the sun, so the transformation of one kind of sorrow into the other can only take place through correct knowledge and comprehension. And as at the rising of the sun everything becomes light as far as the eye can reach, so with the dawning of true knowledge all becomes sorrow as far as thought extends. And as no one can say: "Here let it be day, and there, night!" so none can say: "Here in this heaven, beside this God, transiency and sorrow shall not intrude!" The transformation is only fruitful when it is complete. Upon the completeness of this transformation of mutability into sorrow depends the transformation of sorrow into salvation. Sorrow, as being transiency understood, takes its place at the head of the system because proceeding from it as from the proper end of a knot, everything easily and of itself, as it were, becomes untied.

Buddhism is the religion of sorrow only as sorrow is understood to be synonymous with the understanding of sorrow. "All life is sorrow" is not the crowning summit of an experience, but the topmost peak of a clear, dispassionate, mental penetration and comprehension. In this sense also is our introductory quotation to be understood. The Sorrow preached by the Buddha has nothing whatever in common with pessimism and gloom. Nor need we take offence at such passages as these: "And perfection,—has he who rejoices in life or he who sorrows, obtained it? And the correct answer would be: 'He who sorrows over life, not he who rejoices.'" In another passage it is said of the Buddha: "From the race of those that made merry with life, O wonderful! from those that rejoiced in life, that lusted after living, he has cut off life and the root of life." Again, in another place, the Buddha says to his monks: "Go, monks, consider the misery of the body, think of the disgustingness of food; reflect on the absence of joy in the whole world; ponder the fleeting nature of all appearances." Joylessness here is nought else but the purchase-money that must be paid for sorrowlessness.

But it is not joy of itself that is impeached, but only joy in so far as it is an expression of will. Joy that is innocent and free from will is quite permissible, and the proof of this is that serene enjoyment of natural beauty which we so often meet with in Buddhist literature.

The peace-bestowing shadows of the woods, the wide, lovely forest that the Buddha praised; the cool, clear lotus-pond; the play of the waves; the majesty of the sun, the charm of the moonlight—all these might fill the hearts of the disciples with sweet delight, with cheerful repose. "Enchanting, O Brother, is this Gosiṅga Wood; splendid the clear moonlight; the trees stand in all their bloom; heavenly odours, as it were, are wafted around," says one monk to another in one of the Suttas.

It is expressly said: "All the ascetics and Brahmins who, hating, and embittered in mind, seek out retired places in the wood, just because they are hating, and embittered in mind, will experience guilty fear and terror." Bitterness and pessimism are inconsistent with the thought of the Buddha, and it is expressly laid down that correct comprehension, in order that it may bring forth its proper fruit in the deliverance of the mind, must possess the characteristic of tranquillity, the characteristic of cheerfulness. Not without reason could the Buddha vaunt of himself: "Of such as live happily in the world, I also am one." With good right also, it is said in the Dhammapada: "We who call nothing our own, saturated with happiness, we beam like the radiant gods."

The Buddha presents us with the sorrow-idea only as being a mask of the transiency-idea; something to ponder over and penetrate, not something over which to bewail and go distracted. He gives us mutability in sorrow as one might give gold in a purse. And as one man might say to another, "I give thee here a thousand gold pieces," at the same time reaching him a purse, so the Buddha says: "Here I give you sorrow," and so saying, gives us the transiency-idea. That in doing this he gives us something better than gold—yea, better than the costliest treasure,—this is so because, as by a magic stroke, sorrow at its culminating point suddenly passes over into salvation; through understanding and comprehension, *becomes* salvation, neither road nor footway from one to the other remaining. "Knowing this, ye monks, the pious, the comprehending disciple is sick and tired of the body, and feeling weariness and disgust at all existence, by his righteous way of life he delivers himself. 'In delivering lies deliverance,' this perception arises. 'Abolished is birth; completed the ascetic life; done what was to do; this world is no more': this he knows." Yea, this he knows, and knowing this is what is meant by knowing sorrow.

V

NIBBĀNA[1]

In its conception of Nibbāna, more than anywhere else, we are constrained into wonder at the iron, logical consistency of this system; its unyielding stand upon the basis of sorrow and transiency. In Brahmanism the highest knowledge is the knowledge of the identity of myself with deity—with the highest Brahman. This consciousness, as being the product of supreme comprehension, was at the same time supreme bliss. It was the natural conclusion of the system; a conclusion which, spite of all its grandiosity, still referred to faith the weightiest and most ultimate questions of all. Moreover, this consciousness of identity, making me as god, could not be attained to by morality, could not be seized by meditation; both indeed must be practised to the fullest extent, but the fruit of it all is obtained only by a sort of act of grace. The highest Atman must himself give himself to the fortunate devotee. "Where, friends, is then that great Brahma?" a Bhikkhu asks, and receives this answer: "We, O monk, do not know where Brahma is or how one gets to Brahma, or which is the way

[1] Skt. Nirvāṇa. Literally: "Freedom from desire"; or "The Ceasing"; or "The Becoming Extinguished."

to Brahma. If, however, O monk, the signs of Brahma's nearness are visible, if it becomes light, if beaming brightness appears, then will Brahma appear. These, namely, are the specific tokens of Brahma's becoming visible, that it becomes light, that beaming brightness appears."

At Gautama's time the speculation of the Upanishads had not yet opened out into full bloom, but the beginnings of this noble system certainly were sending forth their first young shoots. And it is with astonishment that we see the Buddha venture to pass over this highest idea of bliss founded upon knowledge, and aim at a new and hitherto unheard-of goal.

So long as the basis of sorrow is not abandoned, logically, the highest knowledge for the Buddhist is nothing but the keenest, most penetrating recognition of this sorrow, and the highest bliss nothing else but freedom from this sorrow. Hence this highest bliss becomes something that can be reached without the intervention of any act of grace; it becomes something that can be taught.

Moreover, in spite of its completest renunciation, there always remained in Brahmanism the longing for this union with Brahman. For him the Muni longed "as the pilgrim longs for home" and "as the tired eagle for its nest." The highest, however, to which Buddhist thought could soar was given in the idea of absolute freedom from every sort of desire. For desire, even where directed towards the highest, worked sorrow. But the highest good of the Buddhist is sorrowlessness; consequently, the Vedanta's conception of bliss must fall to the ground. There was no place for it in the system.

To the Buddha, unification with the highest Brahman only meant "to change the locality of sorrow"; it meant nothing but life under special modifications. In the popular speech, it was frankly said: "Ah, that shines as if beside the two-and-thirty gods"; the Buddha, however, turned but a cold eye upon this sheen. "And should I also," he says to Sāriputta, "only circle among the pure gods, I might not again return to this world." Hence he took one last stride over and away from this Brahministic ideal and posited as the highest goal, the getting loose, not only from everything sensuous, but also, giant-like, from everything supersensuous. And doing so he required of men the greatest that has ever been required of them: the renunciation not only of earthly joys but also of the joys of heaven. Only when a man succeeds in detecting for himself the taint of sorrow and transiency in the joys of the beyond, and, renouncing, turns away from them, only then does he catch a glimpse of Nibbāna.

Nibbāna means nothing but a condition of perfect freedom from desire. That heart has reached the final goal of all which, upon the ground of a perception of the true nature of things, through the knowledge of Not-*I*, has so completely loosed itself from everything that it no longer has any desires. Where there is no desire in the heart, there is no attachment either. Where there is no attachment, there is also no parting, no sorrow. Where there is no sorrow, there is also no transiency, no change. And thus with Nibbāna the true condition of eternal rest and changeless, birthless safety is eternally attained. "Nibbāna, Nibbāna, so they say, friend

Sāriputta, but what, friend, is this Nibbāna?" "The destruction of greed, the destruction of hate, the destruction of illusion;—this, O friend, is what is called Nibbāna."

Because the Buddha sets out from the fact of sorrow in the shape of greed, hate, and illusion, and so proceeds with the course of his thought, his system naturally eventuates in freedom from sorrow, the negation of all these three. Non-sorrow is the conclusion, is the highest. By this transformation of sorrow into freedom from sorrow, nothing of the old is destroyed, nothing new is built up. All of the old remains, only it is looked at from another and from a fresh point of view.

The transition in our understanding from an erroneous view to a correct one has been carried out, completed, and with that transition, even as transiency is transmuted into sorrow, so sorrow is transmuted into sorrowlessness. Our whole being seems to bear the likeness of a sum in arithmetic, which, incorrectly stated at the very outset, with a plus sign instead of a minus, is hence quite insoluble, and yet is worked out *ad infinitum* with the greatest industry, the resultant error being the whole vast universe. The Tathāgata, however, like an able arithmetical master, puts his finger immediately upon the initial blunder and says: "O man, in this problem of life, put a minus here instead of this plus, put non-willing in the place of willing, and everything will be smoothly solved to the last fraction. This monstrous product of thy first mistake, this universe with its god and *I*, disappears with the correction of the signs as in a sum in arithmetic." The problem of life, which, with the great "to will" becomes infinite, is completely solved with the great "not to will."

Nibbāna is simply sorrow destroyed. This destruction, however, is not a real destruction; it is nothing but sorrow looked at from another point of view; it is nothing but the destruction of an illusion that has its basis in me, and has arisen simultaneously with my arising.

In our inmost depths this tremendous revulsion is effected, as it were, in a twinkling of our mind's eye. All indeed lies in us; the entire world, with its arising and its passing away. Hence every man makes his own Nibbāna. As the beginning of the world is individual, so also is its ending. Nibbāna is a purely relative idea. Where hitherto sorrow had been perceived, it is now no longer perceived. Herein precisely lies the stroke of genius in this system, that everything remains relative, that all depends upon my individuality. Sorrow and Nibbāna are nothing else but forms of my apprehension projected into the distance. As a man throwing light-images upon a far, far distant wall, by a slight turning round of his apparatus can throw his picture into empty space,—that is, can make it disappear; so the perceiver who in ignorance has caused the production of the picture of this world—that is, of sorrow—by turning to knowledge, can cause to disappear the picture of this world—the picture of sorrow. "The world, sorrow, is present," and "The world, sorrow, is no longer present," is only the *volte-face* of our inward being projected upon the universe.

Once more: Nibbāna is a relative conception, and implies nothing more than that where hitherto sorrow has been felt and cognised, it is now no longer cognised. The idea of a state of blessedness, of real blessedness, is a perverted one, because issuing in the absolute. The imaging of a *place* of blessedness is a still greater perversion, for, as already said, Nibbāna is individual. As every man through ignorance creates his own world, his own sorrow, so also every man brings to pass through knowledge his own world-cessation, his own ending of sorrow, his own Nibbāna.

Nibbāna implies nothing else but the clear, pure condition of freedom from sorrow, based upon freedom from desire, this in turn being founded upon the highest apprehension of the being of things, the cognition of Not-*I*. As the lamp goes out that is no longer supplied with oil, so that embodied being expires which no longer from any quarter receives food. In this sense, Nagasena says to King Milinda: "Cessation is Nibbāna." It is a condition which by itself is quite unexplainable, quite undefinable. As darkness can only be explained by light, as the opposite of light; as rest can only be explained by motion, as the opposite of motion; so also Nibbāna can only be explained by sorrow, as the opposite of sorrow. As darkness prevails wherever there is no light, as rest prevails wherever there is no motion, so also Nibbāna is everywhere present where sorrow and change do not prevail.

Nibbāna is the only thing which does not arise as the effect of a cause, and which as cause again does not give rise to any effect. It stands above, or rather outside the law of cause and effect, not, however, as an absolute, as god, but only as exhibiting the end of all relations. Since it has not arisen, it is also not subject to transiency. It is the only thing which does not consist of a continual becoming, which is not conceived of as made up of separate component parts; which is not Saṅkhārā;[1] it is therefore the only thing that is unchangeable and eternal; free from all admixture of pain. "Of Nibbāna," says the venerable Nagasena, "we cannot say that it has arisen or that it has not arisen, or that it can arise; that it is past, or future, or present."

"Is there a place for Nibbāna?" the King Milinda asks.

"A place for Nibbāna there is not, O King, and yet Nibbāna exists, exactly as fire exists and yet there is no place where it is stored up. If, however, one rubs two pieces of wood together it makes its appearance."

"Is there no standing place from which one may reach out to Nibbāna?"

"Yes, O King, there is such a place. It is virtue."

As every one who wishes to obtain a good view of the distance must climb to the top of the mountain, so the Bhikkhu who wishes to catch

[1] Saṅkhārā (saṁskāra) means something that weaves together as well as something that is woven together. It is one of the twelve Nidānas as well as one of the five Khandhas. Its translation into "differentiations" corresponds to the most usual division of the world into subject and object, the "differentiator" and the "differentiated," *par excellence*. Practically, it means the world in its entirety, as being that which is "woven together" by the interaction of object and subject. Only where there is a putting together can there be differentiation. In this sense it becomes synonymous with Anattā. Everything is Anattā, everything is Saṅkhārā, except Nibbāna. In this sense it is likewise synonymous with Saṁsāra, the world of birth and death.

a glimpse of Nibbāna must climb, and toil, and struggle to the topmost peak of virtue.

"Warriors, warriors, Master, we call ourselves; in what way then are we warriors?" a monk asks of the Buddha.

"We make war, O Bhikkhu! therefore do we call ourselves warriors."

"For what do we wage war, Master?"

"For perfect virtue, for lofty endeavour, for sublime wisdom. Therefore, O Bhikkhu, do we call ourselves warriors."

Now this struggle and striving requires correct explanation. Nibbāna itself, because complete negation, cannot be obtained by striving. It is, so to say, nothing but the inevitable consequence of striving. If one reproaches the monks in Ceylon thus: "You say that all striving, all desire, is a hindrance on the way to Nibbāna; the striving for Nibbāna itself must then be such a hindrance, and the more one strives, the farther it flees from him," they only laugh at the over-wise European. Desire can really only exist where there is something to which to be attached. In Nibbāna, however, as being that which is utterly beyond all perception and cognition, there is nothing to which to be attached. "Where there is no anything; where there is no clinging; the island; the unique;—that I call Nibbāna, the end of old age and death."

Hence there can be no striving after Nibbāna. There is only a striving for the abolition of sorrow. Upon this latter, Nibbāna follows as naturally and inevitably as darkness follows when the light is extinguished. "A pure heart, free from the hindrances and from desire,—this beholds Nibbāna." And in another place: "And how is Nibbāna to be known? By its freedom from want and misery; by its peace, its quietude, its purity."

This is "Nibbāna in this life."

This expression also, like the "striving after Nibbāna," stands in need of a little explanation. Nibbāna cannot be handled, it can only be looked upon. We can no more lay hold of Nibbāna than light can lay hold of darkness. I can only seize my individuality, my *I*, in so far as it is Not-*I*; I can only lay hold of illusion. Just because there is no *I*-self present, on that very account I can seize my individuality *in toto*, and therefore deny it *in toto*. This perfect negation of individuality, this complete letting go of the illusion of life, this is the giving up of sorrow, for individuality is sorrow. What, however, follows upon the abolition of individuality,—of this no Buddha can say anything, of this no Buddha *need* say anything, for his task is completed with the removal of individuality—that is, of sorrow. It is only possible to lay hold with the forces that reside in this individuality. Nibbāna, however, is only there where individuality no longer exists. Hence also, "to look upon Nibbāna" is not mental vision, in our sense of the word;—that, for the Buddha, would only be sensuous vision, and would drag Nibbāna in its entirety into transiency, to take a place there alongside of God. "To look upon Nibbāna," like Nibbāna itself, is founded upon negation. "To look upon Nibbāna" is nothing else but "not-to-look-upon Sorrow," as I see darkness simply by not-seeing!

Only by the results which this freedom from sorrow calls forth, can I make clear to myself that

"I have Nibbāna," as a man does not see his eyes and yet knows "I have eyes," because he recognises the results of such possession. So Nibbāna is not to be touched, and yet there is Nibbāna in this life, and in four stages, the four Dhyanas (Pāli: Jhāna, meditation); ever and again, mounting upwards, I can assure myself of the fact. For, from the last and highest of these Jhānas, I get a full outlook upon Nibbāna.

Many are inclined to call the Jhānas—"the already-in-this-life-beatifying"—mystic visions. And to judge by the frequency with which they are alluded to in the Sutta Pitaka, it would seem as if no religion attached as much value to the states of ecstasy as does Buddhism. Nothing, however, is farther from the truth than this view. Everything proceeds in proper order, strictly according to regulation. The Jhānas are nothing but an important, ever and again renewed self-examination on the part of each adherent of the system; a skilful recalling of that sweetest of all cognitions: "In delivering lies deliverance." They are "the blessedly serene practice of good, which the monk has to practise day and night."

As the freed galley-slave ever and again feels his ankles to convince himself that there are really no chains there, so the delivered from the bondage of life ever and again tries himself: "Have I comprehended? Am I free?" And as the erstwhile galley-slave with ever fresh delight demonstrates the freedom of his limbs, so he who was formerly the thrall of lust, hate, and error demonstrates with rapture ever renewed: "I have comprehended. I am free."

In the Suttas we continually find the Buddha, often almost without any preliminaries, passing on to these Jhānas. As the loaded ship, gliding into deep water, suddenly shows no further sign of weight, so the Buddha's speech, suddenly lightened of its burden of offering proofs, glides into the smooth track of Jhāna description. With slight modifications, the following schema is repeated over and over again.

"He has now got rid of the five fetters; he has learnt to recognise the dross of passion, the crippling;—dead to desires, escaped from evil, he lives in thoughtful recollectedness, in the peace-born sacred serenity of the First Trance.

"And further. After the consummation of thoughtfulness and recollectedness, the monk attains inward stillness, unity of mind, free from sensation and thought, in the blessed serenity, born of self-absorption,—the consecration of the Second Trance.

"And further. In peace serene dwells the monk, even-minded, full of insight, with consciousness clear; and experiences that happiness in the body of which the saintly say: 'He of even-minded insight lives happily.' And so he wins to the Third Trance."

As, however, the ship from the waves of the open sea glides into the quiet haven, so the mind from the third trance that is still disturbed by desire, passes into the perfectly unperturbed peace of the highest, last trance of all.

"And further. After the rejection of joy and sorrow; after the annihilation of personal pleasures and pains, the monk reaches the consecration of the sorrowless, joyless, even-minded, charged with insight, perfectly pure, Fourth Trance."

Here now he apprehends the highest that can be apprehended. He apprehends: "This is sorrow. This is the arising of sorrow. This is the annihilation of sorrow. This is the path that leads to the annihilation of sorrow." And this is called perceiving Nibbāna.

Inasmuch as my willing becomes known to me and is felt as sorrow, so my non-willing becomes known to me and is felt as peace, quietness, purity. To know Nibbāna, my Non-willing must become known to me, and for that to be possible I must be in a body. Hence this body is not only the chalice and the wine of sorrow, but also the chalice and the wine of blessedness. Only out of this cup can I taste blessedness, perceive Nibbāna, as I can only look out upon freedom from the confines of a prison.

Does non-willing, then, of necessity lead to Nibbāna?

Non-willing, abolished willing, as necessarily leads to Nibbāna as a balloon, when freed of its retaining bonds, inevitably mounts upwards. As a balloon freed of its bonds can go no other way but upwards, so the mind, freed from the fetters of egoism, can go no other way but to Nibbāna. Here is no *cul de sac*, no false path. In the last analysis, salvation is really nothing else but sorrow seen from another point of view. To him who knows, they coalesce and become as one in not-*I*. Not-*I* is sorrow. Not-*I* is salvation. Nothing verily is necessary but the removal of an illusion, just as nothing but correct information is needed for the morning and evening star to be identified as one and the same. No transition is necessary from non-willing to Nibbāna; these are merely different expressions for the same identical thing. Nibbāna is present so soon as our willing functions upon the basis of "Knowing," of "Not-*I*"—that is, so soon as there is no more possibility of our will setting itself in motion, so soon as it has become will abrogated—non-willing. Here nothing, absolutely nothing, is required as preceding condition but that our cognition, instead of taking the form of ignorance, should, through instruction and reflection, take the form of knowledge. With this, willing of necessity becomes non-willing. What, however, seen through the burning glass of willing, was sorrow, seen through the medium of "non-willing" is freedom from sorrow. And this is all that can be said of Nibbāna,—that it is freedom from sorrow.

As our corporeality is in a state of continual struggle with the law of gravitation, so in the moral realm also there obtains a similar law of gravitation, to which our egoism as will—as the craving for life—stands in perpetual contradiction. And as, wherever there is continual strife, there can be no peace, and where there is no peace, misery and sorrow prevail, so in the last analysis, this *I*-consciousness that is founded upon my ignorance, this egoism that separates me from the universe, is the one source of all sorrow.

Whoso apprehends: "This body is not my I," has discovered the source of endless peace. Whoso has annihilated every motion of *I*-ness; whoever has made an end of every delusion of desire, every delusion of existence, for whom the *I*, as it were, has been reduced to vapour, and is only present in order to make his non-willing clear to him—to re-echo, as it were, the rapture of non-willing;—he has "done all that was to do," he sees Nibbāna. With the fall of *I*-consciousness falls also the will to live, and with this latter every differentiation, and hence every cause for sorrow.

"And how, ye monks, does a monk become an Holy One?"

"The dark night of *I*-ness, ye monks, is renounced by the monk; is cut off at the root; is made like a palm-tree stump, so that it can never more sprout again, can never more unfold itself."

> Bliss of all bliss, joy of all joy it is,
> To leave behind the lie that says: "I am."

No more henceforth do I cross the sea of life like some swimmer that wrestles with the waves in mortal agony; but, like the sea-gull, I let myself be rocked up and down on the waves in the huge swing of the law of cause and effect, without fear, unresisting, unafraid. This is the longed-for, supreme state of absolute equanimity; the elevation over all sorrow and joy, of earth or of heaven; above youth and old age, health and sickness, life and death. This is the perfect vision of Nibbāna in this life. Such an one desires neither being nor non-being. Such an one has made his own that patience "as of the round earth" of which the Buddha speaks. Such an one has gained the highest reward of asceticism. But that unshakable deliverance of the mind, monks, is verily the goal, the kernel, the end of all."

To one who once has scented the odour of Nibbāna, naught any more tastes good in earth or heaven. He clings to nothing; nothing clings to him. In peace profound and blest, he goes his way, like the clouds through the blue of heaven. He lives in one single thought: "I am free; I am utterly delivered from this delusion of desire, from this delusion of existence. For me the round of re-birth is wholly at an end." For so the Blessed One taught: "For those who are delivered by perfect wisdom—for these there is change no more for ever."

And when for such an one the moment comes that this "Saṅkhārā group," these five Khandhas, which, unified by the action of Kamma, produced the appearance of an *I*, obedient to the law of nature, dissolve, and that supervenes which we are accustomed to call death, then nothing is left behind which can serve as root or seed to any kind of fresh arising. Such an one is extinguished like a flame when the last drop of oil in the wick is burnt up. He disappears like the cloud after it has bestowed all its moisture upon the earth beneath. From the day when he attained to understanding, he has looked upon life as the grown-up person looks upon a puppet-show; and not only upon the life round about him, but most of all upon life as it exhibits itself in this his corporeality, which formerly he had erroneously regarded as a separate, real *I*. Through understanding, this his seeming *I* has been dissolved and done away both in spectacle and in spectator. Thus, with double meaning the converted Vītasoka said: "For him who has set his heart free from everything, this human world resembles a perpetual festival." As at a conjuring entertainment, or a snake-charming performance in the open street, the onlookers, drawn by the attraction of the performance, group themselves together into one compact body of spectators, so by the power of Kamma have these Khandhas grouped themselves together into the illusion of a body. This he apprehends. And as in such an audience, here some arrive and there some depart, and yet the group as a whole remains unchanged, so this his seeming *I* is also in a state of perpetual ebb and flow, come and go. This he apprehends. And again, as after the conclusion of the performance the spectators disperse, and the conjuror himself takes up his basket and goes away and nothing remains, so also the body of such an one as has apprehended melts away—that is, he goes to Parinibbāna. This he knows.

Parinibbāna is only Nibbāna free of this corporeality; Nibbāna, from which this body has been dried up, withered away; sorrowlessness without an organ by which to become aware of itself—that is, the transition of sorrowlessness into timelessness, changelessness, perfect peace. As the world always arises wherever transiency becomes sorrow, so the world always passes away wherever sorrow turns to sorrowlessness. As sorrow is simply the concept of transiency as coloured by the individual, so sorrowlessness is nothing but the concept of timelessness while still coloured by the last dregs of this individuality. Nibbāna is the timeless, so long as it finds its echo in the individual. Parinibbāna is the timeless—pure, uncoloured, unbesmirched of individuality. But it must be carefully noted that it stands to arising and passing away—to *Becoming*—not as *Being*, as Brahman, as

God, but solely as "No-more-becoming." This system does nothing but abolish, negate. It sets up no new gods in the places of those destroyed.

Whether "Not-becoming" resembles "Being" or whether it does not resemble it, who can know? who needs to know? It is only *Becoming* that can be seized; it is only *Becoming* that is life; it is only *Becoming* that is sorrow. Hence the problem is solved with the transformation of *Becoming* into *No-more-becoming*. To speak of this Parinibbāna is a contradiction in terms, for to speak of anything means to call it into life, to make it a *Becoming*, and to think of anything implies the same thing.

How then do I arrive at all at the conception of Parinibbāna?

By proceeding from the conception of Nibbāna; by the indirect way of Nibbāna. As I can only make clear to myself the idea of "remainderlessness" under the figure of an example in arithmetic, so only upon the basis of this corporeality can I arrive at the idea of Parinibbāna. Nibbāna in this life is remainderlessness blent with corporeality; it is the sum which, in being worked out, is steadily hastening towards solution. Similarly, Nibbāna after this life, Parinibbāna, is the completion of the solution—remainderlessness free from any corporeal basis. As, however, an arithmetician already sees beforehand that the sum will be solved, with no remainder over, so the man who already in this life comprehends, knows that there is Nibbāna. But since he is equally sure that sooner or later the form will perish, he also knows, already in this life, that Parinibbāna will follow upon Nibbāna. Hence the chief function of this seeming *I*, this embodied transiency, is to demonstrate timelessness to us.

"There is, disciples," says the Buddha, "a condition where there is neither earth nor water, neither air nor light, neither limitless space nor limitless time, nor any kind of being, neither ideation nor non-ideation, neither this world nor that world. There is neither arising, nor passing away, nor dying; neither cause nor effect; neither change nor standing still." This is Parinibbāna. It is here with the man of knowledge even as with some traveller in a deep ravine, who thinks he hears the tree-tops rustling over his head but cannot see them. Even to the man of knowledge it has never been raised—the curtain that conceals the "other side." By no stress of thinking can it be reached, for it lies beyond all thought. By no comparison is it to be come at, because it is beyond all comparing. Here no juggler gives his performance. Why indeed should he? There are none present to behold!

VI

GOD

GODS there are in hosts in the system of the Buddha, but the concept of God is absent. Buddhism is the only completely atheistical system in the world. Those systems which expressly deny deity, yet stand related to the god-idea, and are subject to it, in so far as they arm themselves against it, range themselves in opposition to this god-idea. The denier of God recognises the existence of a God by his very denial of it. Buddhism, however, stands so very far removed from the idea of God that it is simply beyond any necessity of denying it. As the eagle wheels its flight high in the heavens, unhindered of any, so the Buddha takes his powerful flights of thought, soaring high above all heavens whatsoever. In every other religion, by the word "god" is understood the residue that is not resolved in the arithmetic of infinitude. Because in Buddhism—as the only religion which sets out with the present, and the fact of sorrow—the sum is solved with no remainder over, there is no necessity of introducing any god-factor into the equation.

The Buddha never denied the existence of a deity; such denial did not come within the scope of his system, inasmuch as it had nothing to do with deliverance. No system in the world holds so strenuously to the *quod erat demonstrandum* as does that of the Buddha. Alone among all the founders of world-religions, the Buddha only speaks of things which he can prove. The non-existence of a god is not demonstrable because the beginning of the world is unknowable. Hence the Buddha contents himself with maintaining that in everything of a deific nature, so far as it is accessible to any kind of human thought, life, the affirmation of life, transiency, lie concealed, and that hence it must be abandoned by him who would obtain true deliverance. The Buddha expressly teaches: "If a monk clings to this world, his heart is yet in bonds. If a monk clings to that world, his heart is yet in bonds." Yet concerning that which lies beyond our powers of comprehension, no one in the world, neither sage, nor ascetic, nor Buddha, can tell anything. Why then puzzle and ponder, and advance useless hypotheses about something that has nothing to do with deliverance? It is only a waste of valuable time—diverting thought from its proper channel, and damaging it, like a knife that is used to cut things for which it was not made.

In correspondence with this also was the position which the Buddha of necessity had to assign to the divine. All the gods, such as Indra, Brahma, Ishwara, were only mythological figures, intentionally taken over from Hinduism, in order that the weak plants among the newly converted might be able to remain undisturbed in their native soil. All these gods take a place infinitely far beneath the Buddha. They pray to the Buddha and are taught by him. The legend tells that when the young Siddartha (later the Buddha) was brought to the temple in Kapilavastu, the statues of Siva, Narayana, Indra, and all the other gods got down from their pedestals and bowed themselves before him. In the Buddha's system the gods take the rank of laymen. What a lofty standpoint, but how dearly bought! For Buddhism is lacking in that highest of all beings to which, under countlessly varied names, the adherents of all the other religions may resort, entitled in their direst need to throw themselves into its arms.

How entitled?

Because they have faith in such a being. Faith is the unwilling sacrifice of my understanding, and to it, as being the greatest sacrifice that man can bring, belongs also the greatest recompense.

Sooth to say there is no such being. The Buddhist has no prayers whatever of a petitioning nature; all he has are prayers of thanks—if such can be called "prayers"—to the Buddha, for that he has shown to all beings the path that leads to deliverance. The Buddhist, in fact, is the only adult among religionists. All the others are children with respect to their god, and beg just as children do. The Buddhist is the only one who seeks the truth, regardless of aught else.

The line of thought pursued by the Buddha is perhaps the most astounding that has ever been pursued by man. The whole world may be pictured as running a great race. All press, and strive, and struggle onwards to the one goal: happiness. And one man, one single man, says: "What all seek to reach by willing, by pressing onwards, that will I seek to reach by non-willing, by stepping back." Under such a guise does the Buddha come before us. In the huge, forward-whirling stream, to be the only one, undeluded, to take the backward step, was a display of courage at which we can scarcely marvel too much. Many an one already had felt that all was illusion, and that the best of all was to abandon it. But they were all people who had, as it were, only clipped one piece from the robe of the eternal, and swaggered over this piece like a thief who waxes merry, although he has only taken one handful of gold from the chest that was full of gold; or like David, who cut off a piece of Saul's garment in order to show that he could have taken him prisoner if only he had wished.

But why did he not wish?

Because his courage failed him; because of timidity. The Buddha, however, stepped unfalteringly up to the divine, the eternal, the mysterious, the concealed, the bemantled, and with divine boldness plucked away the whole mantle, together with all that it contained. And when he had unfolded his capture, what did he find in it? Something of which, as of everything else, he could say with smiling scorn: "Not for me!" Admonishingly he demands of his disciples: "Did you ever hear of a faith in immortality which brought its possessor deliverance from woe, distress, sorrow, grief, and despair?" To him, devoid of faith, everything pertaining to deity became simply a world formed and fashioned by mankind for themselves. We are not only the supporters of this world, but also the supporters of heaven and hell. In this fathom-long body are compassed all the heights of heaven and all the depths of hell. In the thought of the Buddha, as this world, so also heaven and hell become mere forms of our perception, forms of delusion. In a Sutta of the Dīgha Nikāya there is a wonderful passage, full of wit, full of delicate humour, but every word of it a shattering, bludgeon-blow at the idea of a god in heaven. A monk, not satisfied with the relative ending of the world, the ending of the Buddha's world, seeks to know the absolute ending of the world. "Where does the total, remainderless annihilation of the four elements set in?" Leaving the Buddha, he comes with his question before the gods, but there none can answer his query. Sent from one heaven to another in an ever-ascending scale, he at length comes into the presence of the most high Brahma, and perseveringly puts his question to him also. Brahma, however, replies: "I, O monk, am Brahma, great Brahma, the Highest, the Unconquered, the All-seeing, the Lord, the Master, the Creator, the Fashioner, the Perfect, the Guide, the Judge, the Father of all that have been and that are to be." The monk, however, replies: "I am not inquiring, friend, about this; what I am really asking you is, 'Where does the total, remainderless annihilation of the principal elements, earth, water, fire, and air, set in?'" Brahma, however, makes answer again: "I am Brahma, great Brahma," and so forth, and again the monk makes his reply, and so for a third time. "But now this great Brahma took the monk by the arm and led him aside and spoke thus to him: 'The gods of the Brahma-world think of me that nothing is hidden from Brahma, that nothing is unknown to Brahma, that all is open to Brahma's eyes. For this reason I did not reply before to them. But I, too, O monk, I do not know where these four leading elements remainderless come to an end. Wherefore, O monk, it was not right of you, that you left the Exalted One, and outside his understanding sought a solution of this problem. Go, O monk, and put this question to the Exalted One, and as the Exalted One shall explain it, so believe.'"

In another Sutta the Buddha is represented as in contest with this highest Brahma, and one of the deity's retinue calls out to him warningly: "Monkling! monkling! look out for yourself! This is Brahma, the Great Brahma," and so forth.

But the Buddha knew no fear. He alone, dauntless and undismayed, confronted that before which all others bowed the knee in servile fear. With good cause was he called "The Lion of the Sakyas." He alone dared force his way into the dwelling-place of that mysterious being before whose portals, as in the fable, two warriors were posted with swords ever brandished. At the very moment, however, that he ventured to press his way through, the whirling arms were stayed and the flashing swords hung motionless.

What was it that endowed the Buddha with such superhuman courage? Resolute renunciation: naught else. "Through renunciation have I reached the heights," he informs his disciples. Not only does he renounce this world, but also that other, and his own *I* along with it. Thus he became the only non-partisan; the only incorruptible; the one man unhampered by thoughts of heavenly joys. He was the unique man who stepped naked into the arena to wage combat for the truth.

Whoso like him is also stripped of all desires—him neither man nor god can any more touch at all; he is become invincible. And because he has become invincible, therefore is he without fear. But it is through fear that the gods come to be; with the disappearance of fear they also disappear, as ghosts depart along with darkness. For every fear—the fear of God included—arises on one hand out of possession and desire, and upon the other, out of a sentiment of the unknown.

Thus the supreme courage of the Buddha was the courage of renunciation. This endowed him with the courage to grapple and seize, and, grappling and seizing it, the unknown disappeared, and with it all fear, the fear of God included. Therefore is it said: "Every fear that arises flourishes only in the foolish, not in the wise." That is to say, fear flourishes only in those who do not comprehend. In another place it is said: "A monk has heard the words, 'Nothing is worth the trouble.' When a monk has so heard, he carefully regards everything; when he regards everything, he sees through everything; and when he has seen through everything and now experiences a sensation, he observes in this sensation the law of transiency, of abolition, of dissolution, of privation; and so observing, he clings to nothing whatsoever in all the world; clinging to nothing, he does not tremble and shrink; untrembling, unshrinking, he verily obtains the extinction of his illusion. In this way, in brief, a monk is delivered by the annihilation of the lust for life; wholly set free; wholly assured; wholly sanctified; wholly perfected; highest among gods and men."

Whoso will be free from all domination, even

that of the divine, gains nothing by loud-lunged denial of God. Perfect freedom is only to be found in perfect renunciation. He is a fool confessed, and will come to a bad end, who affirms life and denies God. Life is God. The god-idea disappeared for the Buddha, because, abandoning life, he held fast to sorrow. And as a man on a threshing-floor puts grain and chaff into a sieve, and shaking and tossing, throws away the chaff and keeps the grain, so the Buddha, with one tremendous throw, flung the whole world into the sieve of his thought, and, shaking and shaking again, and tossing and tossing again, deliberately threw away the chaff of the formless, the supersensuous; all that lay beyond the range of apprehension. And when with clear and scrutinising eye he looked into the sieve, behold! there was naught therein but the transient and the sorrowful. In it was neither an eternal, nor a soul, nor a true *I*, nor a god. And as an hungry man, before whom is set a meal of disgusting food, turns away from it despite his hunger, so the Buddha, over his great sieve, uttered his: "Not for me!" In it there was indeed nothing of that which he sought.

For the Buddha there is only one world, that which he constructed with the *I* as centre, and perception as radius; only that one world, which reaches as far as reaches the sun of *I*-consciousness, the sun of sorrow. When the radius fails, the circle of life fails also. When the sun is extinguished, extinguished also is the sorrow-world which it has lighted. "This world is no more," the man of wisdom comprehends, but, along with the world, disappears also God.

Only that which resides in us, which is conditioned by us, can entirely cease with our ceasing; only thus has renunciation sense and meaning. If, however, we recognise something which stands behind nature as an unconditioned, an unperceivable, an eternal; something corresponding to an eternal principle, a soul in us; renunciation of life were impossible, unthinkable, an utter contradiction. To deny God were perfectly futile. God, however, is not only what religions so denominate, but also that which the Upanishads, the philosophies, call Brahman, the Absolute. Gautama alone, with unprecedented logic, keeps away from all that lies beyond the reach of the comprehension. Only so could he become the great denier. He did not deny for denying's sake, like the pessimist, but under his hands his search became denial; because he did not find the god he sought, therefore he denied. Or rather: he only denied that wherein God was not to be found. God, however, was not to be found anywhere, and hence this denial itself has nothing absolute about it, but is only relative with a sort of express reservation. The Buddha merely says: "Despite all search I have not found any God, but in this search for God I have found the way to deliverance. Whether there really is a God or no—of that I cannot say anything; of that I do not need to say anything; but, comprehending the true nature of life, I have discovered that salvation is possible without God, altogether apart from God. I can give you salvation from sorrow. Be content with that, and 'the place of peace serene is open to you.' 'Whoso learns my art of swimming—it will always make for his health and well-being.'" Candidly, the Buddha has nothing to say to any one who wishes to overleap the boundaries that divide from the unknown. The Tathāgata teaches nothing but sorrow and the uprooting of sorrow. And the persistency with which he himself withstood all attempts to overstep his limits and dally with the unknown, gives to his teaching that stamp of consistency and uniformity which belongs only to truth. This teaching demands no distinctions, requires no distinctions. Mercilessly it reduces all, even God, to the one common level of Non-*I*.

But since the removal of the god-idea was impossible to the Buddha because of the inexplicability of the being of the world, why does he teach us to ignore the god-idea, to pass it over? Why does he teach us to despise heaven? The existence of the world is more than its cessation, and the Buddha-thought becomes either a jest or sheer frivolity, if there is no necessity for it!

In that very inexplicability of the being of the world—that is, in the very possibility of a god-idea—lies the necessity for the Buddha's thought. The inexplicability of the world is based upon the eternity, the beginninglessness of the world; this beginninglessness in turn is founded upon the fact that everything that exists is only the effect of a preceding cause. Wherever the law of cause and effect holds undisputed sway—there no beginning is to be found. More than this: because this world is *in toto* cause-effect, therefore is this world a *Becoming*; therefore is it an arising and passing away; therefore is it sorrow. And because it is sorrow, therefore there resides in its very nature the incitement, nay, the compulsion towards the removal of this existence. In the inexplicability of this existing world—that is, in the possibility of the god-idea—is to be found the necessity for the Buddha-thought. For the Buddha-thought is the truth in the shape of religion. But there is no "possibility" about truth. Where there is true religion, unalloyed truth, there is no room for "possibility"—that is to say, for the idea of God.

VII

KAMMA,[1] THE JUDGE OF THE WORLD

If there is no god over all, who then punishes and rewards?

Kamma punishes and rewards.

But how if the god-idea lies concealed behind this expression also?

In Buddhism everything is individual: sorrow, salvation, Saṁsāra, Nibbāna; all alike have their basis in the individual, are conditioned by the individual. This individual Kamma alone seems to stand over the individual, seems with sinister might to rule and master him. All of us groan under the stress of this compelling power, all save the Arahan, who, perfect in holiness, is free from the power of Kamma.

Hence there must be a possibility of becoming master of this power which we represent under the name of Kamma?

Yes, there is such a possibility, and it consists in comprehending this Kamma; for we can only abolish what we comprehend. Kamma is master only so long as it is not understood.

According to the Buddhist view, this body is

[1] Skt.: Karma. Deed, action.

compounded of the five Khandhas—body, sensation, perception, differentiations, and consciousness. These five, so far as our powers of perception go, are the final and ultimate substratum of the body; they are the genuinely existent. They only come within the domain of our senses when unified into Bhava, into this phenomenal appearance, the body. This latter is illusion, as the body of the rainbow is illusion, the raindrops and the light-beams being the reality. To put it another way: Our body arises as wind arises, but in reality there is no wind; there is no such positive thing as wind in existence; the realities are the atmosphere and the sun. Wind arises through difference of barometric pressure in two different localities, and it disappears with the disappearance of such difference. It is simply a disturbance of atmospheric equilibrium, and subsides with the restoration of that equilibrium. He only who can represent corporeality to himself in this way can think Buddhistically.

Hence this seeming form consists of the five Khandhas and yet is not identical with them, for the five are real, and the form ideal—an illusion. It is only when the Khandhas are actively woven together and arranged in a specific manner that they exhibit a bodily form. This weaving together is the work of Kamma; it groups the five together into name and form, making them perceptible to mind and sense.

And now what is Kamma?

It is the force, in virtue of which reaction follows action; it is the energy which makes it that out of the present existing life, new life in an inexhaustible stream continually flows forth.

In another place we have seen that the apparent being of this body is in truth an ever-changing *Becoming*, a constant succession of Becoming-moments, that follow one another, endlessly, countlessly—imperceptible to all ordinary sense. Hence the apparent continuity of the body is destroyed by knowledge, and dissolved into a palpitating, pulsating Arising and Passing-away, just as the lightning flash for the instructed is resolved into a succession of sparks that follow upon one another with a rapidity that puts them beyond the power of being perceived separately by the human retina. That which forms the connecting link between one Becoming-moment and another—the force which makes it that one Becoming-moment as its due reaction proceeds from the one that preceded it in point of time—this force is called Kamma.

Thus it is Kamma that conditions the apparent continuity of the bodily form. But just as one Becoming-moment gives birth to another, so one embodied form gives birth to the next that follows it. And in the same way that Kamma binds one Becoming-moment to another, in exactly the same way it binds one existence to another—out of this permits the next to arise; as from action proceeds reaction.

This power, which we represent as Kamma, is not something existing alongside of the Khandhas—standing over them. It is contained in the Khandhas—so the Abhidhamma teaches—in the form of will (*cetanā*). It resides in them as the power which binds action and reaction together, which is not apart from both but is *in* both, is a constituent of both, and is the one as much as it is the other.

Now there must be something which keeps this endless play of action and reaction in perpetual motion. There must be some electric current which keeps perpetually going this vibrator—the best simile for this life of ours. This current is desire, which, clinging to objects, taking delight in objects, absorbs ever fresh nourishment from them, as plants suck water from the earth; as the wick sucks up oil from out of the cup. Trishna (in Pāli, *Taṇhā*)—the thirst for life, and Upādāna, the clinging to life—these are the inexhaustible sources whence flows the stream of sorrow; these two make the resilient force, which, as its due reaction, causes the arising of new life, and with it, new willing. This mechanism of sorrow can never come to rest so long as desire is present; for this latter ever and again supplies fresh nourishment, in the same way that the flame can never be extinguished so long as fresh oil is continually being poured into the cup. Desire gives rise to deed; deed gives rise to result; result exhibits itself as new corporeality endowed with new desire. Deed is as inevitably followed by result as the body by its shadow. This is merely the universal natural law of the conservation of energy extended to the moral domain. As in the universe no energy can ever be lost, so also in the individual nothing can be lost of the resilient force accumulated by desire. This resilient energy is always transmuted into fresh life, and we live eternally through our lust to live. The medium, however, that makes all existence possible is Kamma.

How the law of the conservation of energy in the sorrow-world of the Buddha becomes deed, with its punishment and reward; how the law of cause and effect, as soon as it is transferred to the sphere of beings endowed with consciousness, to the sphere of individuality, becomes Kamma, the supreme judge of the world,—all this is shown in another place.

Indeed, Kamma takes the place filled by God in the monotheistic religions in this respect, that the individual judged by it is also its creature; through its power the five Khandhas have been woven together into name and form, have become an individual—something which has the capacity of experiencing sorrow, of receiving punishment and reward. The only difference between it and God seems to be that Kamma is absolutely pitiless and impartial in its working. As a smooth-polished mirror gives back in its smallest detail any picture we may bring opposite its surface, so does Kamma, with equal exactitude, throw back the consequence of deed upon the doer. Not a quiver of an eyelash but is followed by its due effect—that is, is punished or rewarded. Not a thought can be "lost in time or space." "Neither in the kingdom of air, nor in the depths of the sea, nor even if thou dive into the recesses of the mountains, shalt thou find anywhere on earth a state where thou mayest escape the fruit of thine actions."

In religions, the faithful really think that they can bribe God with prayers; Kamma, however, can as little be bribed as the stone falling to the ground can, by wishing, be diverted from its downward path. Since the Buddhist universe is a piece of self-actuating machinery, since a kindly disposed god is awanting, so also is wanting the possibility of such a thing as the forgiveness of sins. The whole process of the committing and the cancelling of sin has about it something of the cold accuracy of commercial book-keeping. Every past deed is like a loan from eternity. The sum loaned is booked in pounds, shillings, and pence, and in pounds, shillings, and pence it must be repaid. Only one coinage, however, is legal tender, and that coinage is life! The consequences of our deeds must be lived through, lived out. Before, however, a balance is struck, innumerable new loans have been issued, and the painful chain of rebirths drags endlessly on. Nowhere at all can the despairing glance see possibility of escape from liability.

So we are riveted eternally to life?

Not eternally, but so long as ignorance remains in us; so long as we fail to recognise the true nature of Kamma. On the surface we are the creatures of this Kamma, and lie under its dreadful power, but ultimately this Kamma, which drives us from birth to birth, is nothing but a product of our own manufacture. At every moment we have the power to break the endless chain. When deed ceases, ceases also the consequence of deed, and where no bridge exists leading to a next, there also no "next" exists, as there is no beating of the heart where there is no connection between systole and diastole. Systole by itself is unthinkable, as also is diastole by itself. It is only the passage from the one to the other that creates both, that creates life.

Only so long as I am performing actions have I to groan under life-producing—that is, sorrow-producing consequences. Deeds, however, happen as long as there is the will to do deeds. The will, however, can only disappear in true knowledge, in knowledge of transiency, of Not-*I*. In it expires not only the love of life, the will, but also the possibility of willing, and with it the possibility of action, and hence the possibility of consequence.

Hence I am lord of Kamma as soon as my will is converted into non-willing. This resolution born of knowledge, this non-willing, denial of life, is the greatest of all deeds—"the deed that leads to the cessation of deed." And because this resolve lies in my power, therefore am I myself the fashioner of my fate. I myself forge my fetters, I myself file them through, and look to no god for help. In no religion does humanity stand in a position of such sublime, unhampered greatness as in the system of the Buddha. In this sense also Buddhism is the most human of all religions; everything here depends upon us. If we are intelligent, to us alone is the reward; if we are fools, the blame is entirely our own, for

> Has ever fire been known to say:
> "Methinks I'll go and burn that fool"?

Knowledge, however, makes us lords of Kamma, not only by bringing Kamma to an end in non-willing, but also by teaching us that even as the *I*, so also Kamma is illusion. As sorrow disappears in non-willing and in comprehension, so also in non-willing as well as in comprehension Kamma is done away.

The force which unites action and reaction is, on one hand, wholly action inasmuch as it takes its rise in action, but, on the other hand, it is wholly reaction, because it is transmuted into it, comes to blossom in it, as it were. But the *I* also is, on one hand, wholly deed, and, upon the other, wholly the consequence of deed.

Kamma is nothing but an expression for the *I*, in so far as it practises morality and is itself morality, in the same way that individuality is an expression for the *I*, in so far as it perceives transiency and is itself transiency. If the concept "*I*" disappears, disappears also with it the concept Kamma. And as the *I* can only disappear when it is perceived to be based upon illusion, so also is it with Kamma. Nothing that is real, that has genuine being, can ever in any wise disappear and pass away. Only *Becoming* can cease, and Kamma, as wholly deed, wholly consequence—that is, neither deed nor consequence—is, nothing but the continual process of transition from the one to the other—is nothing but a *Becoming*. If there were something that were deed, apart by itself, there were also something that were consequence of deed apart by itself. Deed apart by itself—that were world-creation, the absolute beginning; consequence of deed apart by itself—that were eternal life in heaven or in hell, life absolute.

Hence the existence of god and soul would be simultaneously admitted. The Kamma-concept devours both. Kamma is the inglorious end which the glorious Ātma-concept of the Upanishads found in the understanding of the Buddha. The Ātman (The Self, the Soul), which, like a flash, unites in one, heaven and earth, god and man, in the anatomising thought of the Buddha, became only that flickering spark which, ever and again generating itself from itself, presents the appearance of a closed curve. The soul can be apprehended, the incomprehensible comprehended, only in their abrogation. Abrogation, however, is only possible where there is *Becoming*. To apprehend the *I*, the soul, means to apprehend them as illusion; to apprehend Being as *Becoming*.

Now we ask once more, who rules if there is no god?

The *I* rules, but in such a way that it is at the same time the ruled! The *I* is that which results from the blending of deed and consequence; it is that which does not *do* the deed but *is* the deed. Its domination is illusion, but so also is its subjection to domination! I can only be free of the illusion of subjection to domination when I get free of the illusion of domination. As soon as I perceive: "Here is no doer"—only then can I perceive: "Here is no consequence of doing, of deed." "I dissolve Kamma" means "I dissolve the *I*." It is only when I recognise myself as entirely the product of Kamma, entirely the effect of a previous cause—it is only then that I become completely and without reserve the master of Kamma, the master of the world. For if I am nothing but the effect of a cause, then is the all only the effect of a cause. I understand the law: "The world is the fruit of works," and I understand that the cessation of the world must go along with the cessation of works, of deed. I am deed. With the fall of the *I* falls the world. The possibility of the abrogation of the world resides in me—yea, in me! This possibility, however, is only another way of expressing the truth: "All life is sorrow." For where the possibility of dissolution is present—there also is present

Becoming, transiency; there is found neither Being, nor eternal, nor divine, nor peace, nor delight. Hence the possibility of the abolition of the world is the necessity of its abolition; for as the stream hastens from the mountain to the valley, so the human heart hastens from sorrow to sorrowlessness. To understand Kamma is to be compelled to seek its abolition.

As in one single thought the *I* becomes the central point of support for the whole world, the world-begetter, world-bearer, and withal only a seeming *I*; so, in one thought, Kamma becomes the master of the world and the product of illusion, and to understand it means to become its master. The combat with illusion, with falsehood, is the only natural, necessary combat. In the phrase "Kamma is illusion" lies the necessity of becoming its master, and in the phrase "The removal of Kamma is compulsory" resides the necessity for Kamma being illusion.

Kamma is like the breath in my bosom. So long as I keep it in me as a thought, I am its master; but as soon as I let it escape me in the form of a word, it becomes my master—something outside of me, from the consequences of which I cannot any longer escape. As by silence I maintain my mastery over my thought and hence over myself, so by mental silence do I maintain mastery over Kamma—that is, over the *I*, so far as it represents the endless, beginningless process of the *Becoming* of the world. Through mental silence I become master of the world.

Kamma again is like the heart in my breast, which ceaselessly hastens from systole to diastole independent of my will. If, however, I cease from breathing, this tireless worker, who from moment to moment brings to birth new life, finally comes to rest. As the heart is only to be got at through the breathing, and not directly, so Kamma is only approachable by way of the will, by way of Trishna-Upādāna. And as the heart cannot be regulated by breathing but only brought to a standstill, so I am unable by willing to alter old Kamma, but I can bring to an end the play of action and reaction, the continual renewal of fresh Kamma. I am not master of the past, but I am master of the future. I am not master of the beginning of the world, but I am master of its ending.

As each heart-beat is the final product of a countless number of past heart-beats, and the transmitter, the producing medium for the endless series of heart-beats that are to follow; and as the "now" is the product, the final result of the endless past, and the producer, the bearer of the endless future, so is Kamma the product, the outcome, the consequence of past deeds, and is the bearer, the begetter, the mother's womb of all future deeds. Corporeality, "Now," Kamma, are each the same thing, seen from separate and different points of view. As the *I* first completely becomes the supporter of the world when it is recognised as wholly illusion, so also Kamma first becomes the judge of the world when it is recognised as wholly illusion. To recognise Kamma as illusion does not mean to despise it, but to recognise it in all its horror, in its everlastingness. Where there is nothing but cause-effect, *Becoming*, we also have present the *endlessness* of Becoming. To posit a *beginning* of Becoming means to posit Being, God.

If there is no beginning to *Becoming*, there is also no end to it, and every moment, every "now," is the beginning of an endless series. Every "now," every deed, every thought, is the sculptor of the future in its entirety. There is nothing before us of the nature of a fixed point; nothing waiting for us at the other end; no god with open arms, no jaws of hell; life is no race towards a goal. The path the traveller goes upon he first forms out of himself, as the working spider out of itself spins the track upon which it afterwards travels. Nothing is here but the "now," which, because it is illusion, eternally brings to birth out of itself a fresh "now." Life is not progress towards a future. There is only a future where there is a god. Where there is nothing but cause-effect, where Kamma rules, there is only the "now," and life is nothing but a continual stepping out of one "now" into another. Life is the "now," an eternally becoming "now." The "now" is our present support, the "now" is our future. And as a man walking a tight-rope at each step he takes thinks only of that one step, so the wise man thinks only of one "now" at a time. At every "now" he thinks, "I am building the world afresh"; he knows, "anew I lay down the line of direction upon which the endless future will run its course." Hence he walks with care, like the man upon the tight-rope. He dare not allow his mental eye to rove from the present. Beyond the "now" there is nothing. The "now" behind the "now" has first to be made. To turn his eye from the present to the future, from earth to heaven, simply means stepping into nothingness, into the abyss. The fabrication of planes is also a step into the void.

He only goes safely who, keeping his eye firmly fixed upon the "now," neither leering at heaven nor shying at hell, knows at every step that he takes, "It bears my future." He only travels in surety who, gaping neither to right nor left, neither in front nor behind, but fixedly looking to himself, at every deed, and word, and thought knows, "Now sow I the seed of the future. Now, even now, am I making the heavens, building the hells that later will receive me." This thought, if it has taken good root in the *I*, makes the hand slow, the tongue prudent, the brain thoughtful. Such an one is to be lured neither by fame, nor by gold, nor by love. Home and heaven to him are empty words, seeing that he thinks all this, and in thought it all melts away. Where there is thought there can be no willing, as where there is light, darkness cannot be. Wherever love is thought, it cannot be felt; wherever riches are thought, there they cannot be earned; wherever heaven is thought, there it is impossible that it can be longed after. Yea, even for Nibbāna itself the man does not look. Standing wholly in the "now," looking only upon sorrow, arising and passing away, he steps from "now" to "now," every step being at once the way to the goal and the goal itself. Thus, great, still, and alone, he proceeds upon his way, like the sun which at the same time makes and enlightens the path upon which it goes.

But to what purpose is all this?

"Whoso observes the arising of effects from causes, observes the truth; whoso observes the truth, observes the arising of effects from causes," says the Buddha. Thoughtfulness and reflectiveness bear their reward in themselves, from moment to moment create their own recompense. To understand the law of cause and effect, of transiency, of *Becoming*, is to recognise the truth. To perceive the truth is to have salvation. To perceive cause-effect is to cease to will, and non-willing leads to Nibbāna and is Nibbāna. Every step in non-willing is the way to the goal and the goal itself. Whoso perceives the truth, perceives: "This Kamma, that chains me to painful life, can frighten me no more. I have feared its face as a little child fears its reflection in the looking-glass, unwitting that it is its own face that it looks upon. I not only am the product of this Kamma, but I am also its creator. It can be abolished by my own will, and nothing is needed but the removal of that illusion which pictures the *I* as a substantial being."

Thus everywhere have I sought this master-builder who ever and always puts together a new house of life, and finally, O wonderful! in my own self, in my heart of hearts, I have found him. Therefore says the Buddha:—

> O master-builder, thou art known.
> No more shalt thou the house rebuild.
> Thy beams and bars are all destroyed.
> The house is laid in ruins quite.
> Glad and released the heart hath reached
> The final ending of the will.
>
> (Dhammapada.)

But here a question arises. Is the being reborn through Kamma the same or something different from the old being?

"How does the case stand, O Gautama? Does the self that now lives experience the results of his deeds in rebirth?" a Brahmin asks of the Buddha.

"The self that now lives, that self experiences the results of his doing:—this, Brahmin, is one extreme."

"Does the case stand thus then, O Gautama? Another than the now living person experiences the results of his doing?"

"Another than the now living person experiences the results of his doing;—this, Brahmin, is the second extreme. Avoiding both these extremes, the Perfect One points out the truth that lies between these two." And then follows the series of the twelve Nidānas, from ignorance down to birth, death, and sorrow.

That means: It is neither the same self nor yet another, and yet it is as much the same self as it is another; in somewhat the same fashion that the *I* as deed, as action, is different from the *I* as consequence of deed, as reaction, and yet is not different. That is to say: Life is not at all Being, neither in the form of a "self" nor yet in the form of an "other;" there is absolutely no *I* present; there is nothing present but a process, the endless self-generating play of action and reaction. Of this we cannot say: "Upon this side that belongs, and upon that side that belongs,"—with its very existence is given its endless past, its endless future. As a flame that has burnt through the night, at the night's end is the same and yet not the same as it was at the beginning of the night, so the new being is the same and yet not the same as the old. As reaction is not the same as action, and yet is not different, so also this existence is not exactly the same as the next, and yet it is not another. It is the "now," here as there, and to all eternity.

And now another question arises. If Kamma can be abolished only by the abolition of deed, good deeds also must cease, for they also are followed by their due results—they also bring life to birth? It is quite true. Good actions also must cease, but not in such a fashion that one can say: "I must not do good deeds, so that I may not any more make new Kamma, new life." This rejection of good action would itself be action, and would produce its due effects. That such sayings of the Buddha as: "They are delivered from evil and from good," or "Ye have to leave righteousness behind, to say nothing of unrighteousness," must be thus understood seems perfectly clear.

Good and evil cleave to the individual, to the *I*-thought. Just as soon as the *I*-thought is dissolved in true knowledge, "good" and "evil" have no longer any meaning, become void of sense. One so awakened, who already in this life has attained to the vision of Nibbāna, stands beyond and above both; he spends the time he yet has to pass in this seeming-form, like to the sun. As the sun travels impartially over hill and dale, over beauteous and hateful things alike, so his action and thoughts glide with equal indifference over good and evil, without any clinging arising from will, without the stirring up of any emotion. For where there is no longer any ignorance, there is no longer any differentiation. He does what is to do, but he cleaves to nothing. It is only in the *I*, in the individuality, that the effects of causes are transmuted into reward and punishment, and hence into the concepts "good" and "evil." With the fall of the *I*-thought, both concepts together disappear in indifference. The ideas "good" and "evil," like the ideas "object and subject," "cause and effect," "past and future," are distinctions that have their sole foundation in the illusion of an *I*.

The man perfect in knowledge truly performs actions, for this body still exists, but it is not deed in itself that makes Kamma, life, sorrow, but deed that springs from will. It is not the laying alongside one another of flint and steel that produces fire, but the striking of one against the other. Will, however, can only exist where there is an *I* that wills.

That which the Buddha calls Kamma is not the common force which leads from cause to effect, which actualises the effect; Kamma is that process only so far as it takes place in beings endowed with consciousness—that is, capable of suffering pain. And necessarily so, for it is only here that the result of action—that is, life—is synonymous with sorrow. The Buddha's word, however, holds good only for the world wherein sorrow reigns, wherein sorrow is felt and comprehended. As sorrow is nothing but the law of mutability as applied to the individuality, and as worked out by the individuality, so also Kamma is nothing else but the law of the conservation of energy as applied to the individuality, and as worked out by the individuality. As something founded in individuality, with the fall of individuality it also falls. The man of knowledge can go free.

But not also that other who says: "There is no such thing as Kamma; and the talk of reward and punishment is an old wives' fable. To what purpose the restraint men impose upon themselves? Free will I live, treading upon the necks of men!"

No! Only the wise man is free; no other. So long as there is will, there is deed. So long as there are deeds, so long is Kamma a grim reality, and reward and punishment no empty words. Freedom from Kamma cannot be taught, it can only be lived; it cannot be acquired by learning, it can only be acquired by living. Kamma is not only my creation; it is also my creator. It is my *I*. For him only for whom Kamma is entirely creator, for him only is it entirely creature. He only can get free from Kamma who has set himself free from the *I*, who has renounced the *I*. Boundless freedom can only exist where there is no longer any possibility of such freedom from bounds being taken advantage of.

But why no possibility?

Upon this *I* is based the world. With the *I* the world also comes to an end. Where there no longer is any world, any *I*, there also the world can no longer be either esteemed or despised. On the other hand, where there no longer exists any world, any *I*, there also the *I* can no more be esteemed by the world, lured by the world from life to life, from sorrow to sorrow. Such an one as has abolished his *I* has become master of the world by retreating. This is what the Buddha means when he says: "He has blinded nature; utterly extirpated her eye; he has disappeared from that evil one." No more beholds he the world. No more the world beholds him.

VIII

MORALITY IN BUDDHISM

BUDDHISM, although the most sympathetic of all religions, is not the religion of love, but of knowledge. Christ teaches: "Love thy neighbour as thyself." The Indian religions, Buddhism and the Vedanta, teach the same, but along with the teaching they give the reason for it. We are given to understand why we *must* love our neighbours as ourselves. With scientific exactitude the laws are developed under which this, the most striking phenomenon in the moral domain, takes place.

The mind of Prince Siddhartha, called Gautama, became entirely occupied with this one fact, that all life is sorrow, and in the strenuous concentration of all his powers of thought upon this one point, he seeks to save himself from this sorrow. This, briefly, is the primal source of the whole of Buddhism. Gautama, who later became the Buddha, does not begin his career as a saviour of the world; he does not set out on his life's journey as one endowed from above with supernatural powers towards this high end. Nothing lies farther from his mind than the welfare of others. He seeks his own salvation, and that only. It is a purely egoistical impulse, but what more natural than that one who suddenly finds himself in a burning house should seek first of all to save himself?

However, after he has attained this salvation, after he has worked his own way out of the sea of sorrow to the shore of safety, after he has reached the blest apprehension, "I am saved," his mind turns back to his suffering fellowmen, and only now in this retrospective motion do we see love emerge in the shape of the compassion that comprehends. He himself characteristically says: "There are two reasons why I follow this manner of life: my own wellbeing in this present life, and sympathy with those that follow me."

The Buddha pointed out to a world in pain: "This way have I gone; upon this path have I reached the goal; this is the way to deliverance." This is his great gift of love; hence is he called the "Great Compassionate One." It is not merely the awakening to true apprehension that makes the Buddha; but the combination of such awakening with sympathy for humanity,—that constitutes the Buddha. In Buddhism it has always been the greatest gift of love to point out the true path; a gift assuring to the bestower thereof the richest reward. "Far above the greatest gift stands the reward of those who take only a verse of four lines of this doctrine, and, explaining it, make it clear to others in all its purity," says a passage in a Sutra of the Mahāyāna. Upbraidingly the Buddha says to his monks: "In what way, monks, does a monk not kindle any fire? By not showing to another the doctrine, visible afar off, as he has heard it and learnt it. In this way, monks, a monk kindles no fire."

Here it must be noted that this greatest gift of

love is not bestowed in the interest of the receiver thereof; the giver bestows it in his own interest. That the receiver at the same time becomes the possessor of an infinite treasure is only a secondary consideration. This is the—to our eyes—degenerate shape which love assumes in this system; nothing is left but the bony skeleton of action. That cordiality which forgets itself for others, that affection which breeds tenderness and emotion, is entirely wanting here. The whole moral scheme in Buddhism is nothing but a sum in arithmetic set down by a clear, cold egoism; as much as I give to others, as much will come again to me. Kamma is the most exact arithmetician in the world.

Once, however, that we have overcome our first feeling of discouragement at this apparent misuse of love, which love is the highest we can conceive of, we are forced to admit that in the Buddha's system love can occupy no other place. Here is wanting that great centre of love, that father-god, with whom, in loving, I become one; that father-god who loves me and whom I love in return; whose children all men are, and who thus through his all-fatherhood changes the whole world into one vast family of brothers and sisters, whose natural duty it is to love one another. In Buddhism only Kamma reigns—the relationship between cause and effect, between deed and result, which, with the exactitude of a piece of mechanism, regulates reward and punishment.

God truly is awanting, but perhaps the Buddha can be substituted for him as a centre of love?

The Buddha is in Nibbāna. The concept of fatherhood is so entirely out of harmony with the direction of thought of this system that the already existing bonds of such a relationship are unloosed in the newly acquired comprehension of things. The individual is absolved of all connection with parents, children, or brothers and sisters. These are only the outward connections peculiar to humankind. As birds at evening gather together upon one lonely-standing tree and in the morning all fly away each upon his own road again, so, under the compulsion of Kamma, do the various members of a family gather together and again part from one another when the Kamma which has determined this form is entirely exhausted.

Here there is only one fatherhood: my deed! only one sonship: the consequence of my deed! "My deed is my possession; my deed is mine inheritance; my deed is the mother's womb that bore me. My deed is the race to which I belong. My deed is my refuge." Thus teaches the Buddha. It is no god that is my refuge; my deed is my refuge—that only. Since in all the world I am tied to nothing else but to this my deed, all other ties, whether they have to do with god or with man, are recognised as illusion and given up. Released through the power of strenuous thought from all ties, I stand in the universe quite alone, travelling in utter solitude the path of Saṁsāra. My deed alone goes with me, but not as a companion, only as my shadow. Thus I travel on like a man at evening wending his way eastwards over an infinite stretch of snowy plain or through an endless waste of sand, with nothing behind him but the long trail of his own footsteps, nothing before him but a giant shadow; beside himself—nothing.

Thus does the Buddha teach in the Aṅguttara

Nikāya: "Two joys there are, disciples. What two? The joy of the family life, and the joy of the homeless life. These, disciples, are the two kinds of joy. The nobler of these two joys is the joy of the homeless life." And farther on, "Independence, I say, is the greatest comfort of the mind." The Buddha began his own career with the great renunciation, by stepping behind out of the circle of all those whom he loved, and by whom he in turn was loved. This was the princely earnest-money which he gave to truth in order to bind her to him for ever. In this combat for the supreme good a single act of self-denying renunciation has always been of more value than years of laborious investigation and questioning. Whosoever lacks the courage to burn his ships behind him will never take possession of the new kingdom of the mind. Whoso is firmly resolved to take part in the crusade of truth, of him the Buddha requires that he too, without one backward glance, shall forsake his house together with all those to whom his heart has hitherto clung,

> The bonds of love
> Off-shaking, like an elephant set free.

For father and mother (however much to be honoured), and wife and child too, are only so many fetters which hinder the mind that seeks to soar. When the birth of his son was announced to the Buddha he said: "A new fetter has been born to me." The following passage is often repeated: "With fetters bound is household life, a state of impurity, but like the freedom of the open sky is the life of the ascetic."

The supreme goal of the Buddhist consists in freedom from the sorrow of the world. This condition of sorrowlessness is to be attained by a complete breaking loose, a complete stripping of himself, on the part of each man, from the world that surrounds him, with which he stands through our six senses in continual contact. "Whoso bears love to nothing, he also sorrows over nothing," says the Buddha; and again, "To leave the beloved is the greatest sorrow."

From this view of things there results a confining of one's self to one's self, a withdrawal, which sets its specific mark upon all our intercourse with our former relations and neighbours. Active love, spontaneous sorrow for one's nearest, dies away. The Christ was under compulsion to do deeds of love, to be physician to the sick in mind, to sit among tax-gatherers and sinners, to leave all the others and go after the one sheep that had gone astray. Love is the goal of his religion, its perfect fulfilment. God is love. For the Buddhist there is no necessity for such a course of action. In all matters there is for him only one rule and guiding line: Does this tend toward my deliverance or does it not? Or, to put it better, perhaps: Will this prove a hindrance to my salvation or will it not?

Regarding himself from this point of view, he makes himself the centre of the universe. With anxious care he sees to it that his spiritual centre of gravity shall always lie within his own *I*, and that on this sure foundation all violent vibration is avoided. Even in the activities of love he may never forget why he so acts, he may never forget his own *I*; for every such act of forgetfulness here is a slip backwards upon the steep road to Nibbāna. Virtue is not something to be striven after for its own sake; it is merely the ladder to the highest. Doing good is simply avoiding evil. "If the Exalted One," says the monk Puṇṇa to the monk Sāriputta, "if the Exalted One had indicated pure virtue as being immaterial, as being the perfect extinction of illusion, the Exalted One would then have indicated the material as being immaterial, the material as being perfect extinction of illusion." The material, however, is the inferior.

But why is it sufficient to confine one's self to one's self?

Because the entire world changes with every change in me. The existence of the world depends upon me; my six senses create this world anew from moment to moment. As is fashioned the *I*, the producer, so also is fashioned the world, the product. The world, because it is not a being but only a *Becoming*, is not something firm established for ever, constructed thus and so, but as it exhibits itself to me, so it is; and according as I am inwardly constituted, so the world presents itself to me. My inner constitution, however, is shaped according to the state of my comprehension, my knowledge. Here is found the fulcrum from which the world can be levered up and down, until finally, with one last powerful push, it flies off, and is no longer visible to me, and I no longer visible to it.

Without further demonstration, it is clear that in such a system meditation is of more importance than love of the neighbour. No Buddhist would consider it right to break off meditation, Dhyāna, in order to do something.

> Turn not aside from thine own task
> For others, be they ne'er so great.

Here one can scarcely avoid making a comparison with Christian mysticism. "Whoso busies himself much with external things, even were it in good works, never arrives at true peace of heart," says Tauler. This is, as it were, the introduction to that tremendous word of the Buddha's: "Ye disciples, if ye would understand the highest, ye have to leave righteousness behind, to say nothing of unrighteousness!"

But now we are not to imagine that with this care for one's own *I*, the door is thrown wide open to carelessness and indifference as regards all others: quite the contrary is the case. The Buddhist, indeed, with sober understanding strives strenuously to avoid every contact with his neighbour. If, however, the latter comes in contact with him, then he shall behave toward him as his own best welfare would demand—that is, he shall act as love would act, and not only shall he so act, but he shall also so think. Every thought that proceeds from my mind is as much my deed as the word that falls from my tongue, as a blow from my fist. My neighbour is only the sounding-board for my deed—that whereon my deed actualises itself. As, however, the ball, thrown at the wall, flies back to him who has thrown it, so in consciousness does the deed turn back upon the doer thereof, bringing him as its result punishment or reward. By good deeds I profit myself alone, as by evil I harm myself alone.

And yet from this apparently sterile soil of icy egoism there spring sweet-smelling flowers. We saw above that the sacred bonds of family relationship were burst and broken in this system of comprehension. This, however, is true only of those who have reached perfection, of those for whom, with the disappearance of their own *I*, all those relationships also have taken flight in which this *I* has hitherto stood. With the imperfect, with those still striving, the case is quite different; if my neighbour is to be treated with the utmost benevolence, to this has to be added, in the case of parents, the duty of gratitude. For it was through them that I obtained rebirth into the world of men, and human birth, birth as a man, is more valuable than birth as a god, for it is only out of the former that the way leads to the highest, to Buddhahood. My mother, however, in that she has suckled me and brought me up, has put me in a position to be able to work my way to freedom by following the good Law. Therefore is it said: "If one should take his mother upon one shoulder and his father upon the other, and should so carry them for an hundred years, this would still be a less service than he himself has received from them." As the Buddha himself says: "Whoso properly cares for his parents is greater than a Chakravartin (world-dominating king)." And in another place: "Brahma, O ye disciples, is verily present in those families within whose abodes the father and the mother are venerated by the children." Hence, according to legend, every Buddha mounts up to the Tusita heaven in order to preach the law to his mother there.

Still more tight, however, than the bands that knit me to my earthly parents are those that knit me to my spiritual father, to my teacher who shows me the way to salvation. Spiritual birth is infinitely more important than bodily birth. Hence obedience, humility, love, is the due of the teacher, and as respects homage the Burman Buddhist puts the teacher before the parents.

Friendship is to be kept only in so far as it is able to help us to rise, as it enables us to understand the law.

A friend is good, but right thought is the best friend. Of an earthly friend a word in the Sutta Nipāta says, "Two bracelets of shining gold, however smoothly made, yet rub against one another; wherefore let us wander alone like the rhinoceros."

If now one of those near and dear to us is torn from us by death, weeping and wailing is only a sign that we have not understood the universal law of nature. If there were anything to be gained by lamentation, the man of understanding would most certainly not despise it, but it does no good to the dead and does harm to the living. "Peace comes not into the heart that weeps and mourns." The wise fortify themselves by reflecting upon death. By thought they overcome grief, take food, and attend to their affairs. They know: "What was subject to death has died. What was subject to dissolution has dissolved." The life of a man is indeed like the ripe fruit on a tree, of which we look for some to fall every moment. In plain words the Buddha says in the Sutta Nipāta, "Weeping is useless," and "Try to scatter the grief that possesses you, as the wind drives away the cotton (on the bush)."

In Buddhism, as faith is a product of knowledge, so also is love. Clear, shining, but cold and colourless as the sun on a winter morning, this love rises before us. Once, however, that our eyes have become accustomed to the cold glow, once we have reconciled ourselves to the lack of those beautiful half-tones which in Christianity play around us from faith, hope, and, above all, from love, we cannot help observing how much more firmly and solidly everything here is woven together than in the religions founded upon revelation. Certainly it is a tremendous risk to leave love, which in Christianity is the road to the highest, and indeed that highest itself, completely at the mercy of vague feelings and instincts. It is quite true that it is frequently and emphatically laid down: "Love your neighbour as yourself," "Love your enemies," but these injunctions are completely opposed to human nature so long as I do not understand why I should do good to every one, even to my enemy. The "eye for an eye and tooth for a tooth" lies easier to our hand and requires no explanation.

But all those who act contrary to these injunctions will some time or another be punished for it.

Quite true, but there is always a kind god, and if here and there, now and again, we have gone against the commands of love, we may always hope that everything will be smoothed out again by an act of divine mercy. We lightly say "now and again," and never suspect how infinitely often, day after day, we neglect these precepts. If we looked after the state of our morality with as much interest as we look after the state of our purse, we would be horrified at the huge pile of our accumulated guilt. And if we knew that everything had to be paid back again in pounds, shillings, and pence, we would simply despair.

How different here it is with the god-less

Buddhist! From his childhood the idea is impressed upon his very bones that every deed, the good as well as evil, is followed by its due recompense, as the body by its shadow. The doctrine of Kamma is the law of the conservation of energy, the most universal of all the laws of nature, extended to the moral domain. Nothing can ever be lost; in some shape or another, be it as punishment or as reward, everything inevitably, at some time or another, comes to the light of day. This is the iron, everlasting law of nature. Here neither god nor Buddha avails aught. One thing only avails: forsake the deed, and consequences of themselves will cease. That, however, which now befalls thee as the result of former deeds—because it is unalterable meet it like a man. Yet bear it not with indifference but with recollectedness, with reflection, so that thou mayst fully understand: "So bitter is sorrow, how sweet must sorrowlessness be, how well worth striving after! What a fool I should be if even once again, for the sake of brief enjoyment, I should do things that drag after them such a long and weary train of woes, which no god can lighten for me or make easier to bear."

The Buddhist stands in the position of the man who has had some experience of the world and is well aware of his responsibility. The adherent of religions founded upon revelation in more than one respect resembles a child. The grown-up man knows that in this world nothing is to be had gratis; everything that I take must be paid for in hard cash. The child, on the contrary, stretches out his hand for this and that without ever reflecting: "I shall have to pay for this." By appeals and flattery it tries to avoid punishment or obtain a favour. What, however, in a child is charming, is odious in the grown-up man. Because the adherent of the revealed religions feels toward his god as a child might feel, his worship is on a level with his request for pardon and protection, in its childish charm and *naïveté*. The old Athenians prayed: "Let it rain, dearest Jupiter, let it rain upon the fields of the Athenians!" and Marcus Aurelius adds: "If men pray at all they should pray with the same frank simplicity that the Athenians prayed." And certainly every genuine prayer is such an Athenian prayer.

In Buddhism this veneer of childishness is absent. Petitionary prayer to the Buddhist is an illusion, which would be amusing if it were not so serious. With merciless mockery the Buddha says to a Brahmin: "What would you think, Vasettha, if this stream were swollen up to the very edge, and a man whose business called him to the other side came up here, and, standing on the bank, shouted out: 'Come over here, O thou other shore! Come over to my side!' What would you think? would all his calling and praying and beseeching and hoping bring over here to him that other shore? Even like this man are ye Brahmins when ye say: 'Indra, we call to thee! Soma, Varuna, Brahma! we call to ye!'"

It is thus that the Buddhist looks upon prayer. He is the real adult; an infant at the mother's breast, he also in earlier births a thousand times has lived through all the sorrow and woe of human life. The Buddhist is in the world as one who lies in prison and in chains, without friend or relative or helper. Such an one makes the brave resolve to gain his freedom by his own efforts, and with all the force of mind and body at his disposal sets himself to his task. He knows "there is none to help me." With arms and legs, with fingers and toes, with nails and teeth, he works, always works. Day and night his mind dwells on nothing else until he has broken through the crust that encloses the heart, as the chicken in the egg with claws and beak chops its way through the shell and breaks forth into safety. More than for the Christian, life for the "supine" Buddhist is a perpetual struggle: there is no forgiving god for him. "Strive unceasingly!" were the last words the Buddha spoke.

Thus the Buddhist wages the greatest warfare that man can wage: that fierce, inward battle of renunciation and self-mastery. In silent struggle he wrestles with his own *I*, as Jacob in the night with the unknown. Here beckons nor fame nor gold, nor even love, in that alluring form which supplies the Christian with his greatest inspiration. This fight is fought for sorrowlessness alone; for that assured eternal Peace which no god has given, and hence no god can take away.

A certain cold earnestness seems to pervade the whole of this teaching. Every deed, every word, every thought is treated, as it were, with the dissecting knife. Of so much importance does the Buddha regard its discipline that he calls it the straight path "that leads to the purification of beings, to the overcoming of pain and woe, to the destruction of sorrow and care." It was to this discipline that he referred when he declared to his monks: "By unceasing heedfulness, by steadfastness and endurance, I have reached the highest goal."

In everything the first and only question is: How can I make capital out of this for myself? How can I make this serve my own salvation?" If injustice is done to me, I know that I am not the one who is harmed by it but he, the evil-doer. I know that already his punishment awaits him, and remain serene. Yea, I bestir myself indeed to feel a motion of love towards him, for only then does my peace become perfect. Hence, if I am a true egoist I behave accordingly, and meet the man who injures me with love and meekness. "For not by hate is hate destroyed; by love alone is hate destroyed," teaches the Exalted One. And, "Kindly thought is the best kind of retaliation." And again, "If also, ye monks, robbers and murderers with a saw should sever your joints and limbs, he who fell into anger thereat would not be fulfilling my instructions." "Patience, as of the round earth"—that is the highest goal, the supreme adornment of the true disciple. Whoso has made this his own, of him one may say, "He has accomplished much."

It is not because he knows that the eye of an all-seeing god is upon him that the Buddhist does all this, but only because he is continually thinking of his own true well-being. "To whom is his own self dear? To whom is his own self not dear?" asks King Pasenadi of the Exalted One, who replies: "Those who travel with body, speech, or mind the way of sin, to these their self is not dear; even though they say, 'We love our self,' yet do they not love it." (Saṁyuttaka Nikāya.)

If only we have learnt to think of things in the right way, we shall be able to extract the greatest advantage out of whatsoever wrong may be done to us, and in perfect reasonableness, and not by a forced belying of our nature, we shall give thanks to our enemies as being our greatest benefactors. The legends narrate that the king's son, Kuṇāla, through the malice of his stepmother, who had fallen in love with him, but had been repulsed, had both his eyes put out. When, with collected mind, after the first eye had been torn out, he had it put in his hand by the executioner, as he held it and looked at it with his remaining eye, suddenly there arose in him the comprehension of the transiency of all that has arisen. True knowledge awoke in him, and, throwing off every feeling of *I*, he broke out into the exulting words: "May she long enjoy life, power, and happiness who has made use of this means in order to make me a participator in this great boon."

Another legend tells that the Buddha once heard from a monk named Purna that he wished to settle in a land whose inhabitants were noted for their violence.

"If they abuse and injure thee, what then shalt thou think?"

"I shall then think: 'These people are really good in that they only abuse me, but do not beat me and throw stones at me.'"

"But if they beat thee and throw stones at thee?"

"Then I shall think: 'They are really good in that they only beat me and throw stones at me, but do not attack me with sticks and swords.'"

"But if they attack thee with sticks and swords?"

"Then I shall think: 'They are really good in that they do not rob me of life outright.'"

"But if they rob thee of thy life?"

"Then I shall think: 'These people are really good to me in that they have freed me from the burden of this life.'"

Whereupon the Buddha says: "Well hast thou spoken, Purna! Go and deliver, thou self-deliverer! Lead to the other shore, thou that thyself hast reached that shore! Comfort, thou that already art comforted! Guide to Nibbāna, thou that art already entered into Nibbāna!"

A deliberate martyrdom is, however, unthinkable, for there is no merit in itself in loving one's enemy, but in the contrary case of hating him there would be harm for me. The law is not fulfilled by love, but it is destroyed by hate. The centre of gravity of everything remains immovably fixed in me.

But is it not verging rather close upon the impossible that I should not only restrain hand and tongue but also thought?

The control of thought, sooth to say, is only possible where true knowledge has been attained to, where the injured one knows that this body here, to which hurt has been done, does not belong to me, is not at all my *I*. Why then need I get angry when anything is done to it? This body in itself is an entirely worthless thing. Its only, its indispensable worth lies in this, that my salvation is bound up with it; by it is my salvation conditioned, as the violin string, worthless in itself, becomes invaluable when it permits itself to be set vibrating, and thus provides outward expression for the conceptions of genius.

So in this most wonderful of all systems no true morality is possible without knowledge; no true knowledge is possible without morality, and both morality and knowledge are bound up with one another, as are light and warmth in a flame, or rather each is the complement of the other, like the zinc and the copper plate in the voltaic pile; each is strengthened through the other in an ascending scale without it being possible to assign to either of them the place of primary importance.

But the Buddha does not despise that, I might almost say, vulgar, line of reasoning, which finds expression in the popular saying: "Do unto others as you would that they should do to you," as is shown by the following episode from the Saṁyuttaka Nikāya. The king Pasenadi asks his wife Mallikā, "Is there any one at all who is dearer to thee than thyself?" With rare candour she answers, "Truly, great king, there is none at all dearer to me than myself." And, undismayed, the great king confesses the like of himself also. Apparently out of pure tedium they tell the Buddha of their profound colloquy, who is good-natured enough to answer them with a verse:

> Far have I wandered, over many lands,
> And yet that man I never yet have found
> Who loved aught dearer than he loved himself,
> So dear to every creature is itself.
> Hence unto others he will do no wrong
> Who ceases not to love his own dear self.

But this is only a digression. In specific Buddhist thought, morality in the strictest sense is bound up with egotism—is, in fact, disguised egoism. Hence love of the neighbour is placed upon what is indeed the coldest but also the soundest basis the world can offer.

In the other great Indian religion also, the system of Vedanta, love is founded upon knowledge. The man of knowledge recognises himself to be Brahman, to be the universe. Hence if I am the All, if All is *I*, my neighbour is identical with myself. I must love him not merely as I love myself, but as being my very own self. The unhappy, the diseased, the miserable, that come before mine eyes—these I myself am; what they suffer, that I suffer. In big letters stands written over the entrance-door to Indian morality, "That thou art"—"Tat tvam asi." It is a pure delusion that brings the picture of duality before me. To the wise man all distinctions are wiped out in the great *I*, are merged together into unity. And who does not love his own *I*?

However strange may appear to the Occidental the line of thought that lies at the base of Vedanta, to him who follows it up, and, so doing, arrives at an understanding of it, love of the neighbour becomes a sheer matter of necessity. We are here confronted with egoism's leap for life. Even if the entire phenomenon, in the language of Schopenhauer, depends upon the penetration of the *principii individuationis*, upon the surrender of *I*-will, yet I surrender my *I*, only to find it again in all other beings. In reality egoism is not destroyed, it is only the conception of the *I* that has changed, that has undergone a metamorphosis, which, alongside that other that leads from *I* to Not-*I*, is the most astounding phenomenon which the world can present to us. If we consider it rightly, there are only two thoughts that are worthy of being thought, of being carried to their ultimate—that is, lived out: the thought, "All is *I*," maintaining life in perpetuity, and the thought, "All is not-*I*," for ever abolishing life.

Buddhism, in so far as it is founded upon the "All is not-*I*," stands diametrically opposed to Vedanta. In spite of the tenderest care devoted to this seeming *I*, all actual egoism is here done away with, because all possibility of egoism is also banished. Here there is only an apparent egoism, as there is only an apparent *I*. In Vedanta the path to morality, and morality itself, is given with the phrase: "All is *I*." In Buddhism the apprehension: "All is not-*I*" is only the path that leads to the summit of morality, not that summit itself. In itself the apprehension of myself—and my neighbour of course—as "not-*I*," as illusion, can furnish no basis upon which morality can actualise itself, whilst with the "All is *I*" of the Vedanta the whole of morality is given in a nutshell.

In Buddhism morality is conditioned only by the conclusions drawn from the "All is not-*I*." Only when I perceive that this *I*, precisely by becoming a seeming-*I*, becomes transformed into the central point of support of the world; only when I recognise that this *I*, precisely by becoming a seeming-*I*, eternally chains me to Saṁsāra, and that only a certain specific treatment of this seeming-*I* can set me free;—only then can I soar to genuine, that is, fruitful, morality. In the light of this morality my neighbours become merely objects from which my deeds rebound, to come back upon myself. As sunlight can be seen and made use of only when reflected, so my inner nature only becomes clear after it has been reflected as deed and word—and of course, thought—from my neighbour upon myself (in not-*I* all difference between my neighbour and myself disappears, and deed and thought become one), and only in the rebound is there given me the possibility of self-recognition, and, with it, of deliverance.

All moral requirement remains based upon me, has its beginning and end in me. The idea of transgression against another has no place in the system. I transgress only against myself, or, more correctly expressed, I hurt and harm myself only. Strictly speaking, we have no right to talk of transgression or guilt. Morality is knowledge; vice is ignorance—stupidity. Thus, from the standpoint of morality also, I become the centre of the world, and the absolute, the pure form of this seeming-egotism makes the entire universe nothing but a powerful sounding-board which catches the vibrations that proceed from me and sends them back to me again as the harmony of deliverance. Of this sounding-board, however, the most sensitive part is formed of one's own seeming-*I*. From it the most delicate vibration echoes back in endless reverberation; hence it is clear with what extraordinary care this most sensitive of all instruments must be handled so that it may send forth no confused and deafening din, but instead, the clear harmonious rhythm of deliverance. The profoundest, the ultimate object of the universe and of this seeming-*I* within it, is to help its central pivot—the suffering being—to salvation; to be the means of his deliverance.

Buddhism thus stands along with Vedanta in opposition to Christianity with its despotic, because incomprehensible, moral requirements. Both are apotheoses of egoism, yet each is so in an entirely different manner and fashion.

IX

CHARITY

Charity in a certain sense is the seconds-hand on the moral horologe of Buddhism. Charity is the readiest, most immediately applicable standard of measurement we have for the moral condition of each man. In charity the course of morality can be followed step by step, as by the motion of the seconds-hand on a clock the course of the hours can be followed. The finer and the finest moral movements are almost imperceptible to our senses, like the motion of the hour-hand on a clock; hence it is only with difficulty that they can be made to serve as indices of morality. But we have a perfect right to say: "Whoever cannot give has failed to grasp the A B C of the Buddha's doctrine." For as water under the influence of fire, as its first reaction, yields up its store of absorbed air, so the individual who has been under the influence of the Buddha's doctrine, before all else, seeks to rid himself of his stored-up treasures. This is the first and surest sign that that inversion of all his ideas has taken place in the man, inevitable in those who comprehend—that unprecedented conversion from the affirmation of life to its negation.

Two considerations constrain to charity; but the

most outstanding is the desire to make one's self as free and light as possible, so as not to be hindered needlessly upon the steep path towards the highest. It is enough, and more than enough, that I am obliged to drag this seeming form, my body, along with me. Like the wrestler in the Olympic games, naked must I also enter upon this great struggle, the struggle for truth, if I would not in advance destroy every chance of success. In this sense it was that Jesus said to the rich young man, "If thou wouldst be perfect, go sell all that thou hast and give to the poor." That means: "If thou wouldst be a warrior, put on thine armour." The stripping one's self of everything is the sword in this combat; endurance is the helmet; true humility the breastplate.

A mysterious strength must lie hidden in this apparently purely external act, and every one who has been in earnest about truth has always begun his course with this procedure. So far, there is nothing specifically Buddhistic about this "renouncing charity." In every religion, at all periods of the world's history, this great renunciation has been indispensable for every one who strove for the highest, whether that highest lay in the affirmation or in the denial of god. Many an one may play the prophet, but as long as he lacks the courage to make this renunciation, he has no just title to such an office.

The other form of charity may be called "receptive charity," and it is the specifically Indian, yea, the specifically Buddhistic form. Every action is followed by its corresponding results. The reward for that which I give to my fellowman comes back to me as certainly as the stone, which

I have raised from the earth, falls back to earth again when I let it go. There is no easier or more convenient way of earning merit than by giving. Again and again the Buddha unwearyingly preaches giving. When a Brahmin asks him: "Does Gautama approve of offerings?" he answers: "I do not approve of every offering, but I do not also disapprove of every offering. A blood-offering I do not approve of, but a blameless offering I approve of, Brahmin, and it is inexhaustible giving." And, speaking to his monks, he says: "If beings, O ye monks, knew the fruits of almsgiving, as I know it, most surely they would not eat the least, last mouthful without sharing a portion thereof." Almsgiving is one of the six great perfections of a Buddha.

By far the most meritorious form of giving, however, is giving in support of the religion. "To give" and "to give in the service of religion" are almost synonymous terms. The Indian has but little mind for our kind of giving—giving for generally useful and worldly purposes. The whole of life for him ultimately becomes religion.

The Buddha who freed all the concepts of Brahmanism from the bondage of books and set them in active operation, left this concept of charity, as perhaps the only exception, in the fetters in which it came to him from Brahmanism; nay, in his hands the centre of gravity of giving was transferred perhaps even more definitely than in Brahmanism perhaps, to the religious side of life. When the reward of giving or the punishment of not giving is to be shown, it is always the beggar-monks who furnish the subject matter of the discourse. Here the Buddha indulges himself in an unadulterated *naïveté*, such as we are nowhere else accustomed to hear from his lips. When the queen Mallikā asks him whence it comes that there are women who are ugly and poor, he answers that their ugliness has its cause in their former ill-nature, but that they are poor because in previous lives they did not give to monks.

The Buddha was constrained to maintain the duty of giving by an idea so unspiritual as this, for the Dhamma could only be exhibited in its purity by the monkhood, and the monkhood was wholly vowed to benevolence. It was here a question of nothing less than the existence of the Dhamma in its concrete form. Hence the tremendous emphasis laid upon the duty of giving to the monks; hence the, I had almost said, unscrupulousness of the means adopted to keep perpetually alive the feeling of the necessity for fulfilling this duty. Legend and the borderland of legend and history vie with one another in spurring on both high and low. King Asoka, the great ruler of India, received his kingdom, it was said, because in one of his former births he had, as a child, offered to the Buddha Kassapa, for lack of something better, a handful of earth. The same Asoka three times presented entire Jambudīpa (India) to the Buddhist priesthood and three times bought it back again. And when, nigh to death, and already stripped of everything by his successor, he had nothing else to present, he sent half of the Āmalaka fruit of which he was just about to partake to the monkhood as a present.

In historical Ceylon the legends became reality.

Never, perhaps, as long as the world has stood, has a race of rulers given themselves so completely to the service of religion as this long succession of kings of the Sun Dynasty, one after another of whom sought to outdo his predecessor in his gifts to the monkhood. There were times in which the land supported sixty thousand monks. One single cloister in the capital Anurādhapura[1] numbered three thousand inmates, who all lived upon the bounty of the kings.

It was not fear which incited to such immense gifts, for there was none here like the Brahmin priest who held the key of heaven in his hands, and to whom of necessity one had to make gifts. In spite of all the emphasis that was laid upon charity, it still remained a purely free-will affair. But perhaps on that very account the giving was all the more liberal. With truly royal, nay, almost unmeasured zeal, the rulers made use of the favourable opportunity which their high position placed in their hands of laying up a treasure of good works, through unceasing beneficence to the monks, which would provide them through many more rebirths with the wherewithal to perform yet other deeds of merit. But not only those of high station, but the common man also was inspired by the same views, and therefore by the same zeal. Even to-day, especially among the Burmese people, gifts towards religious purposes are looked upon as drafts upon eternity. No one has any doubt that these payments will be made good again in later lives with compound interest added. Thus, how

[1] Situated north of Kandy; famous for its .uins. The residence of the "Great Dynasty' from about 250 B.C. o 750 A.C.

much more advantageous it is to lay out one's money in this way than in worldly commerce, from which only cares and worries spring. How much more safely, how much more wisely do I act when I content myself here with the simply necessary, and use what remains over in smoothing for myself beforehand the rugged road of future births. Who knows whether the next birth will leave me the possibility of giving? Whoever really supposes that all ends with the close of the one life can have no proper understanding of his own true wellbeing. The succession of rebirths stretches out endlessly, and if I have a true regard for my own welfare, I must not only look after this one life which my present consciousness is able to compass, but I must have a care for the entire series of rebirths which the Buddha has taught me to apprehend with my understanding.

It is through the thought that in this life the next one has to be looked after before everything else that the possibility of deliverance first opens out before me. For who is in a position to obtain deliverance in one single life? Hence the spiritual outlook of such an one widens, and, surmounting the narrow limits of the single existence, he acquires a view of things corresponding to his new outlook. Of course we comfortable townsmen smile at such a citizen of the world and hold him for a fool who sacrifices his present advantage for the figments of his brain. That, however, is because we have never been taught to break through those confining barriers which the *I*-thought has built up all round us. That this reversal of our current modes of thought has remained no mere play of words but has been realised in actual life, the best proofs are precisely these gifts over which the Buddhist church has had to rejoice in such peculiarly abundant measure.

That in this theory of deed and its corresponding consequences, charity came into danger of being worked out like a sum in arithmetic, is quite clear. All the more pleasing it is to find that alongside the quantitative side, the qualitative side was not entirely forgotten. If for long, through force of circumstances, this did not come into notice as prominently as it did in Christianity, we have in Buddhism, all the same, the complement of the parable of the widow's mite. The Chinese Fa-Hien tells that in Purushapura stood the alms-bowl of the Buddha, which was filled to the brim when a poor person only put in a flower, whilst the rich might throw in thousands without ever filling it. Certainly we have here the true views of the Buddha as regards giving, and here, as everywhere, we see that nothing that is human was alien to this Great One of the world.

X

KNOWLEDGE

IN Buddhism and Vedanta, the two great religions of India, this world—life in general—on one hand is sorrow, and upon the other, delusion; hence naturally the desire to get rid of delusion, since every creature flees sorrow. The removal of delusion, however, is only possible through knowledge. Both of these great Indian religions, in contradistinction to all others, are religions not of faith but of knowledge, Vedanta being really a wonderful combination of both, but Buddhism the religion of knowledge unalloyed. In the Vedanta knowledge *leads* to deliverance, to Brahman; in Buddhism knowledge *is* deliverance.

Knowledge, as here spoken of, is the specifically Indian knowledge, the Great Knowledge. Only where life is delusion can this great knowledge exist which brings deliverance and *is* deliverance. Nothing analogous to it can be developed out of worship as found in monotheistic religions. Since the world around me is the handiwork of a god, it cannot be any delusion. Where life is no illusion, the highest wellbeing cannot reside in knowledge, but must be founded upon faith, for if the world is a piece of handiwork, there must be a creation of the world, an absolute beginning. This, however, can never be got at by knowledge, but only by faith. Only ending, cessation, can be known or understood. A beginning of the world, god, faith—these are inseparable concepts. The place that knowledge takes in the monotheistic world is to be seen from these words of the Preacher: "Much learning is a weariness of the flesh, and he that increaseth knowledge increaseth sorrow." Here knowledge is merely a designation of that something, unsatisfying in itself, insufficient for itself, with whose increase care increases; with the increase of which care, increases also the passion for redemption, and with this, the unfitness for redemption! This kind of knowledge only half leads to the goal; it beckons and allures into the depths of sorrow only to leave the searcher to stand there helpless in the darkness. This knowledge lacks the power to lift one out of sorrow into salvation; it lacks the fermentative quality by which sorrow is transformed into salvation.

That knowledge, however, which is specific to Indian spiritual life possesses this quality. Knowledge, in so far as it fulfils the function of leading to salvation, is knowledge *par excellence*, the Great Knowledge. Every other kind of knowledge, however high it may stand in the eyes of the world, is inferior knowledge, a species of ignorance indeed, if on account of it the sense of the greater knowledge is lost.

The idea of this salvation-producing knowledge was taken over from Brahmanism by the Buddha, but as any one who brings to act one and the same reagent upon totally different bases obtains totally different resultant products in each case, so it was here also. In Brahminism this knowledge of life as illusion was brought to bear upon Ātman, as based upon a solid foundation of faith; with the Buddha the knowledge was made to act upon a base of total absence of faith. The substratum here was not soul or Ātman, but the iron law of cause and effect. Hence the wide divergence in the nature of the ultimate products: there, deification; here, cessation and extinction, as of a lamp whereof the oil is spent. This much at least is certain, that only in Buddhism is knowledge to be seen at its absolute altitude in that unalloyed clearness, free of all admixture of faith, in which it bears in itself the proof of its own perfection.

What now is knowledge in Buddhism? The Buddha himself supplies us with the definition. Knowledge is nothing else but the knowledge of the Four Holy Laws of Sorrow; ignorance is nothing but the failure to apprehend these four fundamental laws. Knowledge is the knowing of sorrow. Knowing sorrow, however, is synonymous with knowing salvation. But since knowing sorrow is synonymous with being free from sorrow, so to know redemption is synonymous with being redeemed. Hence to know sorrow is synonymous with being redeemed.

But now, how can the knowing of sorrow mean the same thing as salvation? Thus: by the proposition "All is transient" being translated on one hand into the proposition "All is sorrowful," and upon the other hand into the proposition "All is not-*I*." The transition from transiency to Sorrow is bespoken. It is now time to show how the law of transiency can be transformed into the law of not-*I*.

When the Buddha for the first time set forth his new teaching to the five ascetics of Benares, he clothed it in the form of the four-fold law of sorrow. Koṇḍañña is the first to apprehend, but he does not react by simply saying: "I have apprehended," but he proves his newly awakened knowledge in that he apprehends that "All that is subject by the law of its nature to arising, according to the law of its nature is also subject to decay." And when the Brahmin Sāriputta, who later became the Buddha's chief disciple, asks the monk Assaji to lay the doctrine of the Exalted One before him in a few words, the latter answers: "Of all things that have arisen from a cause, the Tathāgata has declared that cause, and its destruction also he has likewise made clear." The pure, cloudless eye of wisdom opens for Sāriputta, and he apprehends: "Whatsoever by the law of its nature is subject to arising is also according to its nature subject to decay." Despite the fact that one has the law of sorrow and the other the law of cause and effect brought before him, both answer in the selfsame words.

We have here, then, a new form in which the transiency idea clothes itself; everything that has arisen is only the effect of a previous cause; this cause itself is only the effect of a still earlier cause, and so on *ad infinitum.* All that we are able to compass with our six senses, the entire universe, consists of nothing but an endless chain of causes and effects, and hence of an endless arising and passing away again; for everything that owes its existence to the action of a previous cause must cease to be so soon as the force which led to its actualisation is exhausted.

Now no one can maintain that my personality in any sense whatever was, before my parents begot me. In my totality I have arisen as "name and form"—that is, I am the effect of a cause; hence I must in my totality disappear so soon as the force which led to actualisation has become exhausted. If, however, in death I go in my totality down to the dust, there can be no thread, no permanent something, no soul, binding one existence to another. I go on living only in the sense that as I myself am only the effect of a previous cause, so I now become the cause of a later effect. My *I* is that wherein cause and effect, appearing as deed and result, merge into one another; on one hand it is wholly cause; upon the other, wholly effect. It is for this reason that Kamma, the one-word formula for the *I* in activity, is defined as "cause and effect." A connection between the earlier and the later existence there is not, and yet on the one depends the other, and is contained in the other as the reaction is contained in the action. Thus stretches out the tremendous chain of existences, without beginning and without end, and yet each stands out separately by itself, as the heart makes every beat separately and yet produces the finished organism.

From the influence of the idea of cause and effect upon apprehension we get this result: Individuality, *in toto* arisen, must also consequently *in toto* pass away again. Hence there cannot lurk concealed in it any eternal core, any soul. The soul, however, was called in ancient India the Ātman, the self, the true *I*, because it was held to be imperishable. This body, as being transient and perishable, cannot be considered as the true *I*. Because the Buddha found no soul in the body, because he perceived this corporeality together with all its functions, together with perception and consciousness, to be a thing conditioned—that is, transient—therefore did he say: "This body is Anattā (non-self), is not my *I*, it does not belong to me." The course of the argument runs: "Thou that sayest, 'This body is my self,' are such wishes of thine as these fulfilled: 'Let my body be thus; let my body be not so!' or, 'Let my sensations, my perceptions, my differentiations, my consciousness be thus; let them not be so'?" How can this body belong to me when I have no power over it? How can it be the true *I* when it does not at all belong to me?

The Buddha never said: "There exists no such thing as the soul," any more than he said: "There is no god." He only said: "Redemption from the sorrow of life is not to be reached through this god-idea." Further, he only said: "In this bodily form there is no soul, as there is not in anything else that can be seized by the six senses, because all, all is nothing but an endless succession of causes and effects." He was not obliged to go any further, for his task consisted merely in leading from sorrow to salvation, and in the thought: "This body is not my I; it is Anattā," salvation lay concealed, as the sweet ripe fruit in the bitter hull. Hence, when the wandering ascetic Vacchagotta directly asked him: "Is there an *I*?" he kept silence. When the ascetic further asked: "How then, honoured Gautama, is there no *I*?" he still kept silence, and the questioner went away. The Buddha did not answer him because the question lay outside the province of sorrow and salvation, and an answer, therefore, would have been superfluous. It suffices for salvation that in this form there is no *I*. This the Buddha clearly laid down. That suffices! The Buddha only teaches how sorrow may be uprooted. To those who wish to know more, the Buddha has nothing to say. Hence it is idle trifling on our part, based upon a misconception of the whole affair, to worry our heads as to which of these two possibilities the Buddha himself privately regarded as the more probable. He himself upbraidingly asks his monks: "Ye monks, thus comprehending, thus understanding, will you now, at this present time, put such questions as these: 'Am I not? what am I? how am I? This my being—whence did it come; whither does it go?'" and the answer comes: "Verily no, Master!" The not-*I*, like everything else in Buddhism, is purely individual. An *I*, an eternal, a soul there is not, so far as my personality is concerned. That suffices. What sort of conditions the *I* presents, apart from this—that we cannot know, and do not need to know.

Thus the understanding transmutes the proposition of cause and effect—which embraces that of transiency—into the proposition of not-*I*. The law of transiency, the law of cause and effect, the law of sorrow, the law of not-*I*,—all these are only various modifications of one and the same thing. The destruction of sorrow and the destruction of the *I*-illusion are laid down as being identical.

"The transient, O Master, the transient, so they say, O Master! But what now, O Master, is the transient?" a monk asks of the Buddha.

"The body, verily; sensation, perception, differentiation, consciousness—these are transient."

"Sorrow, sorrow, men say, O Master; but what now, O Master, is this sorrow?"

"The body, verily; sensation, perception, differentiation, consciousness—these all are sorrow."

"Non-self, non-self (Anattā), so men say, O Master; but what now, O Master, is this non-self?"

"The body, verily; sensation, perception, differentiation, consciousness—these all are non-self."

"Subject to arising and decay, so men say, O Master; but what now, O Master, is subject to arising and decay?"

"The body, verily; sensation, perception, differentiation, consciousness—these all are subject to arising and decay." (Saṁyuttaka Nikāya.)

The law of non-*I*, of the non-possession by me of the body, is the concealed, connecting link in the thought: "All life is transient; consequently, all life is sorrow." It is the hidden third power which supplies the medium for the comparison of the other two and makes them clear. Because all life is transient, only an arising and a passing away, a play of cause and effect—therefore is all life "Anattā," without a soul, lacking an *I*. The thought: "Here is an *I*," has been seen to be illusion, ignorance. And because with this, my own personality—this that I have hitherto regarded as my surest, most precious possession—is robbed from me, as not belonging to me, and reveals itself as something soulless and hence worthless, therefore does transiency turn to sorrow. For as one who has thought himself the possessor of a valuable diamond, upon being informed by the lapidary that it is only a worthless stone, experiences pain, so is it with one who has thought that in the *I* he possessed that imperishable something, charged with all delight, which elevates to Brahman, and then suddenly perceives that it is nothing but a worthless burden, a group of Saṅkhāras, an embodied sorrow, that he is dragging about with him.

Transiency, sorrow, not-*I*—all three mean the same thing, only looked at from a different point of view, and the knowledge of sorrow is no other than the knowledge of transiency and the knowledge of non-*I*. The blending and merging together of these three constitutes the Great Knowledge, the Buddha-knowledge.

To what extent is this knowledge synonymous with salvation?

All the Buddhas that have yet appeared in our world have done so in order to teach three things, and only three—namely, that everything is transitory, that everything is painful, and that nowhere is an *I* to be found. This is the sum, the quintessence of their teaching, and in it all there is no word about redemption. But as the sea is compassed by the land and the land by the sea, so in the teaching of the Exalted One do sorrow and salvation mutually encompass one another. And as one who maps out all the outlines of all the lands on the surface of the earth, with that same operation supplies the boundaries of all the seas, so the Buddha in giving his three laws of transiency, sorrow, and non-*I*, at one and the same time along with them gives salvation. As in the Anattā-idea —in the idea of *I* as not-*I*—subject and object, deed and result, before and behind, merge into one another, so also sorrow and salvation,—sorrow becomes salvation.

Because sorrow and transiency are synonymous, so this individuality, because *in toto* transient, also becomes *in toto* sorrow. Sorrow is thus nothing external, nothing experienced, no product of corporeality, but corporeality itself; even as deed is no product of corporeality but corporeality itself. Personality, rightly understood, is nothing but embodied sorrow. It is saying the same thing to say, "abolish corporeality" and "abolish sorrow." Hence we cannot only say that sorrow disappears along with the bearer thereof, but we must also say that sorrow and the bearer of sorrow are identical, are one and the same thing looked at from different points of view, just like deed and doer of the deed. As in knowledge the doer of the deed disappears, so also the bearer of sorrow. There remain only deed and sorrow. Hence, because I have recognised the *I* to be transient and without permanent residue, so also must sorrow be transitory and void of any permanent residue. Hence, since I recognise the *I* as having arisen from a cause, sorrow also must have arisen from a cause and must disappear with the disappearance of this cause. In Buddhism, however, salvation is nothing else but the disappearing of sorrow.

Hence everything turns upon the finding of the cause of sorrow, and this the Buddha found in the attachment of our senses to objects. Our senses are the continually active mechanism by which transiency is perpetually being transmuted into sorrow. For sorrow is nothing else but the transiency of all that has arisen entering into our consciousness. Inasmuch as our five senses—with the mind as a sixth—seize transiency, they seize sorrow. Since, however, they are not capable of seizing anything else but transiency—since they only react to the *Becoming*, the arising, the passing away—they seize sorrow *only*, and the activity of the senses is identical with the arising of sorrow. For when the eye meets anything visible, it is affected, unites itself with it, and thus arises and is begotten the impression of sight. When the ear encounters anything audible, the organ of smell anything fragrant, the organ of taste anything possessed of flavour, the organ of touch anything tangible, there arises the corresponding impression. Yea, when the mind unites itself with the thinkable, in that union thought is begotten. "Through thought and things arises thought-consciousness; the interblending of the three gives contact." Where there is contact there is arising, birth. Where there is arising, there is passing away, death. Where there is arising and passing away, birth and death, there is sorrow.

All sorrow depends upon our senses, and so far as the senses extend, so far does sorrow extend. The key to Buddhist thought lies in the identity of transiency and sorrow.

We have now seen that this *I*, as being *in toto* a thing arisen, is also *in toto* a thing to be comprehended with the comprehension of the cause that has led to its arising, and "attachment" has been found to be the cause of its arising. This, however, is something within the reach of our understanding. Hence the *I* becomes something *in toto* comprehensible, hence *in toto* a *Becoming*, a something perpetually arising through the interaction of our consciousnesses of seeing, hearing, smelling, tasting, touching, and thinking, and as perpetually passing away again with their dissolution.

"The personality, the personality, it is called; what then has the Exalted One really declared the personality to be?" asks a monk of the nun Dhammadinnā. And the latter answers: "The Five Bases of the Elements of Being are the personality, so the Exalted One has said."

Just as the entire world depends upon the six senses, so also does the *I* depend upon the six senses. As the six senses build up the world, so also do they build up the *I*. Because it is apprehensible by the senses, therefore is the *I* torn from me as not belonging to me, and thrown into the common mass of *Becoming*, made a part of the external world. Only from this point of view do the words of the Buddha become intelligible where he declares: "Everything, ye monks, is a burning fire. And in what wise, ye monks, is everything a burning fire? The eye is a burning; objects are a burning; the mental impressions that depend upon the eye are a burning; the attachment of the eye is a burning; the sensation that arises out of the attachment of the eye is a burning, whether it be pleasant or unpleasant, or neither the one nor the other. And what sort of a fire is it that burns here? Verily, it is the fire of Lust, of Hate, and of Error that burns here; it is the fire of being born, of old age, and of death; the fire of grief, distress, sorrow, misery, and despair."

In this line of thought all apparent being is dissolved in an enormous *Becoming*, which sucks into its whirling eddy subject as well as object, the seer as well as the thing seen, the thinker and the thought.

If, however, this *I* is cognised as external world, there must yet be something present which transfers the *I* to this position; there must be something which recognises itself as existing in contradistinction to this external world, something of the nature of a true *I* lying behind, concealed in this seeming *I*?

No! Outside this seeming *I* there can be nothing, because we have seized it *in toto*, have watched, as it were, the manner of its arising. It is impossible that something eternal, a soul, can conceal itself in me so far as I am individuality, so far as I am I. The ability to apprehend, the ability to seize this *I* as only an apparent *I*, is only a function of this seeming *I*. Like the other five senses, cognition which produces personality is itself a product of personality. As the cold hand is warmed on the body to which it belongs, so cognition derives its ability to pass out of the form of ignorance into the form of knowledge from that very corporeality out of which it has arisen. This is precisely the distinctive feature in the position assumed by cognition as knowledge, cognition as the apprehension of the *I* as not-*I*, that it does not produce deed—that is, new life—that is, new personality; but instead produces the deed which leads to the *abolition* of deed—that is, to the dissolution of individuality. The transition from cognition as ignorance to cognition as knowledge is synonymous with that activity, that process, in which the individual is dissolved. I produce knowledge, means, I myself dissolve myself, and being saved is nothing else but the unshakable certainty of being saved.

Cognition that performs its own specific functions, cognition as knowledge, is not in itself different from common cognition as life-creating mental activity. The former proceeds from the latter purely by reason of proper instruction. Nothing but receptivity and teachableness on the part of cognition forms the fit soil for the Tathāgata's doctrine of redemption.

Thus, not upon the ground of any mere intuition, but upon the ground of facts of cognition, derived step by step from the working of the universal law of cause and effect, not only this body as a whole, but also in its molecular structure, together with such expressions of life as are based upon the latter, are transformed into a continual *Becoming*, a flame-like arising and passing-away, which excites the impression of a complete corporeality only because the individual pulsations lie wholly outside the range of the perception of our senses. Just as a flame in its individual particles is born and dies a thousand times every moment with a speed totally beyond the power of our senses to perceive, so also is it with our bodies. And as in the flame the sum of these Becoming-moments (each individual one of which lies beyond the boundaries of sense-perception), added up, gives the seeming-form of the body of the flame, so also the mass of the Becoming-moments of the individual adds up into the seeming-form of this body, this thing, in flames through and through, of which hence it is rightly said: "Destruction is its element; in it abides no solid core." (Saṁyuttaka Nikāya.)

It was thus that the Buddha looked upon life. Hence he compared the body to a bubble, perception to the foam of a water-spout, the differentiations to a banana stem, which seems to be wood, but in reality consists of rolled-up leaves. Consciousness, however, he compared to the sleight-of-hand performance of a conjurer. And rightly does the man of knowledge apprehend: "Void is all this of me and mine."

Expressing it in modern language we might say that the whole of corporeality, not only in purely physical but also in its mental activities, was to the Buddha a process of oxidisation of combustion. In one particular Sutta called the "Ant-hill Sutta" it is said: "What it (the personality) ponders and considers during the night as its work for the day—that is the smoke by night. What, after the pondering and considering of the night, it fulfils by day in deeds, words, and thoughts—this is the flame by day."

To be sure, the Brahmins had already comprehended life in similar fashion, but what was specific about the Buddha's view lay in this, that in his thought everything was dragged into this oxidisation-process; in the fiery glow of his thought the eternal substance, the soul, was burnt up and every difference done away; the dualism of body and soul for him merged into a unity, but not into the absolute unity, "spirit," "soul," or "matter," but into the double unity—so to speak—of "Becoming." The only disconcerting thing is that there are two things, matter and Avijjā, out of which this double unity, this life-unity, proceeds. As in arithmetic a minus multiplied by a minus becomes a positive, so, through the mutual interaction of the two impossibilities *par excellence*, the two primary impossibilities, there arises the primary product, the fact *par excellence*, life. But why are matter and Avijjā the two primary impossibilities? Because in their pure and unalloyed form they are unthinkable. Every attempt to formulate them in thought forthwith calls up the fusion of both, the Formed, individuality. Here we have the best expression of the impossibility of life as a genuine unity. All attempts of this nature must end in failure or in—faith!

But let us resume the interrupted threads of our argument.

Now that in thought not only the whole world but also my own *I* has been transmuted from apparent Being into ever-changing Becoming,—only now, after I have not only been dipped but have actually been dissolved in this seething mass of sorrow, have myself actually *become* sorrow,—only now, when the last vestige of *I*-ness under this microscopic scrutiny has taken flight, has disappeared in expiring ignorance, as shadows disappear with the setting of the sun,—only now has that great moment arrived when, as by a magical transformation, that most wonderful of all metamorphoses takes place: the transmutation of sorrow into salvation. For since all sorrow presupposes consciousness and clings to the *I*—to individuality—as rain to the cloud, sorrow also must disappear where there is no longer any *I*. The *I*, however, because recognised in all true thinking as *in toto* sorrow, is recognised as *in toto* non-*I*. To apprehend the *I* as *in toto* non-*I* means to remove it *in toto*, and thus in thought, along with the *I*, sorrow also is done away. To know sorrow means to know the *I* as non-*I*, and this is deliverance. This is the first greeting from that other order of things which, like a gentle, cooling breeze, fans the fevered and tormented mind.

Be it well noted, however, that it is not this body, as consisting of the elements, which has to disappear for sorrow to disappear, but this body in so far as it is "name and form"—in so far as it is individuality. It is not to the elements, to the constituents of the body, that sorrow adheres, but to the consciousness, to the *I*. As sorrow is nothing but the consciousness of sorrow, so salvation is nothing but the consciousness of salvation. With good cause, therefore, the Buddha could say: "Some ascetics and Brahmins, ye monks, accuse me, without due cause, for no reason, falsely, unjustly: 'A denier is this ascetic Gautama; he declares the destruction, the annihilation, the abolition of continuous life.' For what I am not, for what I do not teach—for this, ye monks, these ascetics and Brahmins blame me. One thing, and one thing only, ye monks, do I declare to you, now as always: Sorrow and the uprooting of sorrow."

The wise man perceives: "The door that leads out of the dwelling of sorrow is to be found in myself. I myself have the power to open it. When I dissolve the *I*, I also dissolve sorrow. As the fire goes out when there is no longer anything combustible in it, so is it with sorrow when there is no longer any *I* present. As seeming-*I*, as Becoming, as a product of the six senses, like the entire external world, the *I* must stand and fall with the activity of these senses—it must be possible of dissolution by the senses—that is, by me myself."

But is not all this as if the light should extinguish itself?

No! This dissolution does not correspond to an act of self-extinction, but to the light going out simply for want of fuel. And this lack of fuel is brought about solely through the transition from cognition as ignorance to cognition as knowledge. Because the removal of the *I* is synonymous with the removal of an illusion, therefore is the *I* removable by the *I*. Nothing is destroyed, nothing is denied, nothing is non-willed except ignorance—which simply means that incorrect cognition is brought over to correct cognition through proper instruction. Nay, let us leave our false and true to one side and only say: The old cognition is replaced by the new. Both act after the same fashion; here, as there, we have cognition; only the substrata are changed. The old cognition acts upon the substratum "I" as *Being*; the new, upon the substratum "I" as *Becoming*, as non-*I*. Hence the activity of the former is the eternal creating of life, but the activity of the latter the abolishing of life for ever. The former is, as it were, Deed, but the latter as the deed that leads to the abolition of all doing.

In what sense the body is the product of the six senses we have seen above. The attachment of the senses is the life-giving impetus. This attachment, however, can exist in one of the three forms of Lust (lobha), Hate (dosa), or Illusion (moha). These are the "deepest roots of being." The fire of individuality is kindled through lust, hate, and illusion—that is to say, through the three kinds of willing. Elsewhere it is said: "Four species of nourishment, ye monks, are provided for living beings—for those already arisen, for their support;

for those only now arising, for their development. What are the four? First, the food of the elements, coarse or fine; second, contact; third, mental perception; fourth, consciousness. And where, ye monks, do these four species of nourishment find their root? They find their root in the lust for life."

As one fire ever and again kindles fresh fire, and this in turn fresh fire again, so from the life that once has arisen ever new life flames forth afresh, and from this, new life again, and so on in endless sequence. Like the coming together of tinder and dried grass, so is the contact of the senses with their corresponding objects. Ever anew from the contact flares up the flame of life. And as a fire whose fuel is unexhausted ever burns on, so also is it with this fire of life so long as the senses continue to supply it with new food. Hence we live eternally by reason of our senses; hence is it that from all eternity we have lived by reason of our senses; for contact creates lust, lust creates deed, and deed creates consequence—that is, new life. Here, in our will to live, our attachment to life, lies the force that maintains the eternal play of action and reaction. Therefore "without beginning and without end is this Saṁsāra," this world of sorrow. Ending, deliverance is only possible when the senses cease to bring fresh fuel to the flame of life.

But how is that possible?

The forcible, outward turning away of the senses from objects is not enough; for there is a sixth sense, thought, which goes on working even though the other five have come to cessation, and "all our being depends upon thought; thought is its noblest part." The Buddha himself tells us more than once that no peace or quietude can come to the heart by forcibly imposed restrictions.

"Then the thought came to me," he says, "how if now I subdue, repress, crush down my nature by force of will, with teeth clenched and tongue pinned against the gums. And with clenched teeth and tongue glued to my gums, by force of will I subdued, repressed, and crushed down my nature. Somewhat as when a more powerful man lays hold of a weaker by the shoulder or the head, and subdues, represses, and crushes him down, even so the sweat trickled from the hollows of my arms with my efforts. But my body remained rebellious; it came not to peace through all this grievous asceticism that I practised." Forcible repression of the senses is only a species of action, which must provoke a corresponding reaction. We must go deeper, even to the very roots.

So long as the senses are in existence, so long must they be in activity. Their very existence consists in activity. If this activity in itself were life-bearing—that is, sorrow-bearing—then salvation were only thinkable through the dissolution of our *I* as matter, as composed of the elements. But that sort of salvation is impossible, because we are unable to comprehend the beginning of matter, the beginning of the world. Soluble, because comprehensible, is the *I*, only in so far as it is "name and form," individuality. That, however, suffices for salvation, because it is not to matter but to form, to the *I*-consciousness, that sorrow adheres. Why? Because it is only in *I*-consciousness that will arises, and to willing adheres sorrow—that is, life. Hence, if life, sorrow, is to cease, willing also must cease.

And when willing ceases, ceases also the attachment of the senses to objects. Both lie coldly beside one another, like steel and flint. There is no contact, no fire-producing friction, no willing, no deed. And if there is no deed, there is also no consequence of deed, no arising, no productive Kamma. Where there is no arising, there is also no passing away. Where there is neither arising nor passing away, there is also no being born and dying, no personality, no sorrow.

Blest rest from all arising and decay.

"The arising of personality, the arising of personality, they say, O Venerable One; what then, O Venerable One, has the Exalted One said about the arising of personality?" one asks of the learned nun Ḍhammadinnā.

"This lust of life, that sows repeated being,—this, so the Exalted One has said, is personality."

"The annihilation of personality, the annihilation of personality, they say, Venerable One; what now has the Exalted One been pleased to say about the annihilation of personality?"

"Even the complete, remainderless annihilation, rejection, driving forth, abolition, and disowning of this lust of life,—this, the Exalted One has said, is the annihilation of personality."

Elsewhere in the Saṁyuttaka Nikāya it is recorded that a monk spoke thus to the Buddha:

"Will the Exalted One be pleased to put before me clearly and in brief the essence of the doctrine, so that I, when I so have heard the doctrine, may henceforth remain aloof, withdrawn, watchful, steadfast, and earnest."

"Through attachment, O Monk, man comes to arise; through non-attachment man does not come to arise," was the Buddha's brief reply, but his interlocutor understood.

But do the beginning and end of the argument here agree with one another? It was said above that this body does not belong to me, and the proof adduced was my inability in any wise to effect change in it. Here, however, I am suddenly endowed with the power of completely bringing it to an end?

This body belongs to me in so far as it is my will; it does not belong to me in so far as it is a consequence, the embodying of my will. In the same way my voice belongs to me so long as it remains as a thought, quiet in my breast; but it no longer belongs to me when once it has issued thence. This *I* is nothing else but that in which cause and effect are unified. As effect, I no longer belong to myself; as cause, I am the absolute master of myself. In other words, since this personality is something *becoming*, something that every moment rises anew, and anew passes away again, I have the power to impart a given direction to the newly arising, or to put a check to it, but I have no power to influence in any way the already arisen. That would mean to turn the hands of the clock backwards. But the Buddha never looks behind. With feet firmly planted on the rolling present, he regards it, with gaze steady and unfaltering, as the mother-womb of the endless future. Again, if life—that is, sorrow—ceases, willing also must come to an end. But will, like the activity of the senses, cannot be forcibly turned into non-willing; that would only be a new form of willing. The senses must act, must contact their objects; that is implied in the very fact of their existence. Help is only possible when the substratum of the senses is so changed that these no longer find in objects anything to which they can attach themselves. Help is only possible when the natural process of sense-activity, itself remaining unchanged, no longer produces willing, and with it life, but upon the altered substratum leads to non-willing, and therewith to the abrogation of life. Sense-activity, cognition, are as necessary to the cessation of life as to its arising. The forcible breaking-off of sense-activity is not only useless, but it actually hinders deliverance. In the Buddha's system nothing is broken off, nothing repressed; it is only cognition that is corrected, and cognition once corrected, all the rest follows.

But now, how is the substratum of the senses so changed that they can find nothing more to which to be attached?

Through that precise change which occurs in cognition when ignorance passes into knowledge. Whoso has perceived life, world, *I*, in all their painful transiency, as *Becoming*, nowhere any longer finds anything to which it is possible to become attached. For to what shall he cling when he knows that in truth there is no "self" present that can cling, and no "other" to which it can cling,—that all in this "being-pregnant, flowing world of births" is only a continual, self-changing conglomerate of forms, a pile of Saṅkhāras linked fast to form with the hook of the lust for life. As ants gather together round a piece of booty, and so form an ant-body, so the five Khandhas lump themselves together into the seeming-form of this body that is begotten by the lust for life and born of Kamma. Hence, "Through egoism has arisen this corporeality."

Whoso thus apprehends, finds nothing more to which to be attached. Where there is nothing more to which to be attached, there is not only no willing, but also no possibility of willing. This was what the Buddha meant when he said to his disciples: "When I so apprehended, O ye disciples, all pride of life within me died away." Where there is no possibility of willing, there is no possibility of deed and its consequences; no life, no sorrow. "By the dissolving away of that attachment, the life-impulse is dissolved; by the dissolution of the life-impulse, being is dissolved; by the dissolution of being, birth is dissolved; by the dissolution of birth are dissolved old age and death, woe, distress, sorrow, grief, and despair."

With the removal of the life-impulse, of willing, the endless play of the self-weaving of the Khandhas into new forms comes to an end. The beams, the materials are there, but the master-builder, Kamma, is awanting. As flame does not arise when steel and flint lie beside one another, but only when they are struck together, so this life-flame only arises so long as there is the fire of lust, of hate, of delusion. When these are overthrown by true knowledge, when satiety of perception sets in, so that it can say of the whole world: "Not for me!" just because such apprehension has arisen, the senses may still go on contacting objects; cool and still, they glide off like water-drops from the lotus-leaf without wetting it; like the sesamum seed from the point of the needle without adhering to it. And as the propeller of a steamship turning in air does not drive it forward, as millstones not in contact with one another do not grind grain, so the senses, acting in the absence of willing, do not produce life. This is the true and only valid ending: the ending of "attachments," "when the perceptions of distinction, by whatsoever conditioned, come one after another and find no delight, no response, no support." And so to know sorrow becomes synonymous with salvation.

Even as ignorance and willing, so knowledge and non-willing condition one another, and are involved in one another, bound to one another, like the light and heat of a flame. And as we cannot say of the feet of a man who is running that either the left or the right is the one that is in front, so also here we cannot say whether it is knowledge or non-willing which takes the leading place.

One held in ignorance, driven by the lust for life, is like one driving in a carriage drawn by swift horses who looks down at the spokes of the wheels, which in their rapid revolution present to his eyes the appearance of solid discs. The thinking mind, however, which by thought has weakened the impetuous rush of the life-impulse, is like one who leaves whip and spur alone and allows the horses to go more slowly. Such an one experiences not only the blessedness of rest, but, glancing down at the wheel-spokes, is astonished to see that what had hitherto seemed to him to be perfect discs are only so many whirling spokes. And the more slowly the horses of the senses go, all the more clearly does he recognise, all the more distinctly does he taste "the taste of truth, the taste of the doctrine, the taste of deliverance." And the more clearly he perceives, the more distinctly he tastes, so that he drives ever more slowly, until finally he comes to a standstill. In wondering reflection over the huge marvel of *Becoming*, all willing, all doing, pass from him. An old philosopher called wonder the beginning of all philosophy. All true philosophy, all philosophy that is founded solely upon wonder and deep reflection, leads to the dissolution of life. The Buddha's teaching is one half philosophy of the most unalloyed sort, and the other half a doctrine of conduct. It becomes religion inasmuch as each half is indivisibly intertwined with the other. As in a leaf of paper written upon both sides, one side cannot be taken apart from the other, so is it in the Buddha's system with knowledge and morality. Morality, however, is nothing else but willing brought into certain forms (non-willing). Without morality there is no knowledge; without knowledge there is no morality. With the increase of morality, increases also knowledge; with the increase of knowledge, increases also morality. "As a man washes hand with hand, and foot with foot, so right behaviour is perfected through wisdom, and wisdom through right behaviour." As a man who sets up in business and by industry and ability earns profit, and makes use of this profit to enlarge and extend his business and earn still greater profit, and so on and on, his business becoming ever more extensive and profitable; so is it that with the bridling of the senses comprehension grows greater and greater, and with its increase increase also the inclination and the ability to bridle the senses still more.

But yet there must really be some first shock that turns the mind in this new direction?

There is, and it is the example and the instruction of another.

It is thus that the Buddha is the Awakened One, the Self-taught, the Teacherless, because in him this line of thought was generated spontaneously. Here we would have the genuine arising of the world, the making of something out of nothing, if it were not that the Buddha teaches not only the beginninglessness of the world, but also the beginninglessness of the truth, and of the Buddhas learned in the truth. Numberless as the sands of the Ganges are the Buddhas who came before this Gautama, and who shall come after him. The seed-grain that sprang up in this Gautama was planted countless existences ago by one of the previous Buddhas or by one of his pupils, and after taking countless lives for its development, it has ripened and become fruitful in this existence. Even the arising of the Buddha-thought has nothing to do with supernatural illumination, but is simply the effect of a previous cause. Here again we find ourselves immersed in the waves of this universal law of nature, and like the question as to the arising of the world, this question also finds its answer in the endlessness of the law of cause and effect.

But now, if the *I* is an illusion, if there simply is no *I*, how then can I, upon the knowledge earned in this existence, build into the next, so as finally to reach Nibbāna? For the way to Nibbāna is long and leads through many existences. Along with the *I* have I not likewise abolished the foundation of my building, and hence am only building castles in the air. If there is no *I*, do I not in every new existence begin all over again my struggle towards the highest, unassisted by the resultant residues and attainments of previous lives?

By no means! Inasmuch as Avijjā (ignorance) is abolished, the illusion of individuality done away, that illusion of deed, doer, and result which is founded upon *I*-consciousness, becomes individuality recognised as *in toto* cause-effect. If there is no doer present, I do not perform but *am* the deed. If, however, I am the deed, I am also the consequence of the deed in the same sense that reaction is the same as action, ice the same as water. The *I*, however, as a consequence of deed, is nothing but another expression for the *I* as willing. The thought: "I am not the doer but deed," embraces that other: "I am nothing but deed; I am deed *in toto*." If I am *in toto* deed, I am also *in toto* consequence of deed. That is, I am no willer, but I am will. But "I am will" means that I am nothing but will. Willing and doing here become alike, somewhat like "thinking" and "speaking to one's self." The Buddha himself says: "It is Cetanā (will) that I call Kamma (deed)." Only in the unification of both is the absolute summit of morality attained, which latter is incompatible with a deed-performing *I*, an *I* that can let its willing become deed as it pleases—that is to say, a soul and a god appertaining to it. In the soul and god idea there lies a weakening of morality. When, however, deed and will become as one, I can not only say: "I live out my deed, but "I live out my willing"; I am the creature of my willing. Simultaneously, however, willing becomes comprehensible since deed is comprehensible.

Only in so far as I cognise myself to be entirely will, without an *I* that wills or does not will—only so far do I become master of willing. Only in the perfection of this cognition is its fruit to be found. For only in the perfection of this cognition do will and deed become one and the same. Only where they become alike does will become conditioned, and hence, like all else that is conditioned, accessible to cognition. Willing and cognition in the system of the Buddha mutually condition one another. As is my cognition, so also corresponding to it is my willing made up. Thus the more that my cognition, leaving ignorance, draws nigh to knowledge, all the purer, clearer, more intelligent does my willing also become. The heights of my attainment of knowledge are actualised in my willing, and my willing conditions my next rebirth. If my willing was good, my next rebirth also will be a good one—that is, one in which the mind early turns itself away from longing and desire to reflection upon transiency. In this form is clothed the recompense for the purity of my willing, and inasmuch as this is so, the knowledge acquired in one existence is not lost to the next.

But another question arises. If the *I* is illusion, so also must be the product of this *I*; the force which makes it that the next existence proceeds from this, must be illusion too. If there is no longer any doer, there is no longer any Kamma, any judge of the world, and punishment and reward have ceased to be. Morality would thus become an empty word, and I would be free to sin as I chose against others.

What "I," what "others," what kind of "free"? So long as I perform deeds, possess will, so long is there an *I* present, and so long with iron necessity does consequence follow upon deed, though I repeat ten times over, "There is no *I* and Kamma is a farce." But if no *I* is really any longer to be found, where in that case is there an "other"? With the dissolving of the *I*, is not all else dissolved;—with the doer, the thing done? There is truly no one present upon whom my will can realise itself—that is to say, with the fall of the *I* falls also the possibility of willing, whether good or evil. Just because individuality here is *in toto* cause-effect, without an eternal, without a soul, therefore that "beyond good and evil"—which in Vedanta, with its Ātman exalted above all deeds, threatens knowledge—is here annihilated. Here the good deed constantly remains good, the evil deed perpetually evil. Here the deed is always something real. So long as deeds are done, there is Kamma. Freedom from Kamma is only attained when the possibility of performing deed—willing, of course, included—is done away. Only where there is no longer any *I* is there also no longer any Kamma, as indeed there is also no longer any *thou*. And hence those frightful threatening consequences of a life which through knowledge shakes itself free of all morality, melt into nothing, like a spectre-form in the broad light of day. Thus with the elimination of the *I*-self, this artificial duality of subject and object, willer and thing willed, doer and thing done, this changing world rushes together into immovable unity. The willer as the willed, the knower as the known, the deed and its result, the before and the after, with the taking away of the *I*, which for so long has maintained these artificial distinctions, rush together, each at contact dissolving the other into what is neither "nothing" nor yet "not-nothing." Nought remains over but—as in a mathematical problem that has been successfully solved—remainderlessness.

It is true that there breathes about this system something of the coldness of mathematics; on the other hand, however, there lives in it that purest, sublimest beauty, that taintless beauty, which belongs only to mathematics. And with something of the sound of a mathematical formula rings out that perpetually recurring final summing-up, which serves as an expression for the possession of the highest knowledge: "In delivering lies deliverance; this perception arises: 'Abolished is birth, completed the ascetic life; done what was to do; this world is no more.'"

One who begins to reflect upon the Buddha's instruction, and by knowledge strengthens morality, and by morality knowledge, is like a pilgrim who swiftly, step by step, takes the homeward way. And as such an one, arrived at his journey's end, is no longer a pilgrim—in his character as pilgrim no longer exists,—so he who has attained the final goal of knowledge no longer exists as personality, as individuality.

How, then, does he exist?

That question the Buddha does not answer. The Buddha only shows the way to deliverance, shows deliverance itself, but not what follows after. And it is the token of the genuine, earnest striver that all that does not concern the attaining of his goal has no interest for him.

To this other question also the Buddha vouchsafes no reply: Whence for the first time arose that transformation of cause-effect into doer, deed, and consequence which is founded upon ignorance? Otherwise expressed: Whence springs this Avijjā which at one and the same time is ignorance and illusion?

Here the answer is: Avijjā presupposes individuality, is itself individuality. Anything existent before individuality there is not. This world, this eternal *Becoming*, presupposes the senses, which, deceived deceivers, construct out of it the appearance of *Being*. The senses on their side presuppose this world—that is, this corporeality; for the world, in the Buddhist sense of the word, is nothing but the totality of beings suffering and to be delivered from suffering. Thus we continually run towards that boundary-line where subjective and objective merge together, and can here as little attain to any final end as a man by making haste can reach the horizon. Every moment we imagine we have it within our grasp, but in reality we have only pushed a little farther back that which we fain would seize.

But this is by no means a hiatus in the system. The question, perpetually recurring in a new guise, as to the beginning of the beginning, as to the real "one," has no place in the Buddha's programme. Quite openly and honourably he takes the world, with the riddle of its arising, as a thing given. No wonder that here also we stumble up against the unsolvable as soon as we forsake the way that leads straight to denial, to the way out, to redemption. Lobha, Dosa, Moha (lust, hate, and delusion), the three forms of willing—that is, of ignorance—are the three quantities in which the Buddha's arithmetical sum is stated. They are not to be accounted for, but only worked out—that is, by correct reckoning they are to be solved. That mechanism, which, instead of cause-effect, brings before us the illusion of doer, together with deed and the consequence of deed, is presupposed—is taken as a thing given. The Buddha brings the world before us under the simile of a man found running full speed towards a given goal. We find this inexplicable interchange between subject and object already in full swing. At every stride we suspect that some unity must stand beyond this duality, but we have no power to project into externality such an unity. If we could, it would be God, who can only be believed in, not understood. If, however, we attempt to get this duality blended together, within ourselves, into unity, we come upon self-consciousness as the first point of attack on individuality. "Self," however, is precisely that illusion of all illusions, to banish which the Buddha came into the world. Thus, after all our painful efforts, what we had thought within our grasp slips between our fingers, and in despair we give up the struggle.

Whoso really broods over such questions is like one who broods over the beginning of the world. And as the latter can only reach a conclusion to his broodings by positing a God, the other ponderer also must come to a similar conclusion. But with this he would be snared "in the strong net of the lust for life." For whoever believes in God longs after him, and this longing is the most sublimated form of the craving for life. Hence such an one would for ever be chained to life; for him the way of escape would eternally be barred.

Certainly wherever there is God, life no longer is sorrow. And if life is no longer sorrow, it is also no longer a thing to be renounced. Hence the road to renunciation, and with it the Tathāgata himself, would both be superfluous. But, be it noted, God must be believed in, and not discovered by intellectual ponderings. This God, the one found by intellectual brooding, is nothing but a product of myself, and can never transmute for me the sorrow of life into the joy of life. Hence let every one be on his guard lest he fall out of the solvable illusion into the unsolvable one. The Tathāgata has clearly pointed out the way; the discerning follow him and keep within the limits assigned; the discerning follow him and content themselves with that view, "the holy, the inviting, which invites the thinker to the utter annihilation of sorrow."

Whoso permits himself thus to be led—whoso abides upon the basis provided,—for him the Buddha's system contains nothing obscure, unsolved, or imperfect. From the first step to the last everything lies within our individuality, and is to be mastered by the strength which this individuality itself provides, not by any divine grace, but only by comprehension and by morality. Hence, as this teaching is the only one among all the religions of the world which issues in negation, so also is it the only one which from the first step to the last can be set forth clearly and comprehensibly. Because the Buddha accomplished this task to perfection he had good right to say as he did: "Come! O Bhikkhu! well taught is the Doctrine!" And with good cause also could he call his doctrine that which is "perfect in the beginning, perfect in the middle, and perfect in the end." For as ignorance in this system is synonymous with illusion, so in this system is knowledge synonymous with truth, — a thing that bears in itself the evidence of its own trustworthiness.

XI

AFTER DEATH

Does Buddhism supply any kind of explanation of the life after death? It does indeed. But since here also it adheres to the strictest logic, its explanation is not exactly to every one's taste.

Logically, there are only two alternatives: either life arises with birth and ceases with death, or life is eternal, from eternity and to eternity, for ever persisting. The doctrine of the Semitic-Christian religions, that life comes forth at birth, and thereafter persists eternally, is perhaps the most astounding act of violence that has ever been perpetrated against sane thought,—an act of violence that must always awaken in the thoughtful mind a profound distrust of the religions that teach such doctrine. Wherever there is eternal life, there life is eternal; and never under any conceivable circumstances can I say: "Here, or there, life begins." Eternity is precisely that which has no beginning and no end.

According to the Indian view of things, life is eternal. Because it has not begun with birth, therefore also it cannot cease with death. "This body indeed dies when the life forsakes it, but the life does not die," says the Chandogya Upanishad.

This is the ancient teaching of India regarding the transmigration of the soul. But it belongs not only to ancient India; it was perhaps also the dominant teaching over three-fourths of our globe before Semitism introduced into the mental life of the nations, as into some palimpsest, its teaching of the immortality of an enduring personality.

It must be admitted that to that man for whom life and consciousness are indivisible, for whom life is nothing but loving and hating,—to him the transmigration of the soul is a meaningless phrase: what he craves is the retention of his *I*, his individuality. That is the problem to be worked out, and the fashioning of the Semitic-Christian heaven is its solution; the one exactly fits the other.

To the Indian's way of thinking, however, life and personality, life and consciousness, become quite removable, quite separable one from the other. For the Indian the different phases of the soul's transmigrations are like a bath in which corporeality, together with all its functions, including consciousness, is washed away, and nothing is left over but that purified remainder, the immortal soul, the true *I*. Like the worm that crawls from leaf to leaf, so goes Ātman (the soul, the self) from one existence to another, ever seeking new nourishment, new embodiment, new consciousness.

The doctrine of the transmigration of the soul is simply the sentiment of eternal life, expressed in its most popular form. What, however, might have been a springtime, breathing hope and delight, became in Indian thought, under the sun of India, a pestilence-laden miasma. Because life was felt to be pain, therefore was this ever-renewed entry into life regarded as the summation of all misery, and that life free from personality, that changeless state of being in Brahman, the consummation of all felicity.

This eternal life in Brahman was a life without consciousness; consciousness is in fact nothing but the sense of difference between myself and another; it has its foundation in duality. This duality, however, is nothing but Māyā, the great world-delusion which presents to me the picture of an *I* and a *thou*, where in reality there is only the unity of Ātman-Brahman. If, however, this false picture be destroyed by knowledge and the duality subside into the unity, what becomes of consciousness? Nothing is there, in opposition to which I can feel myself *I*. There is indeed "No one there who says *I*," simply because *all* has become *I*. "There is no consciousness after death," says Yājñavalkya, the spiritual hero of the Upanishads, to his wife Maitreyi. "For where there is doubleness, so to speak, there one sees, smells, tastes, hears, touches, and recognises the other. Where, on the contrary, for any one all has become his own self, how then or whom shall he see, smell, taste, hear, touch, or know? Through Whom all this is known, how should he know Him?" (Brihadaranyaka Upanishad.)

Hence the solution which the problem of life after death found in Brahmanism was:—life in the present, enduring from eternity, lasts to all eternity; and the process by which this life, involved in duality, in consciousness, is transformed in the course of its transmigrations into that which is contained in unity, in Brahman, consists simply in the removal of a delusion. The heavenly life is to be gained only by knowledge.

As in Brahmanism, so in Buddhism each separate existence has its own separate consciousness. No consciousness is carried over from one life to another. The belief in personal continuity is classed as one of the three fetters that hold us back from salvation.

A monk named Sāti has become attached to the view that this our consciousness endures unchanged throughout the cycle of rebirths. The Buddha has him called and asks him: "What sort of consciousness is that, Sāti?"

"That which as self, O Master, again enjoys the fruits of its good or evil deeds."

"From whom then, thou infatuated man, hast thou heard that I teach such a doctrine? Have I not in divers ways made clear the conditioned nature of all consciousness? Have I not shown repeatedly that without sufficient cause no consciousness ever arises?" Then, addressing himself to his monks, he goes on: "From whatsoever cause consciousness arises, through this and only through this comes it into being. Through sight and through forms, consciousness arises—that is, sight-consciousness." After he has in similar fashion explained the hearing, smelling, tasting, touching, and thinking consciousness, he goes on: "Somewhat as a fire, for whatsoever reason it may burn, through this cause and only through this cause comes to be: by wood is fed, and straightway a wood fire comes to be; by twigs, hay, dung, or sweepings is fed, and straightway a twig, hay, dung, or sweepings fire comes to be; even so comes consciousness to be; from whatsoever cause it arises, through this and through this only does it come to be."

More clearly or more distinctly it were impossible to express one's self. Consciousness is, as compared with the whole of the remainder of the body, nothing but a product, a compound, a symptom—the spiritual in us, nothing but a modification of the corporeal. The arising of the Differentiations conditions the arising of Consciousness. The Differentiations on their side, however, have arisen out of Ignorance, and it is nothing but the outcome of defective knowledge to look upon consciousness as something that persists.

Here the relationship is somewhat different from that which obtains in Brahmanism, because the Buddha teaches that nothing is eternal, that no soul lurks in the body. That residue which in Brahmanism is not washed away but remains over; that soul which constitutes the binding thread between the separate existences is here done away with. That which to others was the eternal soul, the true *I*, in the uncorrupted thought of the Buddha became nothing but a form of perception, of consciousness; consequently, subject to transiency. In unequivocal language he teaches his monks: "It were much better if the ignorant regarded as the *I* the body which is compounded of the four chief elements rather than the mind. And why do I say so? Because the body can endure for a year, for ten years, for a hundred years, and longer. That, however, which is called mind, cognition, consciousness, is day and night in an endless process of becoming, subject to an unceasing process of transition."

In the Buddha's thought, that spiritual, eternal part stood in somewhat the same relation to the body as the ultra-violet rays of the spectrum occupy with regard to the yellow rays. The former are perceptible to the senses and the latter imperceptible, yet these last are differentiated from the coloured part of the spectrum solely by the extreme rapidity of their vibrations. With the perception of Becoming, with the perception of life as a process, life had for him become a sort of unity which joined in itself the duality of body and soul. For him the difference between body and soul had become purely quantitative. With the dissolution of corporeality all was dissolved; not only the body, compounded out of the four chief elements, but also that which among others passed for the spiritual part, the soul, the indestructible. It is as if the last little spark among the ashes were extinguished, and doubting we are impelled to ask: "Whence shall new fire come? Out of what shall the new existence arise?"

In Buddhism, as already shown, the part of the soul is assumed by Kamma. It binds one existence to another; or, better put, it causes one existence to arise out of another, as from one swing of the pendulum proceeds the next. The proposition: "Life is eternal," formulates itself in soulless Buddhism, not as a doctrine of the transmigration of the soul, but as the teaching of the cycle of rebirths. This present existence is nothing but the reaction of a previous one, and incontestably gives rise as its necessary reaction to the one that follows it. As inevitably as in the heart's action systole follows diastole, so does existence follow existence one after another; and birth and death are nothing but the flowing transition from this life to the next. Birth and death are to one another as the waxing to the waning moon.

If, however, one life follows another in endless procession, what follows? It is like an awakening, like the taking away of a veil. If there stands no soul, no eternal entity, behind this existence; if this being is something which in its totality has arisen, and in its totality passes away again; if there is nothing here but the repetition *ad infinitum* of the same performance, for what do we wait and hope? This "after death," it goes with us where we go; it is near us—yea, in us. Even now we live this life after death. This world is the theatre of the eternal life. Which, it must be admitted, is rather a disappointing solution of the problem for those to whom eternal life has meant the consummation of bliss.

This is the power, I might almost say the unsuspected artifice, of religions that, like the hypnotiser, they remove from the understanding the facts that lie before everybody's eyes, and so work upon it that the mental eye rests upon a seeming picture instead. Religions, by hindering correct cognition, bind us eternally to that life from which they apparently try to teach us to turn away our eyes. Buddhism, however, in contradiction to all that is usually called religion, teaches the eye to turn from that false picture to the actual world; teaches it to fix itself upon the world that is; in a word, Buddhism teaches us to be thoughtful and heedful. By reflection and observation the man perceives the great *Becoming*, and in the *Becoming* he perceives soullessness. At the same time, however, he sees and knows: "There is no life but this. That 'life after death,' to the ignorant the goal of their deepest longing, is already lived here in want and pain, in lamentation and misery. From all eternity has it thus been lived; to all eternity will it so be lived." And now there rises in him the understanding of those words of the Buddha which he spoke to his disciples: "What do you think? Which is the greater? The floods of tears which, weeping and wailing, you have shed on this long pilgrimage, ever and again hastening toward new birth and new death; united to the undesired, parted from the desired,—this, or the waters of the four great seas?" Now for him life changes into sorrow; that greatest of all transformations, that most stupendous of all dramas has begun, and henceforth shall not cease until all has been played to an end, until the last word has been spoken, and the curtain falls, and peace, Nibbāna, reigns in its stead.

The more life is recognised to be sorrow, the more the desire grows to be rid of it all. The deeper this longing becomes, the more pronounced becomes the tendency towards reflection and attentiveness of mind; and in the depths of reflection the delusion of the *I* is perceived. If, however, there is no *I*, of what use to me is heaven with its eternal life? Like the cackling hen that seeks some place of safety for the egg she wishes to lay, so do we men roam anxiously around, seeking some place in which we can deposit for eternity this precious *I* of ours. Hail then to the man who by force of thought has rid himself of the *I*! He alone is at peace! He alone abides in surety! Heaven and eternal life in God are indeed for him shivered to atoms, but in thinking he has learnt to despise them. Where there is no longer any *I*, there also is there no supplication more for a heaven, and such questions as: "Shall we exist in future periods of time?" collapse upon themselves, fall with the fall of the questioner. Thus it is that the Buddha answers the question: "What after death?"

Now, however, the question arises: "Did the Buddha teach a true death?" And the answer is: Yes, the death of Sorrow. There is only one kind of death here, the death of pain. How is it to be reached? By the death of desire only can it be reached. So long as there is desire, so long is there life—that is, pain. Therefore is it said: "Sad is death to him in whom desire doth live; pitiful is death to him in whom cravings survive." His death is nothing but his being born again to new misery. He lives eternally through his lust to live.

But how does the will to live die? It dies with the thinking of the thought: *Non-I.* So long as I am thinking, I am not willing. To think, *Non-I*, is, however, to make my will itself the object of thought, of cognition. Since, however, a man who beholds his eye—the pupil of his eye—in a mirror sees nothing but this pupil, so does one who perceives his will see nothing but this will. To know the will means not only the dissolution of the will, but also the dissolution of the possibility of willing. And thus "to know the will" is the conclusion of the whole matter.

So far, so good! But now we ask: "What is the afterwards of this true death?"

That question must not be put even to the Buddha himself. The Buddha teaches nothing but how sorrow is born and how it dies. What follows upon the death of sorrow?—that does not concern him who is striving after salvation. It is a question for which one has no leisure *previous* to perfect deliverance, and *after* perfect deliverance, no necessity. Whoso would strive for the fruit of the Buddha's teaching must whole-heartedly resolve to crave nothing, absolutely nothing, but salvation from sorrow.

"What follows upon the extinction of delusion?" asks a monk of the learned nun Dhammadinnā.

"Abandon the question, Brother! I cannot grasp the meaning of the question. If it seem good to thee, go to the Enlightened One and ask him for an explanation of the question."

And the Buddha, asked, makes answer: "Wise is Dhammadinnā, and mighty in understanding. Wouldst thou ask me for an explanation, I would give thee exactly the same answer."

One more question arises: Is not the sentence "I think my *Non-I*," a contradiction in terms? Is it not saying in one breath: I am and I am not? Sooth to say, this is the case: it *is* saying at one and the same time, "I am and I am not," but the state of affairs is as follows. The *I*, as a consequence, as the embodiment of previous willing, already in the present exists in a state of non-willing; that is to say, it recognises itself as *Non-I*. The *I*—existent of necessity, existent purely as a product—has ceased to be a producer, an actively willing. As the monsoon cloud, when it sinks from the mountain ridge down into the hot valley, there steadily melts away, so in the perceiver does every sprouting germ of will steadily disappear in the glow of Anattā, in the conception *Non-I*. But the man is still corporeality: how can he come to an end? how cease to be a producer? He is corporeality only in so far as he steadily produces anew the one, the only thought: "This Self is not my *I* Self"; that is to say, he is and is not at one and the same time. As a sun that has been extinguished for years may still continue to send us its light, and that light may still serve as a source of illumination and energy, so may this *I*, in spite of the fact that it no longer exists, continue to emit the proposition: *There is no I.*

Like a top which, even when it is no longer whipped, still for a time continues to gyrate and show its colours, so does this body for a time present the appearance of an *I*, notwithstanding that the *I*-building energy has already in knowledge been dissipated and done away. The brief period of time during which the *I* pays out the last instalment of the debt contracted through previous ignorance, that is Nibbāna in this life. For, ever and again, in the borrowed light of the perception that has arisen from previous willing, I can make-clear the fact of my final and legitimate freedom. In the light of the new knowledge, the paradox: "This Self is not my Self," becomes perfectly natural, and bears in itself the evidence of its truth.

Yet one question more: Does not Buddhism fall into the very same error, only in an inverted form, that all the monotheistic religions fall into? These latter teach that something that has had a beginning goes on to all eternity; does not the former teach that what is eternal finally passes away?

The parallelism is only an apparent parallelism. The quantities compared are not congruous. To *Being*, upon one side, stands opposed upon the other side, *Becoming*. To the Buddha life all through is nothing but a Becoming; nothing but a self-sustaining, self-evolving process, existent from all eternity. The end of life to him is nothing but the ceasing of this process, the ceasing of Becoming. In the Christian scheme of things Non-being passes into Being. In Buddhist thought, however, Being in no wise passes into Non-being. It is the Becoming only that ceases; that mechanism which in unbroken flow produced the phenomena of life, no longer acts because the propelling force has ceased with the perception of *Non-I*. The end here is not Non-being, but Never-more-becoming! And Becoming is a thing that can come to an end.

XII

THE SPECIFIC IN BUDDHISM

All the Buddhas that have yet appeared in our world have done so in order to teach three things, and three things only: first, that all things are transient; second, that all things are full of pain; and third, that all things are Non-self (Anattā), and that nowhere is to be found a true "self," a true "I," a soul.

The propositions, "All things are transient, all things are full of pain," find an echoing answer in every corner of our globe. The tenet of Non-self alone has a foreign ring about it. And, by contrast, it must in former times have sounded even more alien than it does to-day. The pantheistic thought of India had crystallised itself into that one sentence, "All is I." Ātman, the Self, the soul, was found to be identical with the World-soul, that great Brahman, who ever stands behind the world of appearance ready to gather to his bosom, in rapturous rest and bliss, every individual soul that has won to that highest peak of all knowledge; namely, that Ātman and Brahman are not divided, but are veritably one and the same. All that was necessary was to take away the covering of Ignorance, and all the sorrows of this our life are forthwith transformed into pure Bliss. "To know Brahman is to be Brahman."

To what extent the Buddha adhered to this specific line of Indian thought may be seen from the position which Avijjā (Ignorance) occupies in his system. But how thoroughly peculiar and distinctive his own manner of thinking was, may likewise be perceived from the use which, in his system, he makes of Avijjā; it is, as it were, the mirror of that other. Everywhere it makes a backward step where that other goes a step forward, and pictures to the right what in the other lies to the left. The two systems may be likened to a pair of vessels, whose contents are concealed by similar covers. The immense difference between them only becomes evident when the covers are lifted. The adherent of Vedanta finds therein that rarest of all dishes, that dish for which his hunger is never appeased: eternal life, eternal bliss. The Buddha, however, finds it full of disgusting food, but at the same time he also finds the saving knowledge: "I need no longer food of any kind."

That the removal of the same thing, Avijjā, on either side should eventuate in such totally different results, arises from the difference in the underlying foundations of each. In Vedanta the removal of Avijjā means stripping off the husk that hides the shining kernel of the world, the eternal, the soul. In Buddhism the husk is pierced only that it may be shown that it has served no other purpose than to offer the delusive promise of a kernel. As with dawning day those mists disappear which veil the sun, so in Vedanta, with the coming of knowledge, all those clouds vanish which conceal Brahman.

But since again day itself is only another word for sun, so with the departure of Ignorance not only does the sun of Brahman shine out clearly, but its identity with Ātman, the soul in me, is likewise made clear and plain. The one is never found apart from the other. Brahman can never be cognised without the simultaneous cognition, "I am Brahman." It cannot be cognised if it does not already dwell in the bosom of the seeker. The thing to be proved must coexist with the very axiom by means of which alone it can be proved. Brahman can only be known if it is first incontestably established: "There is a soul, there is an eternal." Brahman can only be known where it is believed in.[1] Knowledge here is nothing but a peculiarly prepared belief.

If there is anything especially characteristic of the Buddha and his system, it is their disability for mere belief, as such, added to a capacity for following to their ultimate issue, and with an unswerving directness, the lines of thought which this characteristic would imply.

Watered by what is specific in Indian thought, from this incapacity for faith, as from a root, springs the plant of the three blossoms: Transiency, Sorrow, Non-self. All three expressions mean the same thing but in an ascending degree of intensity. It is as if a thunderstorm, growling in the distance, draws threateningly nearer, to break over our heads in the lightning flash of Anattā.

"All is transient" is the fundamental thought, the first flower on the tree of lack of faith. Under

[1] Cf. "Ch'ândogya Upanishad," *Sacred Books of the East*, vol. i. p. 122. "When one believes, then one perceives. One who does not believe, does not perceive. Only he who believes, perceives."

the friction of this thought, not only does the external world crumble away, but Great Brahman also, and with him Ātman, the soul, the "I." In the fierce heat developed by the friction, the cold weak phrase, "All is transient," changes into the agonised cry, "All life is Pain." This middle statement, however, differs from the last, the tenet of non-self (which again is the synthesis of the three), only as the bitterness of the unripe fruit differs from the sweetness of the ripe. In the organic unity of the three lies deliverance, and whoso only perseveres in meditation thereupon will surely pass from the Pain of Life to the Peace of Deliverance, as the unripe fruit through time alone attains the sweetness of the ripe.

The proposition, "There is no I-self here," is the fruit, the conclusion, the culmination, but it is a fruit that is still in the rind. As the ripe fruit, so to speak, includes and contains the unripe fruit and the blossom, so also does Non-self encompass and enclose Pain and Transiency, and thus becomes the watchword of Buddhism. It embraces all—the highest morality as well as the highest knowledge. The highest morality, because only in it do will and deed merge and become one; the highest knowledge, because only through it can the Four Holy Truths of suffering be comprehended. The Anattā-thought is thus, in some measure, the spring-board from which the mind takes its leap to Nibbāna. Yea, more, Anattā is Nibbāna itself, come into sight even in this life. All that is needed to make it comprehensible as such is the changed point of view. In the Anattā-idea sorrow and salvation blend and harmonise. As, through this body comprehended as "I," cause and effect exhibit themselves in the guise of will and deed; so, this body being known as "not-I," deed and will change back into cause and effect. The Anattā-idea is that wonderful knot, proceeding from which the whole self-entwined train of the Buddha's thought permits itself to be smoothly unravelled, and indeed not it alone but also the world. For as the thought, "this body is I," constantly causes the world to arise, so that which has arisen again melts away with the knowledge, "this body is not-I." The enormous step from world-arising to world-dissolution is nothing but a shadow in our apprehension cast by correct information.

In the Anattā-idea is mirrored the full depth of the Teaching, as the highest tree is mirrored in the water-pot, as the whole world is reflected in the eye. And as the pupil of the eye gives expression to the human countenance, and lacking the pupil there is a blank, so does the Anattā-idea, the doctrine of *I* as *not-I*, give character to Buddhism. As the pupil of the eye is merely a hollow covered over, so is this body nothing but a concealed *not-I*.

In another place the Buddha gives his disciples the quintessence of his teaching in the following words: "Two things alone I teach, now and always: Pain and the uprooting of Pain." Indeed, we are accustomed in Buddhism to lay the greatest emphasis upon the tenet: "All things are full of Pain." And as in the Anattā-idea, as being the conclusion of the whole matter, everything is solved and seen most clearly, so in the Pain-idea we have, as it were, the highest point of the curve, from which is obtained the best view of beginning and end, Transiency and

Anattā. But it is precisely in the Pain-idea that it is seen how in Buddhism nothing depends upon the words and everything upon the explanation. Only in the explanation thereof furnished by the Buddha, only in its inner connection with Transiency and Anattā, does this most banal of all religious phrases become a sign-manual of Buddhism. Whoso understands what in the Buddha's system is meant by Pain, not merely experiencing Pain but comprehending it, he has sounded the depths of the system. "All life is Pain" is the foundation of the whole. Only he who, like the Buddha, takes his stand here, can, like him, from this foundation proceed to build up into the pure heights. Only where the tenet, "All life is transient," transmutes itself into the proposition, "All life is full of Pain," there only, of a truth, is the Tathāgata apprehended. On the clear, smooth surface of the Transiency-idea the Teaching as yet can find no foothold. It is quite neutral. In pure Transiency, sorrow and joy are of like import, and there would be no sense in the removal of Pain, for it would equally involve the abolition of pleasure.

The tenet of Transiency as yet stands outside of the system, upon that watershed from which the waters of thought can descend on one side to Theism, on the other side to A-Theism. The proposition, "All life is transient," is, as it were, a twilight which may turn into day as well as into night. It can react upon faith as well as upon the incapacity for faith, just as twilight may be a form of night as well as a form of day, as cognition may be either Ignorance or Knowledge. As cognition in the form of Ignorance leads to the perpetual will to live; as cognition in the form of Knowledge leads to the great "I will not," so the Transiency-idea upon the basis of faith leads to Brahman-bliss, and upon the basis of unfaith to the painfulness of Anattā.

Thus, in yet another sense, the Transiency-idea is the specific characteristic of the Teaching, because, considered in conjunction with the other two, it is nothing but the expression of that fundamental characteristic which underlies all three; the incapacity for faith, together with an aptitude for following all inferences to their ultimate issues. For just because the Buddha, in pursuit of the Transiency-idea, halts not before God Himself, but drives straight through Him, as through a mist, therefore is it that for him the Transient changes into the Painful and into Anattā. In other words, he pursues Transiency to that extreme point where it suddenly topples over, out of Sorrow into Salvation. To be a true beacon of Salvation, the Anattā-idea must be simply the transformation of the Pain-idea, and this latter, in its turn, must be merely the transmuted form of the Transiency-proposition. Considered apart, any one of the three is a nothing; only in their organic union do they become all.

Transiency, Pain, Not-self are like some trident that bears sway over the world of the Buddha, and none can be accorded any theoretical superiority over any other. All three issue from a common stock. In practice, it must be owned, the emphasis is laid upon the tenet of Pain. The cause of this is that this tenet was split up by the Buddha into the Four Holy Truths of Sorrow in order to give his Teaching, if not exactly a popular, at least a humanised form. What, however, gives the tenet of

Pain its priority over the other two is this : that in this divided form the tenet of the Middle Path incorporates itself into the whole. The fourth of the Holy Truths is only another expression for this tenet.

The law of moderation, of the Path of the True Mean, is another fundamental characteristic of Buddhism. In one sense running alongside the Doctrine of Pain, that is to say, the trinity "Transiency, Sorrow, Not-self," and regulating them, it is yet, in another sense, nothing but these three in their return flow. As the heart sends forth from itself the arterial blood, so from the heart of the Buddha breaks forth the triple-headed thought of Transiency, Pain, and Not-self. And after it has proved itself on all—world, God, *I*; after it has coursed through all this, become, as it were, capillary, it returns as the tenet of the True Mean to the spot whence it issued; as the pulsing stream of the arteries held in the great *vena cava* flows back to the heart.

As a Cakkavattī (world-conquering king) who has brought the wide world under his sway, even to the four great seas, stopping only at the limits set by nature, is appeased in the thought: "All this is subject to me," so has this triple-headed thought subjugated the whole universe to itself, and the knowledge arises: "There is no more resistance, nothing further to subdue, naught else to loosen ; no world, no God, no I ; security reigns over all." Thus the idea of the True Mean is nothing but the Transiency-idea, as found in its return flow, and which, completely victorious, has now no further opposition to fear from any quarter. Its return in the form of the doctrine of the Middle Path is the proof of the completeness of its victory. Only those still striving and struggling are immoderate, and the search after God, as being the most strenuous and difficult, most readily leads to immoderation. One, however, who knows: "I have reached the conclusion of the whole matter," for him moderation becomes part of the order of nature.

The doctrine of moderation has lent this world-shattering system that peacefulness and quietude which, distorted into indolence and passivity in the eyes of the Western world, has come to be regarded as the peculiar and distinguishing mark of Buddhism. This accusation of indolence, to put it quite frankly, is founded on sheer ignorance of the matter in hand. It is not indolence with which we are here confronted, but the sweet, cool quietude of evening, after the heat of the day's toil. The task, behind which no new one any more makes its appearance, is quite ended. The loud clamour and din of the *Becoming* of the world has been resolved for the wise, with the thought: "For me the world no longer is," into a mere play of the senses. Like a man who sits in stillness on the shore of a clear mountain lake and sees the fish beneath him dart hither and thither, and every pebble and shell on the bottom, so, looking forth from the safe shore, does the wise man perceive the nature of the world and its eternal restlessness. No longer is he himself an actor in the play; henceforth he beholds it merely as spectator. To look on is, however, more honourable than to be engaged therein. Only in our unhealthy perversion of the idea has activity upon this stage obtained that overweening value and importance which we are prone to award it to-day. So praises the grey-haired galley-slave the virtues and excellences of his chain!

The moderation and quietude of Buddhism, the direct result of sorrow and struggle that have come to an end in knowledge, is indeed like some rich, noble hue which at once elevates this wonderful system above the common mass of all other religions. Buddhism is like a dark, clear brook which noiselessly steals between the overhanging shadows. Sweet it is to rest upon its banks; sweet to look and to muse! And it is because it is so deep that it is so still. And if the real value of all religion lies in this, that it teaches me to respect others and to abhor all violence, then is Buddhism not only the highest of all religious systems, but also the highest *conceivable* system. High above those levels where the storms of fanaticism rage, it raises its dazzling ice-crowned summit into the ether, eternally serene.

It was this specific quality of his teaching to which the Buddha alluded when the nun Gotamī asked him: "Will the Exalted One teach me the quintessence of the Dhamma?" and the Buddha answered her: "Of whatsoever teaching thou art sure that it leads to passion and not to peace; to pride and not to humility; to the desiring of much and not to the desiring of little; to the love of society and not to the love of solitude; to idleness and not to earnest striving; to a mind hard to pacify and not to a mind easy to pacify—that, O Gotamī, note well! that is not Dhamma; that is not Vinaya[1]; that is not the teaching of the Master."

Thus, though apparently running parallel and in

[1] Rules of the Order.

contradistinction to one another like artery and vein, the doctrines of Pain and of the True Mean do yet at the end of the circuit merge in each other like the arterial and venous systems of the body. Here once more we meet a fresh, specific characteristic of Buddhism: the sphere-like self-containedness, the mathematical demonstrability, supreme accord with the very nature of things; in a word, the perfection which at every point explains itself by itself. This perfection, however, what is it but the Truth?—a characteristic greater and more profound than any we have yet mentioned! "All other gifts are naught beside the gift of the Truth," says the Buddha.

XIII

THE LAW OF THE MIDDLE PATH

When the Buddha preached for the first time in Benares to the five monks, he began his sermon thus: "There are two extremes, O monks, which he who has renounced the world must equally avoid. Which two? A life given over to lust, which is debasing, vulgar, ignoble, and useless; and a life devoted to self-mortification, which is painful, ignoble, and useless. By the avoidance of these two extremes, the Tathāgata has gained the knowledge of the Middle Path, which leads to Insight, Wisdom, Peace, Knowledge, inward quietude, yea, to Nibbāna. What, however, is this Path of the Mean? It is the Holy Eight-Staged Path."

Now we have already learnt to recognise in the Holy Eight-Staged Path the fourth of the truths concerning Sorrow. The Buddha indeed places the doctrine of the Middle Path as something independent, alongside of, nay, *before* the truth of Sorrow, and afterwards again grafts it upon this truth.

This peculiar position only corresponds with the peculiar functions which this doctrine has to fulfil in the system. With it a man, in some measure, begins to be a Buddhist.

To be a Buddhist, then, is this all that a man has to do—follow the Eight-Staged Path?

One cannot become a Buddhist apart from the Eight-Staged Path. All the study and reflection in the world with regard to the various theses put forth by the Buddha is not Buddhism, except along with such study there be the following of the Path. For the Eight-Staged Path is the morality of this system, and morality here is not a by-product but an integral constituent of the system. Whoso makes his own the philosophy only, and ignores the morality, is like one who should eat the seed of a fruit-tree, thinking that he swallows along with such seed all the refreshing fruit that the tree might have borne.

On the other hand, the following of the Eight-Staged Path does not necessarily involve becoming a Buddhist. Treading the Path is only the preliminary to becoming thoughtful and attentive. Whoso, however, is thoughtful and attentive ceases to oscillate in his mind between past and future, but takes his stand in the present. But he who takes his stand in the present marks the arising of all things from causes. And he who marks the arising of all things from causes, for him all apparent *Being* is dissolved in *Becoming*.

With this, however, we have not yet arrived at Buddhism, but only at the idea of transiency. If the belief in God still lurks in some corner of the heart, the transiency-idea will come to a halt before it; and the result will be that the tortured mind will seek refuge from the illusoriness of this world in the abidingness of that other. The result will thus be merely a strengthening of the God-idea.

If, however, belief in God has no place in the chambers of the heart, and, as a consequence, the mind occupied with the transiency-idea comes to no sudden stop before it, as before some natural boundary; then, perforce, the doctrine of transiency changes into the doctrine of sorrow and not-*I*; in other words, we have arrived at Buddhism. The question then, "How shall I become a Buddhist?" will be answered somewhat after the following fashion.

Buddhism is like some painful cure which no rational person would undergo on its own account, but only because necessity compels. Thus he only can become a Buddhist for whom Buddhism has become a necessity. It is a necessity, however, for him who is without the capacity for faith, and is conscious of this, his lack. For him religion is a matter of necessity; for the believer it is an affair of grace. He, the void of faith, sets forth upon his quest as a sick man goes in search of healing. For him there is no salvation outside of Buddhism. Therefore in him the Eight-Staged Path becomes established; in him that self-renewing process is developed by which knowledge increases with morality, and morality with knowledge.

We thus see that the immediate cause of one's becoming a Buddhist is that one agrees with the requirements of the Eight-Fold Path, and resolves to comply with them. The original cause, however, is inability to *believe*.

The next question that arises is: Can Buddhism work harm in the domain of belief?

However much the teaching of the Buddha is pondered over; however straitly the Eight-Fold Path is followed, the incapacity for mere faith remains the *sine quâ non*. If this incapacity for faith is awanting, the guidance of the Buddha will only vivify deistic belief. Only where it can get a hold is Buddhism really effective. But it only takes hold where it has become a necessary thing to the individual; that is to say, where unfaith is dominant. Thus the influence which the Buddha exerts over the mind may be looked upon as a sort of touchstone. If a man's faith is not vivified by it, then his faith is defective in some particular. Only where truth is feared can the genius of Buddhism be feared, as spirits of wine only causes pain where the skin is broken.

The law of the Path of the True Mean, of the rejection of all extremes, is like a regulating weight attached to the machinery of the law of Sorrow. There is much that is wonderful in the Buddha's system, but the introduction of the functioning of this law is perhaps the most wonderful of all. Only genius can do work like this. Only genius, like nature, produces lifelike forms—not monstrosities that bear in themselves the evidence of their own incongruity and lifelessness.

The vast form into which the sorrow-conception had been shaped in the thought of the Buddha—a form which inevitably must have been destroyed in its own fever-glow—becomes capable of animation only through the law of the Path of the Mean; I might even say thus only is it made adaptable to human needs, as the terrestrial globe becomes capable of supporting life on its surface only when it has sufficiently cooled down. And as the terrestrial globe through over-cooling would again become incapable of supporting life, so the system of the Buddha, through a too great preponderance of the law of the Middle Path over the law of Sorrow, would again become sterile and unproductive.

The system, taken as a whole, has nothing of the limitless or the absolute about it; but in its ideal form always arises through the proper interaction of the law of the Middle Path and the law of Sorrow. That endless *Becoming* of all that has arisen, which the system teaches, holds good of the system itself. Nothing is more erroneous than to suspect in the conceptions of this system—in any one of them—the presence of the unconditioned, the causeless, the absolute; some hidden god-idea. Everything is conditioned by causes, and infallibly disappears with the ceasing of the causes that have led to its arising. Thus the law, in its ideal form, the Dhamma, is conditioned by the perfect recognition of Sorrow on one hand, and perfect moderation on the other.

As on the loom the intercrossing of the threads produces the web, so by the intercrossing of these two laws, and only in so far as they do intercross, is the principle of salvation produced. By their mutual interaction these two cause the Dhamma to issue forth from them in ever-renewed freshness and vigour.

From another point of view, however, the law of moderation is a counter-weight which the law of sorrow has produced out of itself. In it is embodied the impulse of self-preservation of the Buddha-world. For this Buddha-world, unlike the other, has an object, and must endure until this object, salvation from all known sorrow, has been achieved. The law of moderation is meant to inculcate the enduring of sorrow until it has become productive, until it has changed into salvation.

As a planet is maintained in its course round the sun by the equilibrium of contending forces; as every point of its journey at every moment is determined anew by the mutual interaction of the two forces, and as the orbit which thus, as it were, forms itself out of itself is that which is in most perfect correspondence with the conditions necessary to life upon the planet; so, through the controlling influence of Moderation upon Sorrow, arises that manner of living and of envisaging life which, being in strictest harmony with the nature of the being, balances all apparent contradictions, and hence ultimates in the royal path of Salvation. For salvation is nothing but the correct cognition of the law of nature,—nothing but that surrender of all opposition which rests upon the recognition of the necessity of such law. One who has comprehended the Dhamma is a good citizen of the world in the fullest sense of the word, and—to speak frankly—by so much, a bad citizen of the state, for preferences of any kind whatsoever are not consistent with this teaching.

In what fashion the law of the Middle Path influenced the ancient Indian institution of asceticism is pointed out more fully in another place.

Purely by reason of superior knowledge, every incitement was wanting to those frightful penances which the adherents of two other religions, Hinduism and Christianity, lay upon themselves, in order that they may arrive more swiftly and more surely at their God. Upon such penances the Buddha looked with a sort of pitying disdain. The poor creatures truly all strove after the highest good; but so foolishly misdirected were their energies that they only the more obscured their outlook. In their search for the highest, they seemed to him like people looking for some precious object at the bottom of a lake, who scrape about so eagerly that the water becomes turbid, and ever more turbid the more they scrape. And the Buddha himself was just such a foolish stirrer of the mud before enlightenment came to him. But then he resolved to wait patiently and quietly until all the sediment that had been stirred up by irrational asceticism had settled down again. And when everything had become pure and transparent, with clear vision he looked down into the depths to the very bottom, and seeing, spoke thus: "Something there is indeed that glitters here and there, but I perceive therein only worthless potsherds. That jewel which we seek, the *I*—the *soul*—is not there at all. I must just accept the fact." Such was the result he arrived at through the principle of moderation.

His attitude towards suicide similarly follows from this principle; only here other causes are at work along with it. Self-murder, even with a religious motive, was a deadly sin in the eyes of the Buddha. Here also he placed himself in direct opposition to the specific Indian view. Like a moth round a light, so the faithful Hindu fluttered round and round the great divine Being with whom he sought to be united. And as meteor-swarms crash back into the sun, whence they came, so do the souls that thirst for God crash back in multitudes into the fire of the divine central sun, that they may enjoy the bliss of union, of becoming one. Led by faith, this crash brings them into the all-embracing arms of the divine. For the Buddhist, however,—without faith and without God—suicide would only be a most frightful plunge into the abyss; for, since here no longing after that sun of deity attracts, self-murder can only be the expression of a life-despair. But despair of life is Ignorance; where there is knowledge there is no jubilation indeed, but neither is there despair. Where, however, there is Ignorance, there also is life. Otherwise expressed: To break this form only means to give life to another form. Suicide does not mean the end of the drama, but only a change of the scene. Self-murder is Ignorance proving itself by itself, and in its worst form, because here it deprives itself of the opportunity of recognising the results of its own action. And it is only in its results that Ignorance can be recognised and disowned. The self-murderer blocks his own way to salvation, and involves himself ever more deeply in that life from which in such foolish fashion he seeks to escape.

Birth as a man is the most important and the most fortunate of all births. Only in it can be waged that strenuous struggle with the Ignorance which binds us helplessly to life. Thus, what greater foolishness can there be than to shorten even by the tiniest space of time this precious period of all-fruitful strife?

Here again we come upon a deep-lying distinction between the Buddha's doctrine and that of atheist-philosophical systems. With these latter, all ends with the body's death, and suicide is thus the most natural step to take so soon as a living being reaches the point where the joys of life no longer balance the pains. "At all times the door stands open" is the thought with which Stoics make themselves proof against bullet and sword; like one who ventures into danger and disaster with the dose of deadly poison which the seal-ring contains.

And just as deep, be it said, is the gulf that divides the Buddhist from the Christian view. The Christian indeed says, equally with the Buddhist, "This body is not mine." But perhaps nowhere else has such a huge difference in the manner of apprehending life been concealed behind similar words as is here the case. To the Buddhist the body is something that does not belong to him, because it is *not-I*, delusion. To the Christian the body is a gift from God, therefore it is not his. The body is the temple of the Highest; to wound it would be to wound God. Accordingly, all that happens to the body is also a gift from God, and pain is merely purification. Any right to suicide, or rational ground for the same, is here done away with.

When, however, one has followed the Buddha's doctrine to its ultimate and has reached perfect knowledge, has he not then the right to break up this form? Life is sorrow, is it not?

No. For such an one it has ceased any longer to be sorrow; it has become instead a thing of perfect indifference. He can say with the noble Sāriputta: "I desire not life; I desire not death; I wait until mine hour shall come, like a servant that waits for his wage. I long not for life; I long not for death. I await the coming of the hour, conscious and of thoughtful mind." So speaks one in whom the law of the Path of the True Mean has come to fruition. "This, O Bhikkhus," says the Buddha, "is that Middle Path, avoiding these two extremes, discovered by the Tathāgata—that Path which opens the eyes and bestows understanding; which leads to peace of mind, to the higher wisdom, to full enlightenment, to Nibbāna."

XIV

ASCETICISM

THE power and influence of the Brahmins must already have been at their height in the time of Gautama, and nowhere perhaps has the sway of a priestly caste been so complete as in ancient India. Heaven, as it were, was hermetically sealed to the whole people, even to the king himself. The Brahmin alone held the key. The lengthy duration of such an ecclesiastical power, and its revival towards the close of the tenth century, after it had been subdued by Buddhism, can only be explained by the genuine virtues, notably truthfulness, which the priestly caste really possessed. "The Brahmins are remarkable for their knowledge and their love of virtue," says Burnouf.[1] They themselves believed in what they preached to the people. They imposed upon themselves an even stricter rule than that to which they subjected the people. They were like those great generals who, in time of distress, submit to the same hardships as the ordinary soldiers. This earnestness in the common struggle after the highest bound the people to them as with iron chains.

At this period of her history a gloomy religiosity lay over all India. The Brahmins, themselves

[1] *Introduction à l'histoire du Bouddhisme indien.*

most terrified by the miseries—self-imagined—of a future existence, sought safety in an asceticism, the extravagances of which are unique in the history of the world. In every nook and corner there were schools of Brahmins, philosophico-religious sects, which sought to surpass one another in the extremes to which they carried the practice of self-torture. So ardent was their zeal in this direction that few or none took the trouble to inquire whether the foundations, starting from which they tried to build up into the heavens, were quite sound; whether the premises were correct upon which they based their calculations as to their wellbeing for eternity. They went on with their calculations, and, of course, the farther they went, so much the greater was the resultant error. So completely had the idea of torture in the name of religion taken hold of the people, that they were deprived of the power to produce that remedy which here would have been the simplest and most natural of all—namely, satire.

It is not improbable that the Buddha's age was precisely that in which the cult of self-imposed torture reached its zenith. Piety at that time was almost synonymous with self-torture. Spiritual India's line of thought at this time was somewhat as follows:—

Every deed is inevitably followed by its proper consequence: the good deed by reward, the evil by punishment. The offering brought to the gods, as its due reward, brings about the blotting out of my sins. If I compare my offering with the pardoning of the full tale of my sins, a balance of guilt remains against me from which no god can deliver me, and by which accordingly I am brought into direct opposition to the gods, or, at the very least, am put outside the pale of their bounty. Now, self-mortification is that offering which is the highest, and which therefore is the most effectual. If this self-mortification be brought to the necessary pitch of duration and intensity, out of it springs for the performer of penance a store of sovereign power which brings him ever nearer to the gods, makes him ever more like the gods; yea, puts him at last in a position in which he can compel the gods to his will.

Mythology tells of the two brothers, Sunda and Upasunda, who set out to capture the stronghold of the gods. By frightful castigations they seek to vanquish the deities, and already, by the overmastering might of their penance, Vindhya begins to smoke. Already the kingdom of the most high gods begins to tremble; but their tremendous accumulation of merit is swept away at one stroke by sin. In their great need, the gods send the beautiful Tilotamma. All is then over with renunciation and its ways. Love arises in the hearts of both the brothers, and in furious fight they fall together down to earth again.

In some such fashion was asceticism, self-imposed pain, understood in Brahminical India. In it they thought they had found the ladder by which to climb to the divine, and so everything turned upon the practice of penitential expiation as the one means by which to mount to the heights; hence we have that refinement of self-torment at which the Western can only look with an ever-increasing amazement.

The lack of the historical sense, of appreciation of the real, is a peculiar trait in the character of the

Indian. The Indian lives perpetually in a world of phantasies of his own devising. Here he feels most at home. He has always been a bad historian; he has always lacked the critical sense, the capacity of discriminative selection. The Indian, however, has always been great in this respect, that he has always been able to produce something new out of himself, but has had no talent for judging whether his point of departure was a correct one or not. Thus have arisen those elegant air-castles, those clever monstrosities, which may be compared to the banyan-tree that sends out one airy root after another into the soil, and so enlarges its circumference indefinitely. Exactly so does the Indian mind propagate itself in unnatural directions. Vital contact with the earth, with its terrestrial environment, is always wanting.

Herein lies the reason why it has been possible for a whole people to be mastered by this abnormal current of thought, this idea that in asceticism alone is to be found the way from the human to the superhuman. It was with these ascetics, these doers of penance, as it was with our alchemists in the Middle Ages: any little trifle, not explicable by current knowledge, was taken seriously as solid ground on which to rear a fabric of the hugest dimensions. The whole of India was full of such spiritual alchemy. These Indian ascetics were Don Quixotes who in their excursions into spiritual error left the adventures of the worthy knight of La Mancha far behind. But in perfect accord with India and the nature of its people, this period did not, as already said, find its termination in the appearance of any Indian Cervantes; it found religious salvation in the Buddha.

Gautama also followed the beaten track already trodden by millions of his fellow-countrymen. He had set out to find deliverance from the pain of the world, and he too turned to the great Indian panacea, self-imposed pain. He also put the cup of asceticism to his lips—yea, drained it to its dregs. He dived into the very depths of asceticism, to its most profound depths, so that he was able to say: "Greater depth there is none," and behold! with powerful stroke, he suddenly brings himself to the surface, and, like a diver returning from the ocean's floor, out of breath, almost drowned, he brings up with him the precious pearl of the Path of the Mean, the doctrine of the avoidance of all extremes.

In all Buddhism, in its iron logic, in its almost mathematically accurate synthesis, there is always something that seems alien to India; but nothing is more alien than this teaching of the avoidance of extremes, the shunning of all excess. This note was unknown in the India of that day. It was like a transition from sharp to flat in music, but the passage from the one to the other was so sudden that to many the harmony of the Buddha's thought seemed to be merely a harsh discord breaking in upon the rhythm of the spiritual life of his time. Therefore was prudence recommended. Therefore also do we find the Buddha repelling with especial vigour and vehemence accusations of this nature. Sunakkhatta, a prince of Vesali, had entered the Order of the Buddha, only, however, to leave it again in deep discontent; whereupon he taught in Vesali: "This ascetic Gautama does not possess the rich supernatural felicity of clearness of knowledge. A brooding, rugged teaching it is which the monk

Gautama proclaims, which he has thought out and worked out by himself; and its outcome is this: that whosoever ponders and pores deeply enough will attain to the destruction of pain." In our ears this accusation sounds harmless enough, but in the ears of ancient India it was a dreadful thing. The accusation which Sunakkhatta thus brought against the Buddha was that he neglected asceticism and put meditation in its place, and it was all the more dreadful inasmuch as it was perfectly true. The Buddha did indeed assign to asceticism a less exalted position than it had ever before occupied in India.

He had had the daring to reject asceticism as an end in itself, and officially indeed had forbidden it. For, according to Buddhist doctrine, there were three snares in which men's feet were entangled, and these were—belief in continuance of individuality, doubt, and asceticism regarded as an end in itself. In one place it is said in unequivocal language: "A monk who lives the holy life, with a view to receiving some divine embodiment, who says to himself, 'Through these practices or vows, castigations or renunciations, I will become a god or like to the gods,' his mind is far from effort and toil, perseverance and constancy."

"This monk teaches that man by meditation may reach the highest"; this accusation is not to be passed over lightly, and we find the Buddha answering his opponents under this heading with a quite unaccustomed vigour. It ought here to be remarked that it was no faint-heartedness, no mood of half-way hesitation, that had deterred the Buddha from submitting to voluntary pain. It must here be made plain that he, the Perfect One, he alone had pressed on to that ultimate stage of asceticism, to that extreme concentration of ascetic thought which, as its simple and natural conclusion, ultimates in reaction; as in organic life a vital poison finally produces its own antidote.

The picture of his own penances which he brings before the eyes of his disciples is one of such stark realism that the hair stands on end with horror at it.

"I remember when a crab-apple was my only daily food. I remember when a single grain of rice was my only daily food. And by only partaking of a single grain of rice a day as my food, my body became extremely thin and lean; like dried-up withered reeds became my arms and legs; my hips like a camel's hoof; like a pleat of hair my spine. As project the rafters of a house's roof, so raggedly stuck out my ribs. As in a deep-lying brook the watery mirror beneath appears so small as almost to disappear, so in the deep hollows of my eye-pits my eye-balls well-nigh wholly disappeared. As a gourd becomes shrivelled up and hollow in the hot sun, so did the skin of my head become parched and withered. And pressing my stomach, my hand touched my spine, and feeling my spine, my hand felt through to the stomach in front. And when I rubbed my limbs the hair upon them came out rotten at the roots. And yet with all this rigorous mortification I came no jot nearer to the rich supernatural felicity of clearness of knowledge."

Thus was judgment passed upon Brahminical asceticism. In the Buddha-system asceticism became something totally and entirely different.

Here, as everywhere, Buddhism reveals itself to us as engaged in the continual effort to turn from externals to the internal. In the spiritualising of the conception of asceticism its acid sharpness was lost. Not he who castigates his body is the true ascetic, but he who has purified his heart of all vice; the former is only a "word-grubber in asceticism." So long as a man has not put away the evil proclivities of his heart, of what use is asceticism to him? "Like a deadly weapon, ye monks, meant for warfare, two-edged, glittering, wrapped round and enclosed in a cowl, so to me, ye monks, does the pilgrimage of such a monk appear." Again, "A knife, if it be caught by the blade, cuts the hand. Asceticism, wrongly practised, leads to the downward path."

"I preach asceticism," says the Buddha, "inasmuch as I preach the burning away of all conditions of the heart that are evil. One who so does is a true ascetic." The true ascetic, who by true asceticism has burned his heart clean, "he may fitly and properly partake of the food that may be given him in alms, of rice tastily and pleasantly prepared, and it will do him no ill." Such is the monk who has been bathed in the "inward bath."

The Buddha prescribed asceticism only so far as it assisted the forward-striving in his efforts to attain to the highest. In all cases it was to serve as a balancing weight upon the narrow path of virtue, that the scales might be kept even. It did not carry its fruit in itself, as in Brahmanism, neither in any sense was it identical with its fruit. To make use of a simile: In Brahmanism asceticism was the seed-grain; the greater the sowing, the richer the harvest. Here, as in the rice-field, the relationship between penance and reward was reduced to a simple sum in arithmetic. In the Buddha's system, on the contrary, asceticism is rather to be compared to a watering, more or less copious, of the soil.

This inferior position, to which the Buddha of necessity relegated asceticism (since in no other way could he find a place for it in his system), is, as already said, not only un-Brahminical, but also un-Indian. "One cannot, brother Gautama, win to well-being by well-being. It is by woe alone that weal is won," say the "Free Brothers" to the Buddha. This is Indian thought to a hair. Think like this and you think like India.

This renunciation of voluntary pain, we may say, has always remained unpopular in India. For thousands of years India has been the land in which all the lamentableness of man's existence has been manifest in its starkest form. It might even be said that suffering, by dint of unbroken inheritance, had become the peculiar characteristic of the Indian race. And as among many peoples, anomalies in the shape of the skull or the expression of the face are at first prized as a national characteristic, and later regarded as a sign of beauty, and as such subsequently exaggerated in actuality and in pictorial representations, so was it in India with this anomaly in the domain of the mind. The very heroes of the Indian epics are embellished with this capacity for sorrow, as with a precious jewel. Apart from their other qualities they are "divine sufferers," but not after the unwilling fashion of the Homeric Odysseus; with them suffering takes its place as one of the supreme virtues. Of the hero Nāla it is asked: "Is he long-suffering as the earth is long-suffering?"

It is the case that Buddhism in its purer Southern form has remained free from all excess of ascetic practice; only in that corrupt form which it has assumed in Tibet and Nepal, in its fusion with Siva-worship, do we find recalled the practices of the Indian ascetic. But this asceticism of Northern Buddhism comes before us in a special form, a form that is all its own.

As in Brahmanism, penitential practices were carried out in order to obtain supernormal powers; but, as one might expect, conformably with the teachings of pure Buddhism, these Siddhis (Pāli: Iddhis) were not to be devoted to the attainment of individual freedom from pain—that is, for the attainment of Nibbāna—but only in the practice of deeds of compassion on a large scale, in wholesale giving, in spreading the doctrine, and, before all things, in helping to lead living beings from pain to the place of painlessness. Corresponding with this tendency towards the boundless, which runs all through the Mahāyāna, that is to say, through the school of Northern Buddhism—men were not contented with the goal set before them by the Buddha, namely, the reaching oneself the place of safety, Nibbāna; moved by an impulse of boundless compassion, men toiled for the welfare of all living beings; strove themselves to become Buddhas.

When King Sīladitya wished to bestow gifts upon the monk Jayasena, the latter answered: "Whoso receives the necessaries of life from another must concern himself with the troubles of the giver. I am now working in order to save men whom the stream of life and death is ever sweeping away. How can I find time to occupy myself with the affairs of your Majesty?" They did not speak like this in the days of the Buddha and his early disciples.

In those days everything turned upon one's own salvation, not upon the salvation of others.

> Cease not to strive thine own high goal to gain,
> Through thought for others, be they ne'er so great,

says the Dhammapada, that is to say—in all probability—the Buddha.

The Chinese Hiuen Thsang, the most famous of the pilgrims who penetrated India from China in order to study Buddhism at its source, had three ultimate wishes, which he thus expressed as he worshipped before the miraculous statue of the Bodhisatta: "First, I pray that after the completion of my studies I may return to my native land, and there live in perfect peace. Secondly, I pray that after my death I may serve the Metteyya Bodhisatta (the next Buddha that is to be) in the Tusita heaven. Thirdly, it is taught that among the mass of men there are some who are not in touch with the nature of the Buddha. I wish to know whether by the practice of virtue I can become a Buddha."

Thus in the teachings of the Mahāyāna was the supreme goal by sheer strain transferred to the realm of the vast; and vast also were the means by which men sought to reach that goal. The system of meditation, of knowledge, is here blended with the system of works, of self-torture. The latter, however, in agreement with the end aimed at, is called "The Penance of the Great Compassion," and as a phenomenon presents itself in a correspondingly compassionate form. From the legendary book of Taranatha, who wrote a history of Indian Buddhism in the Tibetan language, we cull the following:

"The monk Aryasangha desired to conjure up the Arya Maitreya (future Buddha). Four times, for an unbroken period of three years, he laboured over the magic spell in a cave. But as in the whole twelve years no sign of success appeared, he gave up his attempt in great dejection and left the cave. And in the city that he came to, he saw a certain dog snapping and barking at people, and the lower part of its body was eaten and gnawed by worms. Moved by compassion, Aryasangha thought within himself: 'If I do not rid this dog of these worms, the poor creature will die; if, however, I take the worms from off her and throw them away, the worms will die,' wherefore he resolved to cut some flesh from his own body, upon which to put the worms. From the town of Acinta he procured a shearing knife, and laying his begging-bowl and staff upon the ground, with the knife he cut a piece of flesh from his calf. Then he closed his eyes and felt for the worms in order to take them, but his hand found nothing. Thereupon he opened his eyes again, and found that both dog and worms had disappeared. Before him instead he saw the adorable Maitreya, glowing with light. Tears starting from his eyes, Aryasangha said: 'O Father, my Refuge, although I exhausted myself with toil and labours many, yet did no fruits appear. Why has the rain-cloud, the arm of the sea, come down after I, burnt up with grief, have ceased to thirst? Although so long I tried to conjure thee forth, yet hast thou never shown thy countenance.' Maitreya answered: 'Although thou, darkened by the shadow of thine own deed, hast never seen me, none the less have I ever tarried near thee. Following upon the potency of the words of power, spoken by thee aforetime, now through this deed of penance of great compassion, through the flesh cut from thine own body, are all thy sins and stains purged away, so that now I can be seen by thee.' To the question as to what he (Aryasangha) wishes of him, the latter replies asking him that he might work for the spreading of the Mahāyāna teaching, and the salvation of all creatures."

Here we see penance at an ideally high level, such as it never occupied in Brahmanism. It here possesses that superhuman form given to it by the Buddha in the Jātakas. These latter are the legendary stories of the previous existences of the Buddha and the deeds of love which he then performed. In virtue of his omniscience, the Buddha in them recalls those parts of his career as a Bodhisatta which lie far back in the past, concealed from ordinary mortal vision. One of the best-known stories of the Jātakas is that legend wherein the Bodhisatta (future Buddha) offers his own body to a tigress in order to save her and her young from death by hunger. Equally well known, and the one most prized in Buddhist India, is the Vessantara legend, in which the Bodhisatta as Prince Vessantara carries asceticism in the shape of perfect self-sacrifice to a height only conceivable in the thought of India. Innumerable representations of this legend adorn the walls of Buddhist cloisters, rock temples of Ceylon, and *kyoungs* of Burma, and the tastelessness of their execution is only equalled by their multiplicity. And still after so many hundreds of years, when this legend, a veritable Buddhist passion-play, is played in the rude native theatres of Ceylon and Burma, it never fails to draw floods of tears from the eyes of the spectators. The suffering brought before us in the Jātakas is, as it were, the surrogate for actual pain; it is a kind of crucifixion in effigy.

Perhaps nowhere so much as here does the Buddha show how nothing that is human is alien to him. He stands too much in the centre of the currents of his time for this dead centre in his system to have escaped him. He well knew that in India he stands highest in the popular esteem who submits to the greatest extremes of self-torture. Asceticism was incompatible with his system, for the quintessence of the latter is avoidance of every sort of excess. He thus conceived the happy means of escape which the Jātakas offered him, and put together a career of expiations which surpassed those of the Brahmins as much in their extent as in their duration. He was thus able to say with full justification: "The most that you Brahmins endure here, all that have I also borne; yea, what you only endure for one brief lifetime, or a little part thereof, that have I undergone thousands and thousands of times." He thus made sure his own position in the popular esteem, but not that of his monks, against whom the reproach was constantly brought that they did not allow the way to the highest to be made sufficiently difficult!

And, truth to tell, the teaching of the avoidance of all extremes was in too great contrast to the frightfully strained efforts of Brahminical asceticism for the Buddha's disciples to have been spared this reproach.

The Muni or Brahminical penitent, who sits

naked in the dust, covered with ashes and dirt, publicly exhibiting his mortification of all worldly sense, has never been the Buddhist ideal. In quiet —we might say in respectable monotony—pass the days of the Bhikkhu, the Buddhist beggar-monk. He has no care for his bodily necessities, and the hardships of the weather are unknown in these happy lands. In the quiet yard of the cloister, away from the noise of the streets, lies his little cell. In front of it slim areca palms wave their green crests in the monsoon wind. In a walled-in enclosure stands the Bo-tree, the sacred fig-tree, and through its bright, ever-tremulous foliage a mystic murmur continuously sighs. Everything conspires to give the mind the opportunity to collect its forces, to turn inward upon itself. The monk may only partake of food in the fore part of the day. After twelve o'clock noon he may not partake of nourishment again until the dawn of the next day. Further, he may not sleep during the day, and of the long tropical night only a portion may be spent in sleep. It should be said, however, that those who are lazy of nature can always find an opportunity to evade these rules, and thus can turn what is meant for a course of strenuous self-discipline into a life of torpor and satisfied ease.

Moreover, there is good reason for suspecting that those inward struggles, those tortures of the doubting mind, which play so important a part in the lives of our Western heroes of religion, are here more rare, and more easily quelled when they do arise. For Buddhism is not based upon faith, that wonderful force which, like some tantalising flame, now shrinks to a mere spark, and, flaming forth anon, threatens to destroy its possessor. As we have seen, the Buddha founds his teaching upon a knowledge which, through quiet reflection, may be acquired almost as one acquires a handicraft, little by little. Something substantial, almost prosaic, runs through the whole Buddhist system. Patience and quiet tenacity of purpose are here the wings that bear one upwards. Here is no sudden lightning-flash of illumination from some divine idea. Not one of the Buddha's disciples ever trod the way to Damascus.

Buddhism is simply a subject of instruction, and if a man finds himself making no progress, the way out of the Order always stands open to him. Not the slightest odium attaches to those who so go out. Thus it is quite possible that the teaching of the "Path of the Mean," which the Buddha brought up from the depths of asceticism like some most precious pearl, has become for many merely the doctrine of the path of mediocrity!

XV

WOMEN

NOWHERE, perhaps, has woman occupied so high a position as among the Aryan peoples. Esteem for their womenkind has always been a distinguishing feature of the Aryan stock. The Hindu—at least the higher-caste Hindu—belongs to this Aryan stock. The lower the caste, the greater is the alloy of Turanian, East Asiatic elements. In the two highest, and therefore purest castes, the Brahmin and Kshattriya, the position accorded to woman was always an important one. According to the law of Manu the woman was to be to the man, not only wife, but mother, sister, friend, and slave as well. Noble womanhood has in India been sung in as sincere and heartfelt accents as it ever has in Europe. The forms of a Damayanti, of a Sakuntala, are like fragrant blossoms.

Yea, more: upon the religious side of life—for with the Hindu, religion always forms the standard—woman plays a worthy part. When the householder, after he has looked upon his children's children, forsakes his home in order to devote himself to meditation under ascetic discipline, as Vanaprastha (dweller alone in the forest) he may take his wife with him. She also is thought fit to turn her thoughts toward the highest.

Maitreyi, the wife of the wise Yājñavalkya, says to him: "If now, O Lord, this entire world with all its treasures belonged to me, would I thereby become immortal or would I not?" "By no means," was the reply. "Only as is the life of the opulent—so would thy life be; hope not for immortality through riches!" Then said Maitreyi: "If I may not become immortal—what should I have to do with that? Rather reveal to me the wisdom that thou hast in thy possession."

This passion for renunciation, from of old endemic in India, extended also to the female sex. Indeed, in the polemical tourneys of the Upanishads we find women showing themselves active and vigorous combatants.

There is yet another circumstance of significance as regards the position of women in Brahminical life. In the religion of the Veda a special seal was set upon sensual love, so that the act of generation, together with the organs involved, was deified, as it were, in the subtlest allegories of that allegorical system.

Wedlock was a sacred thing in Brahmanism, and marital duty as binding and universal in that ecclesiastical state as military duty in modern militant states. Yet, be it understood, the compelling force was not an external but an internal one. Unhappy the man—in this world as well as in the next—behind whom stood no children! And to be able as Vanaprastha to devote himself unreservedly to religious meditation, a man was obliged first to discharge his duty as student and then as father of a household.

As the Buddha tore asunder the bonds of caste,

so also did he tear asunder the religious bonds by which the individual was bound to wedlock. Here whosoever feels the impulse thereto may at any time betake himself to the solitary life; and, since the lower must at all times give place to the higher, no odium was incurred when any one, while still involved in the duties proper to the householder, pledged bridegroom, or son, threw these off and entered the Order.

Oft recalled is this passage in the Suttas: "With fetters bound is household life: full of impurity; like the open air of heaven is the life of the ascetic." In the first sentence the Buddha must surely have had married life in his mind when he spoke of the state of impurity. Generation was to him a "den of murder." That particular tang of pain and disgust which, according to the Buddhist way of thinking, belongs to all personality, attaches in more abundant measure to the female personality, as being the least worthy, the more impure. When the Buddha wishes to represent in an especially drastic manner the transition from the height of lust to the depths of sorrow, from the delight of embodied things to the misery of embodied things; when he wishes to show that the most seductive charms are only a covering cloak, an ante-room to the disgusting in its most pronounced forms, he chooses the female body as the object of his deductions. At one stroke of the brush the colours are laid on with such glaring brilliance that the central law of the system, the avoidance of all exaggeration, comes very near to being broken.

"What now, ye monks, is the delight of the embodied? This: a king's daughter, a Brahmin maiden, or a citizen's girl, fresh with the freshness of her sixteen or seventeen years; not too big, not too small; not too slim, not too stout; not too dark, not too fair; does not such shining beauty, ye monks, at that age seem simply entrancing?"

"Indeed yes, O Master!"

"What now, ye monks, is the misery of the embodied? Only let us look upon this sister at a later time, in her eightieth, ninetieth, or hundredth year; broken, crooked, shrunken, tremblingly shuffling along, supported upon crutches; infirm, withered, toothless, with bleached wisps of hair, bare, tottering head, wrinkled, the skin full of spots; what do you think, monks; is not what once was shining beauty wholly departed, and misery now come in its place?"

"Yes, indeed, O Master!"

This is by no means the terrified abhorrence that characterises our modern woman-hating philosophers, with whom it is a matter of principle to look upon the female form from a safe distance, and who strive with angry objurgation to rid themselves as speedily as may be of every tender emotion. It is the deliberate aversion of an expert who has seen behind the scenes; the aversion of one who has made this "human flesh"—for others, merely warmth and lust—the object of cool reflection. The Buddha is incorruptible, and nothing that is human is alien to him.

How very much lower the female form stands in the esteem of Buddhists as compared with the male form is best exemplified in this—that Buddhahood, the state of perfect enlightenment, can only be reached by the man, never by the woman with her "two-fingers-broad feminine understanding."

In the Aṅguttara Nikāya it is said: "Three things there are, disciples, to which secrecy belongs, and not publicity. Which are the three? Secrecy, not publicity, adheres to women. Secrecy, not publicity, adheres to priestly knowledge. Secrecy, not publicity, adheres to false doctrine." In the same breath, the sun, the moon, and the doctrine made known by the Buddha were declared to be the three things that shine before all the world, and not in concealment. Thus the nature of woman was posited as something, in a measure, incompatible with the doctrines of the Buddha, and only under pressure from his foster-mother, Gotamī, did the Buddha finally consent to permit the admission of women into the Order.

When Ânanda asks him how one should conduct oneself towards women, he answers:

"Don't see them, Ânanda!"

"But if we see them, what should we do?"

"Don't speak to them, Ânanda!"

"But if they speak to us, O Master, what shall we do?"

"Keep wide awake, Ânanda!"

This is quite in the style of Thomas à Kempis when he says: "Commend all good women to the care of God. The bad ones do not concern thee!"

In the most emphatic manner it was forbidden to the monk to touch a female form upon any pretext whatsoever. To make clear, by an example, the strictness of this injunction, it is stated that if a monk's own mother falls into a pit he must use a stick in helping her out!

At the first council held after the Buddha's death, the reproach was brought against Ânanda that he had allowed the admission of women to the Order, and that he had permitted women to shed tears over the corpse of the Master, which latter was a sort of defilement. Those delicate and beautiful relationships which attached the founder. of the Christian religion to the other sex, are here awanting, at least the details that have come down to us in vividness fall far behind the episodes narrated in the Gospels. Some rich lay-adherents are noticed, who, by way of offering, place their wealth at the disposal of the Order, to whom in consequence the Buddha grants some favours, and some king's wives are mentioned; but they remain lifeless types, not living individuals.

That specific quality of the feminine character in virtue of which woman becomes the complement of man, was not, and could not be, taken into account, for in Buddhism the entire effort is, out of single separateness, whether of man or woman, to make a self-contained, final whole which no longer requires supplement or completion from any quarter whatsoever. As in chemistry we speak of bodies whose total affinities are satisfied, and which consequently no longer have any tendency to unite with other bodies, so also the affinities of such as have attained to perfection are so fully satisfied in knowledge that even the strongest reagent, the sex distinction, is powerless to affect them. Indeed, where there is no longer any *I*, wherein can reside any attractive force of one for another. At bottom, love is nothing but an opposition. But opposition is based upon difference. As the distinction of sex is the distinction *par excellence*, so is sex-love, love *par excellence*. If, however, all is merged together in

Anattā, every kind of difference disappears, as also every possibility of love. The whole world has become a mist, through which the pendulum of thought oscillates unrestrained; and so also is it with the tokens of separation found therein; they too have disappeared and melted into the mist. In Buddhism it is with love as with some pampered greatness, which a rough but righteous hand suddenly puts back into its proper place.

Theoretically indeed, upon the heights, man and woman stand equal; practically, however, the latter stands much lower, because, with her inferior organisation, it is found in experience to be much more difficult for her to reach the heights.

The position occupied by woman in the Buddha's system is in accord with the place she occupies in the life of those peoples over whom Buddhism has flowed from its Aryan source. Among the peoples of Eastern Asia, women have always been measured by another standard than that in usage amongst us. After all, Buddhism did nothing but fix the colours already prepared. Judge as we may of the position of women among the Mongolian peoples, in their under-estimate of the qualities of the feminine portion of humanity these peoples have assuredly not gone as far astray from the truth as have the Christian peoples of Europe in their over-estimate of these qualities. For this latter the inborn characteristics of the European races are to blame, especially the German stock, as also the peculiar development of social relationships in Europe, where the sexes are continually being drawn still farther and farther apart from one another, with an accompanying intensification of the mutual force of attraction between them. Thus, as by famine the price of grain is raised, so by our system of education the value of one sex to the other has been artificially raised to a quite unwarranted height.

It is characteristic of the mental life of the East that in it that wonderful creature, the pious mistress, has never found a place. Her sickly-sentimental, sweetly-languishing airs are the diametrical opposite of the clear, cold, steel-like atmosphere of Buddhism. The characteristic mode of thought of this system, together with the native tendencies of the peoples of Eastern Asia, make it unthinkable that out of the mist of legend a form could ever have been evolved like to that of Mary, the "mother of God"; notwithstanding that in the person of Yasodharā, the Buddha's wife—the young, the gracious, the forsaken, the sorrowful—all the elements were united which could have elevated her into an object of adoration. The imagination of these peoples has never been able to make anything else out of her but a nun who disappeared into the Order as a drop of water disappears in the sea.

XVI

BEGINNING AND END—THE TWO RIDDLES OF THE WORLD

THAT first of all problems: "How has the world arisen?" does not exist for Buddhists—at least, not in the same form as that in which it presents itself to our minds. Schopenhauer's words are entirely applicable to the Buddha: "My philosophy does not undertake to explain how such a world as this has come into existence; it merely endeavours to indicate our true position therein." The Buddha never even entered upon the attempt to enlighten his disciples as to the arising of the world.

With single-minded, persistent logic he adheres to his problem, salvation from sorrow. He continually repelled all questions as to cosmological beginnings, either by silence or by the constantly recalled advice: "Save thyself; that is the thing of most importance."

Since the Buddhist system sets out from the fact of sorrow, which is found in full flow in the present, the question as to the creation of the world, in our sense of the word, collapses of itself, and discussion of it here were needless, yea, were criminal foolishness, because we are handling a problem which carries in itself the evidence of its insolubility.

When, however, the question as to the first germ of life is brought before him, the Buddha begins with the present and works backward into the past. Like a man following a clue, he goes farther and still farther back, until he is lost in the shadows of infinity. "Exactly as if a man were to cut down all the grasses and growing things, all the twigs and leaves that are in this entire continent of India, and, gathering them together, heap up one handful after another, saying: 'This is my mother; this is the mother of my mother,' and so forth; there would be no perceptible end to the mothers of the mother of this man, until he had actually reached the last handful of all the grasses and growing things, all the twigs and leaves of this continent of India. What is the reason for this? Without beginning and without end is this Saṁsāra; unknowable is the origin of beings enveloped in Ignorance."

Dealing thus with the question, the Buddha is the only one of all the founders of world-religions who has avoided bringing himself into conflict with exact science and the facts of evolutionary history, which latter already for such a long time has juggled before us with the much-sought-for beginning of the beginning. He does not set himself in opposition to these facts, but embraces and comprehends them. If the ascent from the primordial cell up to the evolved present has always happened, what then? It is really only a phase of life within this Saṁsāra, a motion of Saṁsāra's breath. As little as ebbtide lays bare the bed of ocean, just as little does the primordial cell lead us to the beginning of all life. And just as flood both follows and precedes ebb, so does this hollow of life on either side lead to the heights. If Saṁsāra ebbs and flows, what matters that? Like in-breathing and out-breathing, it is only the necessary condition of all life.

This idea of continual ebb and flow exists in Buddhism as the doctrine of the periodic destruction of the world. The inconceivably long period of time which divides one world-catastrophe from another is called a Kalpa; in Pāli, a Kappa. The Kalpas that are past are numberless, as also are those that are yet to come. In each new Kalpa the entire evolutionary process is in a certain measure gone through from beginning to end. But each Kalpa has its root in the previous Kalpa, as each life finds its root in the life preceding, each life-moment its root in the life-moment before it, as the heart's systole has its root in the diastole. The Kalpas are nothing but the hour and year hand of that horologe of eternity upon which the single, separate lives mark the minutes and the seconds. The whole Kalpa indeed consists of nothing but the totality of the deeds of the single beings that exist in it. As in the life of the single being, each existence is linked by Kamma to the one that follows, and itself by Kamma has arisen out of the one that preceded it, so the sum of all the separate Kammas forms the connecting link between one Kalpa and another. Life is eternal, without arising or passing away, and remains untouched alike by birth, or by death, or by the Kalpa conflagration.

And yet the Buddha taught an arising and a passing away of the world.

And what does the Buddha teach? He teaches

that this visible world, this Known, can only exist where there is a Knower. Where there is no subject, no Knower, there can be no object, no Known. This world therefore stands and falls with the knower thereof. Yea, not only does it stand with him, it also arises with him. It is the activity of my six senses that causes the world to arise. This, according to Buddhism, is the arising of the world. Every look, every thought, every heart-beat in our breasts is the arising of the world, and thus has rolled from all eternity the all-o'erflowing stream of this *generatio æquivoca*. In unmistakable language the Buddha says in the Sutta Nipāta: "The world arises where the six senses are," and again, "I tell you of a truth that none can make an end of sorrow until they have reached the end of the world. And now I declare to you that in this fathom-long perishable body, with its perceptions and imaginings, are contained the world, the arising of the world, the cessation of the world, and the way that leads to the cessation of the world" (Saṁyuttaka Nikāya).

There are thus two kinds of world-ending, as there are two kinds of world-beginning: the absolute and the relative. The absolute world-end is that which corresponds to the absolute world-beginning. It is this that is taught by the religions that are founded upon revelation, the which, however, no one understands, for it is the mental impossibility *par excellence*. The relative world-ending is that which corresponds to the relative world-beginning. It is this latter which the Buddha teaches, and it is quite accessible to the understanding, and therefore possible of realisation.

The beginning of the world, in the Buddha's sense of the words, always and everywhere sets in where Will arises or comes into action. The world-end everywhere and always sets in where Non-willing comes into play.

Only he who is able to make this standpoint his own can understand the Buddha. Only he who has succeeded in making this standpoint his own can perceive that it bears fruit only when it has attained the point of perfection. This does not happen with the mere recognition: "I am the maker of the world": that is, the idle diversion of a philosophy as yet unpricked by the goad of necessity. But when I recognise that I am *nothing but* world-creator; that I am *nothing but* activity of the senses, *nothing but* deed; when I can say with full conviction: "An absolute, a soul, has no place in me," then indeed it begins to bear fruit. Only in the perfection of comprehension do we get Buddhism, for only in its perfection does this comprehension come under the constraint of necessity. The constraint of what necessity? The constraint of the necessity for liberation, the necessity of the struggle for liberation. For if I recognise myself to be wholly act—that is, the product of necessity—I at the same time recognise myself to be a thing entirely transient—that is to say, I recognise myself to be sorrow. With this recognition liberation becomes a necessity, and Buddhism only begins where necessity sets in.

So far, so good! "But if now I am wholly sense-activity, wholly act, then every motion of my *I* is itself synonymous with world-creation. How then is the cessation of the world ever to come about?" may be asked, and the answer is, "In the perfection of comprehension is to be found the fruit thereof." Just because I recognise myself to be wholly act, for this reason the cessation of the world can come to pass. How so? If I am not doer—endowed with a soul—but *deed*; if I am not only deed, but *nothing but deed*, then I am nothing else but a *Becoming*, a process, and a process can have an ending. The *I*-picturing process ceases with the cessation of willing. It is not sense-activity by itself that creates the world, but sense-activity in so far as it is regulated by will. How this latter ceases is shown elsewhere.

Now it has just been said that individuality is wholly activity of the senses, *i.e.* deed; and sense-activity, *i.e.* deed, is regulated by will. On the other hand it has also been said that individuality is wholly will. How do these two statements agree with one another?

As the seed lies behind the plant in bloom, so behind the senses, in the depths, lies the will. The activity of the six senses is simply will in a state of division, and will again is sense-activity falling together into unity; while life is nothing but the eternally unfathomable process of the passage from one to the other, nothing but the eternally incomprehensible mechanism which, through the illusion of the succession of deed and will, creates the illusion of time, the illusion of the "I"; and the abrogation of life is nothing but that specific form of cognition which does away with the illusion of time, with the illusion of the succession of deed and will, through the thinking of the Anattā thought. In the Buddha-knowledge deed and will fall into one another, time as well as the "I" being crushed and annihilated between them.

If, however, deed and will are alike, what is the end or aim of the Buddha's whole scheme of liberation? What means the fight against lust, hate, and illusion? The budding thought of lust is already a deed; how still fight against it? To these questions the answer is: Deed and will *are* never at any time alike; they only *become* alike in the Anattā-thought. As on the horizon heaven and earth become one, so in some particular individuality recognised as Anattā, recognised, like the horizon, as something wholly conditioned, do deed and will become as one. So soon and so long as individuality is a thing like the horizon, which at every step forms itself anew, so soon and so long will deed and will be as one.

Is the cessation of the world, then, only a temporary affair? The cessation of the world as something merely temporary were idle playing with words; the case lies thus.

As a glowing stick, whirled around by the hand, produces the appearance of a complete circle, so does corporeality, under the impulsion of will and ignorance, produce the appearance of a complete "*I*." And as when the hand becomes fatigued the circle collapses and nothing remains but the glowing stick, so with the wearying of the will does the *I* collapse, and naught remains but the bare law of cause and effect. And as by the whirling of the stick, not only the fiery circle but the fire itself is fed and maintained, so under the impulsion of will and ignorance, not only the illusion of the *I*, but life itself, is fed and supported.

And as the glowing stick becomes extinguished as soon as it is brought to rest, so is this *I* extinguished in Non-willing—that is, in the thought: Anattā. For, so soon as Ignorance passes into knowledge, willing necessarily passes into non-willing, and the abrogation of life simply means the abrogation of the possibility of life. As the heart that once has come to a stop can never again begin to beat, so the life that has once been annulled by knowledge and non-willing can never begin anew. The cessation of the world, in so far as it is not an empty form of words, comprises in itself the necessity for the cessation of the world, and has about it nothing of the temporary or merely optional. Thus the beginning of the world is found wherever will arises, and wherever willing ends there also ends the world.

We have now to inquire whence springs the will?

Willing is conditioned by Ignorance. Further, if the world arises in will, then Ignorance (Avijjā) must be that which conditions the world, which precedes world-arising. But at this stage do we not step out of the realm of the relative and confront the beginning of the beginning, the Absolute, the hidden deity? Not in the least! In this system, Ignorance is nothing but ignorance of the true nature of the *I*. Even if it exists before the will, it is yet nothing absolute, for this individuality, this will, is unity in duality. Just as the point at which two lines cross one another is one and yet two, so also this individuality is one, but arises from two causes: on the one hand from Avijjā, and upon the other from Cause-effect; Will, individuality, is the product of the mutual action of these two factors. In one sense, a flame is fiery spark and nothing else; and looked at in another light, it is solely the fuel that feeds it. Similarly, individuality in one sense is wholly ignorance, while in another sense it is wholly cause-effect.

Cause-effect, together with Avijjā, would thus seem to precede the beginning of the Buddha's world, and so, if Avijjā were the absolute, there would also have to be a second absolute, which would be a contradiction in itself; or else Avijjā and cause-effect would have to be considered identical, whereby not only individuality, but also its elementary substratum, would be done away with as being illusion. In knowledge then would be dissolved not only the form, but also that upon which form is founded. This, however, is not the case, and cannot be the case, because the world rests upon me only in so far as it, as the *Known*, stands opposed to me, as the *Knower*. Only the form can be known, not that upon which it is based. Wherefore the world can only be done away with through knowledge—that is, only in so far as it is form. Only so far as it is form does it arise and pass away, is it a *Becoming*, and *Becoming* can have an ending. That, however, upon which form is based, the elementary—that is *Being*; and never and nowhere can Being pass into Non-being; never and nowhere can what is eternal come to an end.

Saṁsāra, then, is without beginning or end, eternal; and yet we are to regard its parts, the individuals, as abolishable? By no means. The eternity of Saṁsāra is relative, existing only as the summation of endlessness in time and space. It does not indicate any true eternity, but only the picture, the appearance of eternity. Only in appearance does it pass beyond time and space, even as the single separate *Becoming-moments* out of which this corporeality is built up, also pass beyond time and space, the only difference being that the one (Saṁsāra) is, in a manner of speaking, above, while the other (the embodied *Becoming-moment*) is, so to say, below our time-horizon. This is the trick by which our senses, those deceived deceivers, conjure up, before us and behind us—that is to say, in the place where we are *not*—the illusion of eternity. The real eternity is with us, in us, as matter. Our *I* is a parasite upon eternity.

Then the Buddha also has recognised an Absolute in that upon which form is based—namely, in matter?

The Buddha never said anything at all about matter. He only speaks of cause-effect and of the Khandhas. Cause-effect, however, is only thinkable as something perceived—that is, as something joined to individuality. The Khandhas are, only where there is Kamma—that is, where there is individuality. Thus it is only with matter as it is employed by individuality, with matter held in the fetters of relativity, with perceptible matter, that the Buddha deals. About matter outside of relativity, about an absolute, about God, the Buddha never uttered a word.

But if such a thing is, what is it? The answer is unbroken silence. And this silence is justified; nay, it is necessary. The individual has to find liberation from himself, from individuality. With this liberation alone has he anything to do. The introduction of something lying outside of individuality is illogical because quite unnecessary.

Cause-effect, then, is thinkable there only where it is perceived. Where it is perceived, there is individuality, and where individuality is, there is Avijjā. In other words: Avijjā is thinkable only where there is something that can be made subject to Avijjā—that is to say, Avijjā is only thinkable upon the basis of individuality. Where individuality exists, there also is to be found its substratum, active matter—that is, cause-effect.

Here an objection arises: the Buddha teaches that the entire universe is nothing but this mechanism of cause and effect. I, however, perceive the existence alongside one another of subject and object.

Exactly so! This is precisely the proof that Avijjā is in operation.

Yes, so the Buddha says, but where is the proof of it? Here is the proof. The relations between subject and object are synonymous with the world. Along with the *I* arises the *Thou*, which means that upon the *I* rests the world. Now even the ignorant see that the *I* upon one side is subject, and upon the other, object. The Buddha, however, found that the *I* upon one side is *wholly* subject, and upon the other side *wholly* object. How so? Because in one aspect it is entirely effect, that is, act; and in another aspect it is entirely cause, that is, will; in the same way that a flame from one point of view is naught but fuel, and from another point of view is naught but fire. If, however, I am wholly subject and wholly object, it follows that I am neither subject nor object, as the flame is neither spark nor fuel. Consequently I can be nothing but the perpetually active process of the unification of these two—that is to say, a *Becoming*.

Thus does the Buddha prove the *I* to be a delusion; not, however, on the score that it makes pretensions to *Being* and *is not*, but because it makes pretensions to *Being* and is only a *Becoming*. He drives the *I* into corporeality in order that there he may bring it to the ground. To him the *I* is nothing but the symptom of a deficiency, nothing but the product of lack of knowledge. As a fall in the temperature of the atmosphere produces as its outward effect frost or snow, as a fall in barometric pressure for outward result has wind or tempest, so this lack in knowledge brings forth for outward sign the *I*. Nothing here is left which stands in opposition to the world as subject *par excellence*, as a true *I* not conditioned by the *Thou*, as an absolute, as a permanent soul housed in the impermanent body.

More than this. If the *I* is illusion, so also of necessity is the distinction between *I* and *Thou*, between subject and object. As past and future are the props of the illusion of the "now"—in point of fact there is no "now," but only a perpetual collision of past and future—so are subject and object the supports of the illusion of the *I*. But just as, on the other hand, past and future are only conditioned by the "now," so also subject-object are only conditioned by the *I*. The *I* is at once producer and product of illusion. It is the deceived deceiver: illusion and ignorance in one. This, however, does not mean that the *I possesses* Avijjā, but that it *is* Avijjā, and every actualisation of the

I is nothing but Avijjā actualising itself. The primary function of the *I*, however, is the distinction between *I* and *Thou*; subject-object is nothing but cause-effect actualised in the individuality.

Now it may be granted that what pictures to us subject-object is only illusion and Ignorance, but how do I know that subject-object is simply and solely cause-effect thus transformed and transmuted through Ignorance? Simply because every one, even the ignorant, perceives that cause-effect, action and reaction, reign throughout the universe, while the man of knowledge also perceives that *nothing else* reigns but cause-effect.

But is it not possible that this view of cause-effect may itself be based upon an illusion?

No! The wise man himself furnishes a case in point. In the Anattā thought everything is dissolved, no remainder being left over. As in an arithmetical sum that works out evenly, there can be no doubt as to whether the solution is correct or not, so also is it here. In this system, knowledge is that which bears in itself the witness to its own truth. Here that sentence of Spinoza's entirely holds good: "Whoso has a genuine intuition, also knows that he has one, and cannot doubt the truth of the object." For the Buddha-knowledge to become truth—that is, something that bears fruit—no merely formal demonstration avails anything. It can only be attained to by living it, and by living it to its ultimate.

But to return to our starting-point. The place which Avijjā occupies in the system is best exemplified by the definition of it supplied by the Buddha himself: "A common man, a man uninstructed in the truth, does not perceive this truth with regard to bodies subject to growth and decay: 'The body is subject to arising and to passing away.' This is called Ignorance, and such a man is an ignorant man." In other words, he does not know the four Holy Truths of Sorrow, which means that Avijjā, like everything else, is conditioned.

Thus Avijjā and cause-effect, which apparently, like two blind runners, go out into endlessness, come back again into individuality, and presuppose individuality. In the very moment of their arising both ingeniously produced conceptions close together again upon that through whose collapse they have arisen, as water closes up behind the hand that cuts through it. To decompose individuality into Avijjā and cause-effect is only to build individuality anew, as the dissipation of the Khandhas in death is nothing but the building process of the new Bhava. We are still enclosed within the charmed circle of individuality, like the wanderer who, notwithstanding all his exertions and haste, ever finds himself girt round by the horizon. The question: "How, at the beginning, for the first time, did the union of Avijjā and cause-effect result in individuality?" falls with the weight of its own foolishness to the ground, like a man who falls over his own feet. Avijjā is already just individuality, and the question: "What was before the *I*?" has only one answer: "The *I*."

Here again we stand at that "boundary-line of possible perception" where the phrases, before and after one another, before and behind one another, become void and meaningless. This wonder, *par excellence*, the union of cause-effect and Avijjā in individuality, their transmutation (effected by crossing) into subject and object, their play in space and time, is not a function of the *I*, but the *I* itself. As the mirror does not require first to wait upon the world which is to be reflected in its surface, but is itself that world, so the *I* does not need to wait for union of cause-effect and Avijjā, but is itself the union of both.

Only from this standpoint can those obscure passages be understood in which "before" and "after" appear to be misplaced. Here at the very outset must be mentioned that twelve-linked chain of cause and effect which, under the name of "Paṭiccasamuppāda"[1] or the twelve Nidānas,[2] plays such an important part in the system, the most important next to the Four Holy Truths. It is the "deep, of lustre deep"; upon it, as upon a scale reaching in both directions, up and down, the Buddha took the full measurement of this world of sorrow, as he sat under the Bodhi-tree at Uruvelā, enjoying the bliss of deliverance.

In this chain of causation Avijjā, so to speak, plays its official part. Ignorance is the first link in the chain. "The Differentiations, Sankhārā, are conditioned by Ignorance, Avijjā. Consciousness, Viññāna, is conditioned by the Differentiations. Individuality, Nāma-rūpa, Name and Form, is conditioned by consciousness. The Six-fold Sense-domain is conditioned by individuality. Contact is conditioned by the Six-fold Sense-domain. Sensation is conditioned by Contact. Lust for Life, Tanhā, is conditioned by Sensation. Attachment, Upādāna,

[1] Roughly translated: "Arising simultaneously with, and by the help of something else."

[2] Nidāna means "that which furnishes occasion for"; for example, if I suffer pain from a thorn in the finger, the thorn is "nidānaṁ."

is conditioned by the Lust for Life. Becoming, Bhava, is conditioned by Attachment. Birth, Jāti, is conditioned by Becoming. And old age and death, woe, lamentation, sorrow, grief, and despair are conditioned by Birth. Such is the arising of the entire Sequence of Sorrow."

Nothing in the whole system has given rise to so many hypotheses and learned dissertations as has this list. The fundamental error has consisted in translating the idea, "is conditioned by" (paccaya), by the words, "arises by," thereby importing the idea of succession into the whole series. *Paccaya* really means: "To be through the help of." My teacher in Ceylon explained it thus. If we lean three pieces of wood all against one another, each is held upright by means of the other two. We cannot take one away without the other two falling to the ground. It is because of each one of the three that all three stand upright. That is the meaning of paccaya. This thoroughly understood, we shall not lightly incline to the notion that *Jāti* means birth in the ordinary connotation of that word, and in the attempt to understand the existence of "Lust for Life" before "Birth," as a help towards explanation thereof, we shall not resort to the idea of previous existence, to come finally to a halt before Avijjā, as before something cosmic and unexplained, something constant on the farther side of individuality. "The apprehension of the objects of sense, that is called Birth," it is said, the which "birth," and not the coming forth from the mother's womb, is birth in the Buddha's sense of the word. The entire sequence of causality is run through within the span of one existence. This existence is compounded of innumerable acts of dying and of coming to life again. It is Avijjā in me, which ever and again brings about the revival of will, of thirst for life. With will, however, "arising" sets in, that is to say, the world, rebirth and death. Avijjā already presupposes the entire individuality. It is not, however, that the Differentiations only arise where Avijjā is; they are there already, just as, wherever an object is maintained in a given position, there also exists that which maintains it. Along with Avijjā is given the distinction between subject and object, Knower and Known. (To him who knows, on the contrary, all distinctions are done away in *Not-I.*) Where, however, subject and object are differentiated, there also, and at the same time, is there consciousness of *I.* But where the *I* exists, it exists in activity, and where there is activity, there also its above-mentioned consequences ensue. Sickness, old age, death, misery, and distress, on their side, however, are nothing but another expression for Ignorance.

Here again Avijjā has already set in, which simply means that with the last link of this chain the first link of the next is already given, and so on *ad infinitum.*

The twelve Nidānas are nothing but an expression for the fact that in this single body is represented the full endlessness of Saṁsāra. The very being of Avijjā is synonymous with the beginninglessness and endlessness of its existence. The chain of causality is, so to speak, a life-moment split up into its component parts, and this fatal process of delusion, ever and again reproducing itself from itself, is brought about by the intellect in order to awaken the "disgust of the understanding." Even as sorrow lies in the understanding, so also in the understanding lies the aversion to sorrow, the revolt against the originator of sorrow, Avijjā; and this must not only be felt, it must also be known.

The twelve stages embrace, as it were, the span of an octave. As in this latter the first and last notes are the same and yet different, so is Avijjā the same as suffering and death, and yet between these stages one and twelve there is a distinction conditioned by the illusion of time. The Nidānas do not close up into a circle, so that numbers one and twelve come together again in every aspect; they are simply the exact image of the thread of endlessness.

As the final note of one octave is already the first note of the next, so the final link in the old chain is again the first link in the new. And as with any single octave are also given all the others that can proceed from it, both above and below, so with any one chain of causality are also given those that are past and those that are to follow. And as the succession of octaves never really comes to an end, but only the notes finally come to lie on the farther side of the threshold of sensation, so life, in reality, never vanishes, like something that no more is; it only passes beyond the range of our human sense. Life, as it were, is the entire domain of sound; this existence, the notes of a range of octaves that extends in both directions up and down, to the limits of audibility, and the chain of the twelve Nidānas, simply the span of *one* octave in this range of octaves.

It has been said above that Individuality *has* not Avijjā, but *is* Avijjā. Thus Avijjā is only possible as self-acting. A single stirring of Avijjā, a single moment of the thought "here is an *I*," is as one with the full eternity of Saṁsāra. For wheresoever the *I*-thought is, there also is individuality, and wherever there is individuality, there also is subject-object, the world, the illusion of space and time, and therewith the idea of eternity; for time, the "now" is only thinkable as something in flow,—that is, without beginning and without end. Out of each single "now" we look before and behind us into eternity. Only with time, with the conception of transiency, does the idea of eternity arise. "What is the root of past, present, and future time?" asks King Milinda, in the Milindapañha; "Ignorance," answers Nāgasena. The *I* in a word, is the formula of endable endlessness!

The idea of eternity is in truth nothing but the *I* looking at itself—the very quintessence of all illusion—deception that deceives itself! The possibility of looking at one's self, however, is also the necessity of the same, since the *I* that generates the illusion is also itself the illusion. Hence the possibility of self-contemplation equally involves its beginninglessness and endlessness.

But to contemplate one's self is to reflect, and to reflect upon one's self is to endeavour to comprehend one's self. This, in fact, is the most profound feature of Avijjā, that in it are united the passion to comprehend one's self and the impossibility of ever being able to do so. Life is an endlessly repeated yet ever unsuccessful attempt to comprehend one's self. No one can comprehend his *I*—think his own thinking! Life is a thing that can only be willed; it cannot be understood. To understand one's self is to dissolve one's self, as a light reveals itself only by consuming itself. In other words, the *I* is comprehensible only as *Not-I*; becomes *Not-I* in being comprehended. To desire comprehension of an *I*-self is to desire the impossible; hence the effort to do so must of necessity come to grief, or else end in a compromise;—that is, it will be believed that there is a God, and that eternal life is to be found in Him, which is like a sort of declaration of self-mate on the part of thought. Hence this Avijjā-problem is the most incomprehensible trick which the *I* plays upon itself, for it creates by its power to delude, eternity and allurement towards an eternal life in God, and at the same time presents the possibility of deliverance without God, the possibility of realising the Buddha-idea. For the Buddha-idea can only adhere where, upon one hand, man sees death, and upon the other, the form of eternity.

The Buddha found that the only way which led to the conclusion, to the solving of this Avijjā-problem, lay in the direction of the idea that this personality contains no *I* at all. I am comprehensible only in so far as I am *Not-I*. Just because I am *in toto* comprehensible must it be that I am void of any true *I*. The presupposition of its existence, with which all others have set forth upon their quest for the *I*, is pure weakness. The error already exists in the problem itself, and transfers itself, necessarily, to all its conclusions.

Where there is no *I*, there is also no contemplation of an *I*, no idea of eternity. With the *I* falls the "now," for there is only a "now" where there is consciousness of time. With the disappearance of the *now*, past and future merge in the unity of timelessness, and this is the only true eternity. That image of eternity which our senses bring before themselves is only an apparent eternity, the product of the summation of innumerable apparent *nows*. Timelessness, however, can never be obtained from time even if we extend the summation-process indefinitely; it can only be obtained by the abrogation of that which is created by time, by the abrogation of the *I*. As a ring that turns upon itself, if one half of it be concealed by a stationary one, through its twisting motion presents a delusive appearance of endlessness, so also does life so long as it is impelled by the *I*-illusion. And as the twisting ring, even while its one half is covered, appears to bring to view ever new portions of its circumference *ad infinitum*, so does that part of life's ring which lies in sight between birth and death ever appear to be a new portion *ad infinitum*. The illusion of succession arises, and with it the illusion of eternity. When, however, the gaze of knowledge penetrates the covering, the *I* perishes: the bare ring lies before us, and all is clear, so clear! And with shame and astonishment we perceive that the idea of eternity has arisen in our minds in no other way but as the image of endlessness presented by the revolving ring before our deluded eyes.

Here the question arises: "What precisely is the object of Avijjā?"

Avijjā in the form of self-consciousness is

nothing but a constraint to keep my mental eye fixed upon the apparent *I*, hence nothing but a constraint, an incitement toward reflection, toward the solution of the riddle of life. This Avijjā-problem, *i.e.* the chain of rebirths, ever and again provides new incitements, new possibilities, new opportunities for deliverance. One is tempted to assume that Avijjā comes into play only that it may abolish itself; that individuality only arises in order to provide the possibility of deliverance from individuality. That, however, would be as if one recognised the object of imprisonment to be merely the breaking out of prison again.

No object of Avijjā, *i.e.* of life, can be given, any more than there can be given an object of endlessness. To ponder over the aim of life is as fruitless as to ponder over its beginning as an absolute event. The Buddha never said a word about the aim of life. Life as a whole is always taken as a given fact. Lobha, Dosa, Moha (Lust, Hate, Illusion), that is, will—that is, sorrow—these are present, and nothing beside. Deliverance from them is quite naturally not the aim, but the problem of life, as the removal of pain is the problem of those in torment. Deliverance is an object only as regards asceticism. The end and aim of monkhood is deliverance, as it is the aim of a medicament to relieve pain. To inquire concerning the aim of life is only a disguised fashion of asking about the absolute beginning, about God. Only where there is God is there an aim to life. Avijjā as representative of the empty endlessness of life has no object. Inclusively in one thought I cognise myself as the central pivot of the world, as that upon which the world rests, and also as something objectless, something that were better not to be, as illusion. In other words: There can only be an object to life where creation, an absolute beginning of the world, is recognised. No Buddha, however, can point to an absolute beginning. He also must accept the world and life as things given. But this is not to be considered a lack in the system, for, properly, it does not belong to it. The only task the Buddha undertakes is to show how he who has seen life to be sorrow may bring life to an end.

The Buddha-system is the only one in the world which finds its end in itself, because to it life, in the first place, is something to be denied, and, in the second place, a *Becoming*, a process, a perpetual uniting of two factors (cause-effect and Avijjā), one of which two factors (Avijjā) lies in ourselves. Life ceases as soon as the uniting of these two factors ceases, and thus the abrogation of life rests in our own hands; it depends entirely upon the turning of Ignorance into knowledge. Avijjā produces the specialised individuality out of the universal, the elementary, out of matter; which latter in activity reveals itself as cause-effect. Individuality is nothing but a reflection of the universal, of cause-effect. Just as a reflection in a mirror in one sense is, and in another sense is not, so I, in so far as I am cause-effect, *am*, but in so far as I am individuality, *am not*. I am a unity of Being and Non-being, that is to say, I am a *Becoming*.

In so far as I am individuality, I am the product of lack of knowledge, and disappear with the disappearance of that lack of knowledge. A cloud that has rolled itself up into a form *is*, in respect that it is condensed vapour, but *is not*, in respect that it presents an illusive appearance of form. As in correct perception the form disappears and the condensed vapour remains, so in correct perception does the body disappear and there remains only the material substratum, cause-effect, the elements.

It is precisely this conception of Avijjā which at first sight appears to border most closely upon the cosmic, the unrelated, which in reality leads us most directly back to individuality. Avijjā, which is the one-word formula, the monogram for individuality, as the individual *par excellence*, runs alongside of cause-effect, the universal *par excellence*. Avijjā is nothing but ignorance of life as something wholly and entirely transient; that is, ignorance of life as sorrow, and hence is synonymous with will, the arising of the world.

As a man looking upon a puzzle-picture considers it to be of itself a veritable picture, so, ever and again from all eternity, has the puzzle-picture of subject and object, of world and *I*, been brought before the individual, and ever and always has he affirmed it to be that which it appeared to be, with the words: "This am I, that is the world," without the least suspicion that it was only through each of the innumerable forms of affirmation that that arose which thus confidently he accepted as actual fact, as the already existent. Looking upon such a puzzle-picture, only when an expert points it out to us do we suddenly perceive the lines of the picture in their true significance; only then do we perceive that what we had hitherto regarded as figures placed alongside one another were, in point of fact, only the means by which the true sense of the picture was, on one hand, concealed from us and, upon the other, revealed. The solution once supplied, those shapes quite disappear which alone up till now had caught the eye, and give place to the real picture, becoming merely so many lines whose sole use was to make up the configuration of that proper picture. In precisely similar fashion one who has hearkened to the words of the Buddha perceives the true and proper meaning of the world, that greatest of all picture-puzzles. He perceives that that which has hitherto presented itself in the guise of world and *I*, object and subject, is nothing but a means whereby on one hand the true sense of things has been concealed, and on the other hand the genuine explanation made possible. He perceives that it is only with *I*-consciousness, only with the *I*, that the *Thou*, the world, arises. He perceives, however, at the same time, that it is only with the *I* that the possibility arises of perceiving *I* to be *Not-I*, the which possibility simply means the possibility of world-cessation. The possibility of world-cessation, however, is on one side the acutest pain, because an expression of the transiency of all things, and on the other hand the keenest bliss, because an expression of the possibility of deliverance from sorrow. Hence the possibility of world-cessation becomes the necessity of world-cessation; hence also the struggle against Avijjā becomes a perfectly natural thing. Here the removal of Avijjā simply means the removal of everything. The removal of Avijjā here is like the removal of the rarest treasure. For this each man must know, that in this system no way leads from sorrow to salvation; a man must know that sorrow is itself salvation, unperceived; that sorrow, so to speak, *is* salvation, seen with the eye of Ignorance. Yea, verily, this each man must know!

Hence everything depends upon the dissipation of Ignorance, that wonderful thing which, like zero, of itself is nothing, but yet creates the world so soon as it is united with "being," is placed after "being." Hence, once more, in us, and not outside of us, lie the beginning and the end of the world, with all that lies between these two. Wheresoever Ignorance arises, there is the beginning of the world; and wheresoever Ignorance is done away, there also is the ending of the world.

Now let us once more run through the series of twelve Nidānas, with minus-Ignorance as our starting-point: "Where there is no Ignorance there are no Differentiations; where there are no Differentiations there is no Consciousness; where no Consciousness, no Individuality; where no Individuality, no Six-fold Sense-domain; where no Six-fold Sense-domain, no Contact; where no Contact, no Sensation; where no Sensation, no Lust for Life; where no Lust for Life, no Attachment; where no Attachment, no Becoming; where no Becoming, no Birth; where no Birth, there are no old age and death, no woe and lamentation, no sorrow, grief, and despair. Thus comes to pass the dissolution of the entire sequence of sorrow. And this with the Buddha is called the annihilation, the ending of the world.

But how can Avijjā perish? How can Ignorance be transformed into knowledge if I have not but *am* Avijjā? How can I come to know not-Knowing?—

Ignorance cannot directly pass into Knowledge; that would only be to give rise to Ignorance in a new form. The Buddha-knowledge is not that which is opposed to Ignorance; it is in itself the cessation of Ignorance, the impossibility of Ignorance. For here the possibility of Ignorance is also the necessity of Ignorance, precisely because individuality, as being entirely will, has not, but *is* Ignorance. Hence Ignorance can only cease when the possibility of Ignorance ceases; that is to say, it can only cease with the ceasing of the *I*, *i.e.* in Non-willing.

Here, however, we stumble over the same difficulty. The same question confronts us here as above: "How can willing change into non-willing if I have not but *am* the will? How is it possible to will not to will?" And again we get the same answer as above: "Willing can only cease when the possibility of willing ceases; that is to say, with knowledge."

Behind willing, as behind non-willing, stands knowledge. Only by means of this knowledge can willing, in a settled and natural way, become non-willing. All affections are nothing but the re-action of others upon me, upon the *I*. So long as the *I* is there, willing as well as non-willing is only an affection, a re-action. Willing cannot directly pass into non-willing; that would only mean a change in the willing. Only where the *I* has been dissolved in the Anattā-idea is there no longer any impact; as a stone falls unimpeded through empty, airless space. Where there is no impact, no resistance, there also there can be no rebound, no re-action. Thus willing can be transmuted into non-willing in a natural manner only where the possibility of willing, that is, the *I*, perishes ; in other words, where there is knowledge.

Willing is not something that is the opposite of non-willing ; both alike are deed, only the one is deed joined to ignorance, and the other deed joined to knowledge. The latter, however, is that particular kind of deed which leads to the "annulling of deed." In exactly the same way knowledge is not the contrary of ignorance ; both alike are cognition, only ignorance is cognition united to willing, while knowledge is cognition united with non-willing. Willing can only be dissolved in knowledge, and ignorance can only come to an end in non-willing. Therefore is it said that in this system, morality and knowledge are bound up with one another as in the flame, light and heat. But through what does my solving activity set to work upon this insolvable tangle ? Through the teaching of another and through quiet reflection. These are the beginnings of the transition from ignorance to knowledge, from willing to non-willing. They are the beginnings of world-cessation. But with which of the two does the process begin ? With knowledge, or with non-willing ? With both !

As the full eternity of Saṁsāra is already present in one moment of *I*-consciousness, so in one moment of right reflection already lies *in nuce*, full deliverance. To give ear to the words of the Buddha, and to reflect upon what is heard, is already knowledge and non-willing, each springing up alongside the other. Let a man lay hold of the Buddha's teaching in what fashion he will : through transiency, through sorrow, or through *not-I*, everywhere he lays hold of knowledge and non-willing together. "When the Master lays down the Doctrine, going farther and farther, deeper and deeper, with its parts of good and of evil, it becomes clearer and clearer to the disciple, and sentence by sentence reveals itself to him." As a man, provided with two wooden pegs, from the ground upwards climbs into some giant tree, by driving in one peg and standing upon it, driving in the second, and with this as fresh foothold driving in the first again, higher up, and so on to the top of the tree; in like manner also the disciple proceeds from level earth—that is, from actuality, from the consciousness of sorrow—and works his way upwards by resting his growing knowledge upon his beginnings of non-willing, and supporting his non-willing upon his knowledge. But he must experience the necessity of allowing non-willing and knowledge to act, just as the man, in spite of possessing his two pegs, will not climb the tree until he feels the need of doing so, until hunger drives him. Need, necessity, is here the motive force. Our Bible phrase: "His delight is in the law of the Lord, and on His law doth he meditate day and night," does not apply here. What delight! Here a bitter *must* alone holds sway, and the only play is the play of necessity. Buddhism is necessity as religion, and religion as necessity. Other religions may be put off and on like a garment: to take up the religion of the Buddha and lay it aside again is, however, an absurdity, because it is not a garment but the man himself. I do not possess the teaching; I *become* the teaching; and there is only one way, once it has come into action, of laying it aside again, and that is, to dismiss it along with the *I* after its work is accomplished. This is what the Buddha meant when he said to his disciples: "A raft let my doctrine be to you, useful for escape, not for retention."

The will, if we give heed to the words of the Buddha, is already the beginning of non-willing, and the cognition: "Now do I give ear to the teaching," is already cognition in the form of knowledge. If, however, the process (of the transition from Ignorance to Knowledge) has previously set in, it reproduces itself out of and through itself as necessarily as the converse, the building of the world through Ignorance and through Willing also reproduces itself out of and through itself.

"By whomsoever, ye monks, confidence in the Perfect One finds a footing, strikes root, receives an impulse; with such a hold, in such a manner, under such circumstances, ye monks, this is called confidence in foothold, striking root in contemplation, strength, and neither priest nor penitent, nor god nor devil, nor Brahma nor any one whatsoever in all the world can uproot it."

The distinction between the two kinds of self-reproduction, out of self, and through self, is merely this, that in the former something is continually taken away, whereas in the latter something new is continually added; in the latter, endlessness threatens, while in the former an end beckons. For if the *I* is fully transformed into the *not-I*, the process of itself comes to an end, as a fire goes out when its fuel is exhausted.

The end of the world is no constant entity, no

Being, but exactly as the beginning of the world is an eternal *Becoming*, so also is the world-ending a *no-more-becoming*. The world-ending, like the world-beginning, is a process, and not a stated event, a sudden cutting off, for then indeed the absolute would stand behind the world that had disappeared. As in willing the world arises in unbroken stream, so in non-willing is it dissolved in equally unbroken flow. "And what, disciples, is the destruction of the world? Through the total remainderless destruction of the thirst for being arises the destruction of the impulse towards life; through the destruction of the life-impulse arises the destruction of *becoming*; through the destruction of *becoming* arises the destruction of birth; and through the destruction of birth arises the destruction of old age, and death, sorrow, lamentation, pain, misery, and despair. After such a fashion comes about the destruction of the entire complex of sorrow. This is the destruction of the world."

In itself there is no difference between world-creation and world-cessation, except that in the former case the result is produced by willing, that is, ignorance; and in the latter case by not-willing, that is, knowledge. It is as if a perpetually recurring error in arithmetic were perpetually made good again, perpetually set right. The striver after salvation, therefore, must unweariedly practise in himself this process of setting right, as a man who has a precious plant under his charge is obliged to take continual care for its growth and wellbeing. But this setting-right process, which must ever be kept going (by non-willing), is at the same time a delight, for at every moment is to be seen the ceasing of *Becoming*, the ceasing of sorrow. It therefore is carried on quite as naturally as the world-making process is carried on by willing, while Avijjā is still present. This new life is not continuous denial and combat, but here, as there, we have the flow of life; only, with him who knows, its activity takes the form of negation, the cessation of deed—that is, of the *I*. Yea, in strict truth, life only "flows" with this latter, the man who knows, like a stream that steadily glides down to the sea, whilst others rage and roar in the whirlpools and narrows of egoism.

Thus is world-cessation, the "blessedly peaceful exercise" to which the disciple must devote himself day and night, so long as such devotion is possible; especially so long as a world-cessation can still be spoken of, for only where there is arising, where there is a world, can we think or speak of cessation, of end. What the end of the world is, if it is no longer a continual *Becoming*, of this as little can be said as of a world-beginning, if it is no longer perpetual *Becoming*. What the world-end is, as something actual and constant, we can as little perceive as we can feel a heart that has ceased to beat in death. We can only perceive the motion of the breathing, slower and more slow—that is, the expiry of the will. To that which follows upon the cessation of the will no bridge leads across.

The moment when *Becoming* comes to an end is as one with the entire eternity of *no-more-becoming*, as the moment when the heart's activity ceases is one with the entire eternity of non-action.

If, then, I am so destitute of all control, what sort of guarantee have I got? Am I not then obliged to have *faith* in the world-cessation, in the ending of this *I*? And what have I to do with faith? Faith is the airy pedestal of eternal life. For him who strives after world-cessation, knowledge alone availeth aught—yea, knowledge only. And indeed, just as I know the eternity of life, of *Becoming*, so also do I know the eternity of *no-more-becoming*. Already in this life the process of world-cessation sets in; even here Nibbāna may be known. How will, in continual flow, passes over into non-willing on the basis of knowledge—this I perceive. As I perceive sorrow, so also do I perceive the ceasing of sorrow. I have the cognition: "This process of world-cessation has set in." And as one can foresee the completion of a sum that has been begun without having actually reckoned it all out to its conclusion, in like manner I can foresee the end of the process of world-cessation without having actually realised that end in myself. As, for example, I know that such and such a number will go into another number a certain number of times without having actually worked out the sum, so do I know that life can be dissolved, with no remainder left over, through knowledge, without myself having carried out the solving process. As I know that I shall finally reach a solution, with no remainder over, when I begin to subtract two from any even number, so do I know that life will finally be solved with no remainder over when the process of transition from ignorance to knowledge, the process of world-cessation, has once set in. Its termination is only a question of time, as the destruction of the combustible material of a fire is only a question of time once the fire is set agoing. Thus is it with the knowledge of world-ending, of *no-more-becoming*. It is that immovable, mathematical certainty which looks down upon "faith," as found in current religion, as upon something dubious, something lacking of sure foundation. The certainty of being delivered—that alone is deliverance.

But the process once begun, can it not be renounced before its term, when it is only half way through? Impossible! Just as a ferment begins chemical change in a fluid, and in the product of the change anew creates itself, so does knowledge begin to act in this personality by weakening the will to live, out of the weakened will to live all the more powerfully reproducing itself. As the ferment cannot cease to act until the transforming-process is complete, so likewise knowledge cannot cease to act until all ignorance has been transformed. And as, when there is no longer any more material to transform, the ferment by its own concentration comes to nothing, so does knowledge by itself cancel itself after the completion of the process of transforming ignorance into knowledge. But since ignorance is not a possession of the individual but is itself the individual, so also knowledge is not a possession of the individual but *is* the individual. Knowledge annulling itself by itself, just means that the individuality in whom the knowledge is, abrogates himself. The persistence of the individual, after knowledge has been attained to, is a self-contradiction. Herein lies that immovable certainty already alluded to; for the man who knows, perceives that knowledge and continuance of life, that is, re-birth, can no more exist together than light and darkness, past and future can exist at the same place and time. This is precisely the criterion of perfection in knowledge, this is the perfect fruit of knowledge, even this immovable certainty of *no-more-becoming*. There is no road from the one to the other, even as there is no path from sorrow to salvation.

But is it not possible to content myself with the knowledge that individuality is removable without entering upon the process of its removal? No! Once the statement, "The *I* is removable," is not merely a something learned by the lips, but is actually realised as a genuine possibility, it no longer lies in our power to hinder the process of removal. For the perception that the *I* is removable is sorrow, since transiency is sorrow. To put it another way, such a perception is sorrow because with the possibility of abrogating the *I*, is equally involved the possibility of abrogating the soul and God. If, however, behind this world there stand no divine, no soul, no true blessedness, then does all life become pure sorrow, something wholly "unblest." On the other hand, the perception that the *I* is removable is blessedness, is deliverance; for where there is no *I*, there also there is no sorrow. Hence the perception of the possibility of deliverance implies also an irresistible attraction, impulse, passion towards deliverance. For, as water flows downwards, so does the human mind press from the painful to the painless, from *I*-ness to *I*-less-ness. This impulse it is which the Buddha calls the disgust of ignorance, that disgust for the illusory and the untrue, that passion for truth, which in the intensity of its indifference to consequences shrinks from nothing, not even from the sacrifice of self.

The setting-in of this process is that condition of twilight, that mixture of light and darkness, when young knowledge and old willing meet. As the body cannot rest so long as some limb is pulled out of place, so the mind on which has flashed the thought of the Tathāgata cannot be at peace until confusion has given place to order, until that disturber of the peace, that deceived deceiver, egoism, has been wholly eliminated. This is what the Buddha meant when his monks asked him: "What monk truly lends lustre to Gosiṅga wood?" and he replied: "When a monk, having returned from his begging-round, sits down when he has finished his meal, with crossed legs, body upright, and persists in the resolve: 'I will not rise from this place until my heart is wholly delivered from the illusion of existence'—such a monk truly lends lustre to Gosiṅga wood." Herewith also is answered the question: What object is there in striving to reach such a far-away, superhuman goal? It is only the resolve, the beginning, that is distant. Once we have the beginning, the end also is given. With the struggle the result of the struggle also is given. He who digs a well will surely come to water if only he digs deep enough.

Humanity, as being that *par excellence* which on one hand is endowed with *I*-consciousness, and upon the other with the capacity for thought, is the formula for sorrow as well as for salvation. The instinct of self-preservation, being *I*-consciousness in action, is common to all nature, and the finding of salvation in the God-idea is only this instinct in its most sublimated, as also in its commonest form. Salvation through self-abrogation, however, is something that is possible only where *I*-consciousness and thinking co-exist, and is therefore something specific to humanity. We may put it thus : Thinking in its every form is the unconscious endeavour after self-abrogation, is the beginning of self-abrogation. This self-abrogation becomes conscious and active so soon as Willing becomes an object of thought ; that is, so soon as *Not-knowing* is *not-willed.* As a being endowed with the power of thought, the highest that man holds within himself is this self-abrogation, the which, as being his highest, is also his destiny. This process of the abrogation of ignorance, of Avijjā destroying itself is the most human and, at the same time, the most superhuman of all dramas : it is the "comprehension" and "apprehension" of one's self as man. And this is the ending of the world.

XVII

MIRACLE

In his book on Francis of Assisi the French Sabatier writes: "Miracle, that affable pastime of God, would be immoral, since it would set at naught the equality of all before God, and hence make of God a capricious tyrant." Excellent! But the creation of the world out of nothing is the greatest and chiefest of all miracles, the which miracle God has performed, and in the last analysis *had* to perform; for, as we can only speak of teacher with reference to pupil, so we can only speak of God in relation to a created world. The creation of the world is assuredly His masterpiece, by which, through endless time, He is henceforth duly qualified to act as God. Only it is uncommonly awkward that in this most important and interesting case we should unite in our own persons the bungle and its judge; it is scarcely calculated to arouse much confidence when the pigtail begins to philosophise about the pigtail-maker. Yet no twist, however clever, can deliver us from the dilemma. When all is said and done, the pigtail still persists in hanging behind, not in front. God remains incomprehensible to us; the miracle is an accomplished fact. Consequently, whoever acknowledges the morality of world-creation, along with it acknowledges the morality of miracle itself, for the fire cannot be otherwise constituted than the sparks that fly forth from it. On the contrary, that would be an immoral world which, now that its existence is assured, should disavow the miracle to which it owes that existence; somewhat the same as if all of us, although the product of generation, were to speak slightingly of generative activity.

More than this. If we hold that it is with generation that we first came into existence, then every single conception—which, of course, includes every birth—is precisely as great, as complete a miracle as world-creation. Whoever admits one miracle, the creation of the world, must of necessity concede the other, the creation of the individual. These are the daily bread by which those religions live that are founded upon revelation. The man of faith looks upon this illusion, endlessly repeating itself in time and space, with profound veneration, exactly as a child looks upon the moon it sees in the water, which every fresh wave seems to bring to new birth.

The Buddha put both miracles outside his system by means of a species of infinitude-arithmetic. The Buddha never speaks where silence alone is adequate; hence he never speaks about God. But since he never speaks about God, he has no need to speak of a creation, and because he never speaks about a creation, so also he has no need to speak about birth in our sense of that word. The world is eternal: without beginning, this Saṁsāra; without beginning, the beings therein. "If I pull up all the grasses and growing things in all this Indian continent, and, taking them by handfuls, say at each handful: 'This is the mother of this man; this is the mother of his mother,' and so forth, I might indeed come to an end of the grasses, but not of the mothers." Here the Buddha says as much as reasonably can be said, and pushes back into infinitude that point at which, of necessity, must set in the miracle of arising out of nothing, the so-much-sought-for first link in the chain of cause-effect. Where those religions that are founded upon revelation, like impatient children, leap at one bound out of time and space, and so maintain the miracle of creation, the Buddha moves discreetly, step by step, and gives the mere protocol, so to speak, of his observations in thoroughly scientific fashion, differing from the course of our present-day science only in the fact that his glance reached far out over the whole of this little sphere of ours.

His work would have been very exact, but it would also have been very useless, had he been obliged to say: "Infinitely far have I gone back through the chain of being, yet never an end have I perceived." All might have degenerated into a juggle with numbers, towards which, moreover, there has always been a tendency in Buddhism. But he specified the reason for this miscarriage. By a real stroke of genius he stripped bare this apparent infinitude, and showed it to be an illusion, whose root lies in the deceived person himself. Thus, with regard to this idea of infinitude, he wrote us all down as so many deceived deceivers, and hence that cry of distress, "There is a God," wrung from tortured minds by the foreboding of eternity, never comes from his lips. He showed that the infinitude which extorts this cry of distress from us does not lie an enormous distance away on the farther side of finitude, whither it is constantly being transferred by other religions, but that it actually lies within the finitude, and that it is precisely this body, this sense-picture of transiency, which out of itself produces and presents the illusion of infinitude, as the surface of a puddle reflects the infinitude of the sky. In us lies the infinitude of the world; with us it arises; with us it passes away. It was thus that the Buddha solved the question of world-beginning and world-ending, and we do not hesitate to say that in his train of thought lay the most colossal surprise that has ever been prepared for the world. There is no longer any miracle of creation out of nothing; every moment of my existence is the creation of the world, and that corresponding miracle of religions founded on revelation, the transference into eternity of man who has arisen in time—this also is done away in the same Buddha-thought. As beings have no beginning, so also they have no ending, and their apparent ending, this "behind time and space," continuously arises only *with* "time and space," and time and space arise with me, the *I*, the illusion. There is nothing, however, that is less a miracle than the true ending in Nibbāna, the "timeless and spaceless." Quite the contrary. Nibbāna is the comprehension of that illusion out of which miracles grow for us, that illusion which pictures infinitude to us, and thereby ever fetters us to finitude.

All obligatory miracle is done away with in the Buddha-knowledge. There only remain those facultative, minor miracles which, in religions founded upon revelation, circulate as the small change of faith. But even these small-wares also have no place in Buddhism. From the infinite heights of his knowledge the Buddha, "the great compassionater," lets his Buddha-eye, like some sun, range over the happiness and unhappiness of separate individuals. He only recognises; he cannot, however, assist. His sympathy, his love, are of no avail to the separate beings, but only to the world, and to its sorrow, as a whole. He well knows that the unhappiness of the separate beings is purely the result of an illusion, a lack of true knowledge, and that it will disappear with the disappearance of this, the illusion; that is to say, with the comprehension of the true law. For him who comprehends there is no more any sorrow; along with the sufferer, it is utterly done away, no least trace being left behind. Before his eyes, in whom ignorance has been destroyed, happiness and unhappiness alike are dissolved in the one law of cause and effect, just as iron, as well as gold, is dissolved in *aqua regia*.

Miracles are only asked for where sorrow comes in with such an overwhelming flood that our understanding, and with it all idea of self-help, are drowned beneath the waters. Hence, with the wise—in the Buddha's sense of the word—all need for miracle is abolished. For the ignorant, however, for all the manifold sorrows of the human heart, the Buddha has nothing but the true teaching, the which, with sublime monotony, he unfolds again and yet again before the eyes of the afflicted. Thus do we treat grown-up persons. Only the child requires miracles; the grown-up person is satisfied with an understanding of the inner connection of things. He accommodates himself to necessity.

There is a legend which inevitably suggests comparison with the biblical story of the raising of Lazarus from the dead. Kisā Gotamī, a young mother, has lost her child by death. Unknowing of the nature of death, she carries the corpse of her child from house to house, asking: "Do ye not know of some remedy for my son?" The people answer her: "Surely, daughter, thou hast lost thy wits, wandering about like this, asking for medicine to cure thy dead son." Finally one of them thinks: "I will send her to the Exalted One; he has help for all." So she comes to the Buddha and asks him: "Dost thou know of any medicine that will cure my son, Lord?" "Yes," was the reply, "I know of one. Thou must get a pinch of mustard-seed from a house where neither a son nor any one else has died." So she wandered from house to house, and there was mustard-seed everywhere, but when she asked if any one had ever died in the house, the answer was always: "What dost thou say, honoured one? The living are but a few: the dead, many." All day long she wandered thus about the village. At last towards evening she thought: "Ah, it is not an easy task. I thought that it was only my son that was dead, yet all over the village the dead are more, many more, than the living." And with this thought her heart, that had been weak with love of her son, becomes strong. She leaves the corpse in the wood and goes back to the Buddha. He says to her: "Thou thoughtest that it was only thy son that was dead. But this is the eternal law of living beings. The king of death, like to some raging flood, carries off all living beings, even those whose desires are yet ungratified, into the sea of corruption." And Kisā Gotamī, on the spot, attains to the first stage of the path to Nibbāna.

It was in this manner that the Buddha comforted the distressed,—a constant pointing to the unchangeable law of nature, from which we can only escape by an intelligent submission thereto. The miracle of the raising from the dead is inconceivable in Buddhism, for it would be a contradiction of the fundamental principles of the teaching.

The following, narrated by the Chinese Hiuen Thsang, is characteristic.

The Abbot of Nāḷandā Monastery, tortured by a terribly painful disease, resolves to end his life by abstaining from all food. Three Bodhisattas (candidates for Buddhahood) however appear to him in a dream, and command him—not, as we might suppose, to resort to this or that healing herb, this or that wonder-working relic, but to give himself to quiet meditation upon the Suttas. He does so: his inner being is calmed and the sickness leaves him.

In Buddhism it is with miracle-adjuncts as it is with God-adjuncts: they are a purely ornamental by-product; in any case they merely serve to make minds more open to the comprehension of the doctrine that is afterwards preached to them. It is not consistent with the Buddha's character to perform miracles. He is a man, even as we. The greatest, the only miracle—as he himself says—is the miracle of the Doctrine, that wonderful internal transformation by which an ignorant man becomes a wise man; an unbeliever, a believer. This is the thing which to the Buddha also appears "astoundingly wonderful," and because he accomplishes this, therefore is he called the "will-changer."

Since the Buddha has no desire by miracle to establish a claim to divine nature, there is here an entire absence of those debatable prodigies that just stand upon the border of the barely possible, those occurrences that lie, as it were, in the twilight land of thought. Here every prodigy is so unhesitatingly relegated to the region of the colossal, that discussion, whether possible or not, is never in the question at all. Miracle from the very outset is referred to the legendary. For example, Buddha rises into the air and with his two hands lays hold of "the so mighty" sun and moon; then he lets rays of fire burst forth from him that penetrate the entire universe, and so forth. But, as said, these are things that have nothing to do with his specific quality as Buddha. The self-same powers are attributed to every one who attains to perfect enlightenment. The performing of wonders is a result of a complete understanding of the laws of nature; it is no secret power, no divine grace, but merely a result of knowledge. Yet the Buddha, as an historical personality, regards wonders with disdain. When the king of Kosala required of him that he would permit his monks to perform miracles, he answered: "I do not teach my disciples the law that I may say to them: 'Go, ye monks, and perform miracles before the Brahmins and the elders of households,' but thus I teach them the law: 'Live, O monks, concealing your good deeds and revealing your faults.'"

When young Kevaṭṭa asked the Buddha to turn the rich town of Nāḷandā to the Doctrine by means of a miracle, the Buddha rejected miracle as being inadequate. "For in the land of Gandhāra, for example, there are people who also can perform similar miracles. Seeing clearly the insufficiency of miracles, of magic, I am oppressed by a miracle of magic, I abandon it, I despise it." He was able thus to answer because no one could say to him as —with one word altered—they could say to Christ: "Prove by a miracle that thou art the Buddha." That would be a poor proof if some one who taught us to perfectly understand the eternal laws of nature were obliged to accredit himself by turning these laws upside down. He himself, in spite of his Buddhahood, is subject to these self-same laws. He has only the power of withdrawing from their jurisdiction; he has no power to act in opposition to them. Therefore is it said: "Four things there are, disciples, which neither ascetic, nor Brahmin, nor God, nor Māra, nor Brahma, nor any one else in the world can compass. What are the four? That old age may not come on; that sickness may not afflict; that death may not snatch away; that the fruit of action may not come to ripeness. These four things no one in all the world can compass."

Thus everything proceeds without display, but in a manner that completely satisfies the intelligence. True knowledge is synonymous with deliverance, and this with painlessness. Where, however, there is freedom from pain, there is no reason, no necessity for miracle. The man of knowledge truly possesses all, for he has renounced all!

XVIII

THE ELEMENTS

THE whole course of the Buddha's thought is nothing but a perpetual pointing out that a soul, a true *I*, does not exist in this body. He would have us hold in disdain the discussion of such statements as "Soul and body are one," or "Soul is one thing and body is another." One thing he teaches, and one alone—this, namely, that what I have hitherto regarded as *I*, as a separate *self*, is in truth a *not-I*, an illusion.

Yet this my corporeality is here, and cannot in anywise be argued away; consequently I must be something?

Undoubtedly! I am *not-I* only with reference to my individuality. Only so far as I am an individual do I consist, not of *being* but of *becoming*; so far only am I a process, an illusion. Individuality is the illusion which the *I* assumes along with its own existence; that is to say, individuality is at once illusion and ignorance.

But every illusion must have something real as its basis; as there must be some actuality to correspond to every image in a mirror?

The actuality which lies behind the apparent *I* (Bhava) is the five Khandhas, the five constituents of all life.

At one and the same time I am, and I am not. In so far as I represent myself as *I*, as personality, *I am not*. In so far as I consist of the active elements, the Khandhas, *I am*. This distinction is of the greatest importance because cessation refers, and need refer, only to personality, only to the *I*, since it is only to the *I* that pain attaches.

But if it be true that at one and the same time I am both reality and illusion, then at the dissolution of the form, this reality in some way or another must become manifest?

Exactly! When, at Colombo, I asked the venerable Sumangala, the highest authority in Ceylon, about the relationship between Bhava and the Khandhas, he smilingly showed me his fist: "That is Bhava," he said. Then he opened his hand: "These are the Khandhas." By this he meant to say that the dissolution of the old form is only another expression for the arising of the new. Just as it is possible, by the opening of the closed hand, by the dissolution of the idea "fist," for the perception "five fingers" to arise, and by the closing of the opened hand, by the dissolution of the idea "five fingers," for the perception "fist" to arise, without there being any leap as it were from the one to the other, any perceptible gap between the two ideas; so also is it with the transition from one form to another form, from one life to the next life. Nowhere here, as from some rent, does bare matter protrude itself. Kamma and the Khandhas mutually condition one another; without the one, the other is not possible. Passing away, death, is nothing but arising, birth, seen from another standpoint. Life is eternal; it is merely the form that changes: only "life" must be understood in the Indian, not in the Christo-Judaic sense.

Let us take another comparison. According to the Abhidhamma the five Khandhas do not range themselves alongside one another in the operations of Kamma, but are placed crosswise. It is only this crossing that produces life. They arrange themselves so that on one side only "Form" (Rūpa) is found, and on the other side only "Name" (Nāma), with consciousness (Viññāna) in the leading place at the head of the other four. And as the body is no *Being* but a perpetual *Becoming*, so this union of both is nothing that *is* but only something that perpetually *becomes.* Like so many pearls, the separate points of crossing follow upon one another, producing the appearance of a closed circle—this seeming form. So soon as we try to understand them, we find the Khandhas creeping into matter also, into the appearance of conditioner and conditioned, subject and object, the basis of all thinking.

If now we adopt such a thing as the rainbow by way of illustration, we shall find it fit in exactly with the above presentation of the case, one line of falling raindrops striking in symmetrical, equal flow against one line of light-beams. The line of falling raindrops corresponds to the Rūpa-lines; the line of light-beams to the Nāma-lines. That which brings them into contact is Kamma. The product of the crossing, the rainbow—that is, Bhava, my body, an appearance, an illusion; at one and the same time, existent and yet non-existent—that is, a *Becoming.*

As the *I* stands between subject and object, as Kamma stands between Nāma and Rūpa, so the rainbow stands between the light-beams and the raindrops; on one hand wholly beam, on the other wholly drop, and yet really neither beam nor drop but the perpetual union of both. Thus the process of union is the same as the product of union; the product is nothing but the token of the continuance of the process. The process here is the final fact. But whither shall we here look for the force that unites these two factors? Where shall we find the third great factor in the case, Kamma? Where lurks the power that brings together raindrop and sunbeam?

The answer is: in themselves; in their own being. Matter is synonymous with activity, which is precisely what the Buddha means when he says: "Without Khandhas there is no Kamma." Because raindrop and sunbeam are present, therefore do they join one with the other; no third factor brings them together. Because the material substrata of the body are here, therefore also their union, the form, is here. No Kamma, no third factor, brings them together; their mere being is itself the ground of their union. This precisely is the illusion continually besetting us that we find present, end and means, where in reality there is only cause-effect. Kamma, the eternal righteousness, the eternal punisher and rewarder, only arises with us. We ourselves are at once the originators of Kamma and Kamma itself, as the raindrops and the sunbeams originate the rainbow, and at the same time are themselves the rainbow.

Hence the mere existence of this reality, of these

Khandhas, is likewise the ground of their union to form, to individuality. Their existence of itself, their mere proximity, is also the necessity for their unification, is the unification-process, is the unification-product. The entire comedy of Khandhas, Kamma, and Bhava is only another way of saying that Avijjā is present—that is, that form is present, and that this itself dictates the laws of its conservation. For, in so far as we are Kamma, so far do we represent the force which maintains the world in eternal equilibrium, eternally moral. Without morality there is no world.

May Kamma be apprehended as illusion, seeing that at least there are Khandhas. The Khandhas are only where there is Kamma. Where the latter fails, there also fail the Khandhas. As one complementary colour constantly conditions the other, and both alike have their origin in colourlessness, and as with the disappearance of the one the other also disappears, and both alike fall back into colourlessness, so the concept "Khandhas" only arises with the concept "Kamma," just as, moreover, the notion "components of rainbow" only arises with the notion "rainbow." Matter is the five Constituents (Khandhas) only in so far as it stands behind this apparent form, even as light and water are constituents of the rainbow only in so far as they stand behind the rainbow; no one would think of applying such an expression to either water or light taken by itself. Similarly we cannot denominate matter by itself as the Khandhas. Only where there is Kamma are there Khandhas.

But if the rain-clouds go off in another direction, if the coming together of raindrop and sunbeam ceases, if the Bhava-raindrop dissolves, then we have the Khandhas before our eyes in the shape of light and water! Have we not?

Patience! They stand before us, but only that they may immediately convince us that they do not stand before us! For at the moment of dissolution the water, as also the light, has become Bhava. They themselves are Bhava so soon as they are no longer comprehended in the formation of Bhava. Behind the water-drop, that has now become Bhava, stand as Khandhas water-vapour and the atmospheric influences which have given to it its present shape. Next the drop disappears, but the vapour remains, and immediately this latter assumes the rôle of Bhava, and behind it, as Khandhas, emerge hydrogen and oxygen.

But here we have Khandhas again! The end is still the Khandhas!

Yes, but not the final end, only the end of our science. So soon as we are able to analyse both, they will immediately cease to play the part of fundamental constituents. Behind them also lurk the eager Khandhas, ever ready to force the Bhava-rôle upon them. Thus reality becomes nothing but the constituent of illusion; it is not in itself real, but is so only in contradistinction to illusion. The dissolution of one illusion is only the disclosure of the perspective of another; it is only the removal of the illusion one stratum deeper. Our senses only apprehend *Becoming*, and *Becoming* is a process; the interaction of two agents upon one another; unity in duality; illusion founded upon reality. These realities, however, remain realities only so long as they produce *Becoming*, stand behind

Becoming, lie beyond the reach of our perceptions. So far as our perceptions penetrate, so far enters *Becoming*, and with it illusion. To make anything perceptible to sense means to make it illusion. To make the Khandhas visible is to transfer them to the stage of illusion (Bhava). I can no more reach to this foundationless foundation of all than by diving into the water, however deeply, I can reach to the vaulted sky that mirrors itself therein. The reality retreats before us as the horizon before the traveller, simply because I not only *have* illusion, but *am* illusion. That phrase of Petrarch's about life being a *statio instabilis* is here felt in all its force. Where the process is conclusion, ending, there the end becomes a process! Otherwise expressed: The *I* is comprehensible only as an apparent-*I*, as *Becoming*. To try to comprehend the *I* as *Being* would be to try to dissolve the world by a backwards-going process; it would be turning time wrong way round, setting past in the place of future —the very epitome of all impossibility. Every attempt to think, to comprehend *Being*, Reality, "Soul," or Matter turns them to form—that is, to illusion. Every attempt to comprehend the dissolved form, to comprehend death, only creates new life. All clinging to life after death is nothing but that inexhaustible reservoir from which life, this life here, is fed and nourished. So long as a future lies before us, so long are we in the *now*. Stepping out of one *now* into another, a future life eternally lies before us. The tragic thing about the whole puppet-show is precisely this, that not only is this apparent *I* a delusion, but it is also a deluded delusion, a delusion that deludes itself.

Hence the very existence of the illusion means the eternity of the illusion. As I must understand the *I* to be illusion in order to be able to understand it as the maintainer of the world, as the pivot of the world, which from moment to moment anew creates itself, so also I must understand life to be illusion in order to be able to understand the eternity of life. I must demolish eternity, dissolve it into an endless number of *nows* in order to be able to understand it. "The existence of the illusion is the eternity of the illusion," is only another way of saying that "without Khandhas there is no Kamma."

And now let us return to our starting-point. There we saw that the dissolution of one existence is nothing but the building up of the new, seen from a different standpoint; the endlessness of the series of existences was admitted. For example, as water, in the shape of ice, conceived of *as* ice, disappears, and by this dissolution now exists as water; as next the notion "water" may disappear and the notion "vapour" be left, so disappears one form, one *I*, and unfailingly is left the next, the new *I*. It is not life that ceases, it is only the form that ceases; but its cessation is arising; that is to say, life is the vicissitude of eternity.

As a man digging a pit in the ground, deeper and still deeper, suddenly, when he has passed the central point of the earth, is no longer digging down but up, so the binding and loosing of the Khandhas, arising and passing away, birth and death, are synonymous terms, are one and the same thing looked at merely from different points of view. And the inquiring mind that breaks its way through from one stratum of ideas to the other, finally perceives the absolute relativity of all ideas. As the light of day rolls around the world, so this huge wave of the life-illusion rolls round the supra-sensuous. And as none can say: "Here night begins and here the day," so none can say: "Here this life begins, here that." As a day is only the follower of a past night and the forerunner of the next one, belonging to both, a form of night; as similarly, night is only the successor of the day that has gone before, and the forerunner of the one that is to follow, belonging to both, a form of day; so life is only a form of death, and death merely a form of life. As, however, day in reality eternally revolves between two nights, so Bhava, a veritable phenomenal form, an embodied *now*, eternally inserts itself between those two nights, past and future. And as day has never been in night and will never pass into it, so life has never come from death and will never go into it. Life, *I*-consciousness, alone it is that creates death, the idea "death," as it is only the concept "day" that produces by inversion the concept "night." Both arise together, mutually condition one another, like stroke and counterstroke, "good" and "evil." As the concept "good" only arises with the concept "evil," the idea of "past" with the idea of "future," so the notion "death" only arises with the thought "life"; that is to say, with *I*-consciousness. That life can pass and death remain is as absurd an idea as that of past by itself, or future by itself; light by itself, or shadow by itself.

As day in reality never arises and never passes away, so individuality in strict truth ever is, and the illusion which its arising and passing away conjures up before me is equivalent to that of day when in sunrise and sunset it pictures to me the appearance respectively of a renewal and of a cessation of solar activity. As dawn is nothing but high noon, seen from a particular position, so birth is nothing but full corporeity as regarded from a particular point of view, from the standing ground of illusion. Wherever the illusion of passing away exists, there is formed of the mind itself the binding thread, the "soul," the correlative of illusion. Whoso, however, has understood that Bhava, life's day, is eternal, he knows that no binding thread is needed; he knows that that which here is seen as the evening-red of death is in another place the glow of noonday.

In another place! For others! Quite so, but that does not lighten my fear, my pain!

Patience! For what others? My body is earth, sun, day, all in one. How can sun forsake me when it actually exists in me as *I*-consciousness. But where *I*-consciousness is, there also is somewhat of the elements upon which this *I*-consciousness is based, and where these two are, there also is Kamma—that is, the third factor which brings them into contact, makes them cross one another, causes Bhava to arise, just as day is present whenever earth and sun are present. At one stroke we again stand in the midst of the play of infinitude.

The whole trick is just this, that we, just because we ourselves are light, see ourselves surrounded by darkness; and because we do not know that we ourselves are light, at every step we are afraid of falling into darkness. But as soon might the sun decline into darkness as our life-day into night and death. As well might we step out of the *now* into the future, as out of life into death. Where we are, there is the *now*, there is life. Thus without a break stepping out of one phenomenal form into another, creating one *I*-sun after another, we drive before us, as it were some dark wave, the ever-distant yet also ever-nigh terror, death. As the Khandhas, so soon as they are dissolved, become fresh Bhava, so death as soon as we enter it becomes fresh life, and the question: "When life is over, what?" becomes an idle jest.

What then in our simile corresponds to night?

The Khandhas, standing behind individuality, behind the *I*-sun, these correspond to night. As night is really nothing but past and future day, so the Khandhas are nothing but past and future corporeality (Bhava)—that is, they are nothing but matter as seen from the standpoint of individuality. In fact, as night is only seen as the non-existence of light, so the Khandhas are only seen from *not-to-be-seen-ness*, are perceived only from *not-to-be-perceivedness*!

If now, however, individuality is the life-day which in unbroken flow pours itself all over its substratum, whence comes it that consciousness also does not remain unbroken? Why does not consciousness pass over from one existence to the next?

It is true that I am the day, but it is also true that I am its substratum, and as the present day is never exactly the same as the one that precedes or that follows it, because the substratum upon which it is unfolded is in continual change, because never at any time is the *now* recalled, brought back again; so, also, no life is ever the same as any other either before or after it, because the substratum out of which it is evolved exists in a state of perpetual change. Consciousness, however, is a product, and changes with the changes of the factor that fashions it. "Without sufficient cause no consciousness arises," says the Exalted One.

But every moment of this life is equally different from every other; each produces its own consciousness, and yet there is continuity from birth to death!

Quite so! Every moment in a day is also divided from every other moment, day being nothing more than a composite of day-moments, a perpetual *becoming*, and yet it presents itself to me as a unity from dawn until eventide! And here is the reason. The attachment of the senses to their objects produces the apparent continuity of day as well as the apparent continuity of this corporeality. It is the attachment of the senses which out of the whirling spokes evokes the image of a solid disc. The attachment of the senses, however, is will. The life-impulse itself creates the conditions of its existence; itself prepares the soil upon which it grows, out of which it is able eternally to generate itself anew. The continuity of consciousness reaches just as far as the senses reach. This body, however, is nothing but "sense," therefore consciousness is severed only with the severing of this corporeality, this semblance of form. As, however, the next form does not need to be formed when this has been dissolved, but the dissolution of this *is* the creation of that, so the new consciousness does not first require to be constructed; here also the dissolution of the old is the formation of the new, and ready and waiting stands the new corporeality with its five constituents, the chief of them being consciousness (Viññāna).

But why does not the process of the breaking up and joining together again of the Khandhas cease of itself? Because in willing it continually regenerates itself through itself, as the seed brings the fruit and the fruit the seed. To direct—in willing—our senses towards objects is to scatter before one the seed of new life.

As trees and creatures wither away and die in the course of the day without the day being in any way affected for evil, so the body withers away and dies without the life being any way affected for ill. Life is eternal, but not as bound up with consciousness; this is the ancient wisdom of India. Out of this, it is true, the Brahmin has manufactured his changeless, eternal life in Brahman; to the Buddha, however, the proposition—the cognition: "Life is eternal," became the tenet—the perception: "This life is eternal"—this life endowed with consciousness—that is, with sorrow. Eternal is the *Now*. The abolition of the fear of death was here dearly bought. The proposition: "Life is eternal," became the terror of all terrors. Its precious content, to others the most precious, most desirable of all things, to the Buddhist lacking a God, becomes of all pains the most painful. As one before whom were set some most dainty dish with the injunction: "Of this dish thou must eat for ever" would soon, disgusted, die of hunger; so also would it be with one who was told: "This life thou must live for ever." It is the continual compulsion to life that creates the pain of life—that makes the sounding-board, as it were, for the thought: "Happy were final rest from all arising and passing away"—and so incites us to the combat with Avijjā.

Well and good! But if, with the removal of ignorance, the *I*-sun is done away in the great death, the Buddha-death, perhaps eternal night is there—that is, life without consciousness?

What kind of night? Night only arises with day, as day with night. Where there is no longer any day, there also there is no longer any night. Night really is nothing but past or future day. With the removal of the *I*-sun not only does day disappear, but also the very possibility of imagining either day or night. What, however, night may be apart from day, supposing such a thing possible, or what death is apart from life, supposing that also possible, these things lie beyond us; and neither priest, nor god, nor Buddha can know them, or needs to know them, since they have nothing to do with deliverance.

Quite so, but the fact still remains that in the ruin of the circle of endlessness something is left corresponding to the earth in our simile, upon which no sun acts, on which it is neither night nor day. To put the question in direct fashion: "What becomes of the body of the Buddha, or of the bodies of those of his disciples who have attained to the Perfection of Holiness? What becomes of the elemental residue of all those who have severed for ever the chain of willing, dissolved the form, ended the circle? Where do these elements now reside?"

Listen! A monk with a desire in his heart for the solution of this question had left the Buddha, and, persevering in meditation, had made his way into the presence of that great Brahma who is the Father of All that Are and Are to Be. To his pointed question: "Where does the residueless, total annihilation of the four elements take place?" he received the following answer. "Go, O monk, and put your question to the Exalted One. As the Exalted One shall explain it, so believe." The Buddha, however, when asked by the monk, said: "As the land-seeking bird, set free out at sea, turns back to his ship after he has flown through all the four quarters of heaven, so also thou, O monk, after thou hast searched all through the Brahma world, art come back to me. But not in this fashion, O monk, should the question be put: 'Where does the residueless, total annihilation of the four elements take place?' Verily, O monk, the question can only be put thus:

"'Where, no more, is there earth or water, or fire or wind?'

"'Where are dissolved both long and short, and large and small, and good and bad?'

"'Where are subject and object, wholly, remainderless, melted away?'

"And here is the answer:

"'By the undoing of consciousness, wholly, remainderless, all is melted away.'"

Yes, that is the Buddha's answer to the question. Upon the *I* the world entirely rests; with the *I* it arises, with the *I* it passes away.

And now, on this point, I would like to take one single step farther, but a natural, almost a necessary step.

What becomes of my body, in respect of the elements of which it is built up, when will has forsaken it, when form has been abolished, never again to be renewed, when the word of the Buddha has borne its final fruit?

Hearken! A monk of the name of Yamaka had got the heretical view: "I understand from the doctrine declared by the Exalted One that a monk who has conquered the attachment to existence, when his body breaks up, goes back to nothingness, and on the farther side of death ceases to be."

This view was expressly declared to be heretical.

Then after all there *is* some sort of existence after this great death, the death of the will?

Listen again! A monk named Vaccha asks the Buddha: "Where is that monk reborn who is freed from being's bond?"

"To say that he is reborn is not appropriate to the matter in hand."

"Then, O Gautama, is he not reborn?"

"To say that he is not reborn is not appropriate to the matter in hand."

"Then, O Gautama, is he both reborn and not reborn?"

"That also, O Vaccha, is not appropriate to the matter in hand."

"Then, O Gautama, is he neither reborn nor yet not reborn?"

"That also, O Vaccha, is not appropriate to the matter in hand."

Thus the Buddha.

And now shall we say straight and plain that the Buddha himself did not know?

Hearken! A monk named Māluñkyāputta once came before the Buddha and said: "All those theories which the Exalted One has left unexplained—about whether the world is eternal or not, whether the body of the Perfect One exists after death or not,—about these I would like to have an explanation. If the Exalted One himself knows, might the Exalted One be pleased to tell it to me. If the Exalted One does not himself know, then let him say: 'I do not know.'

"If the Exalted One does not wish to enlighten me on this matter, then I go forth and leave the Order, and turn back to the world."

This was plain speaking, but what was the Buddha's reply? "Māluñkyāputta, did I ever say to thee: 'Come, follow me, and I will explain to thee these matters, whether or not the world is eternal; whether the Perfect One is or is not after death'?"

"Verily, nay, O Master!"

"Or hast thou ever said to me: 'I will follow the Exalted One on condition that he enlightens me with regard to these matters'?"

"Verily, nay, O Lord!"

"Whom then, thou foolish man, dost thou blame? Māluñkyāputta, one who says: 'I will only follow the Exalted One if he enlightens me as to these matters,' is as a man pierced by a poisoned arrow who will not have the arrow removed until he is informed as to whether his enemy belongs to a higher or a lower caste, is tall or short, light or dark, dwells in this or in that town; whether his bow is made thus or thus, and so forth. Māluñkyāputta, one who wants an explanation of such things as: 'Is the world eternal or not eternal?' 'Does the Holy One exist after death or does he not exist?' —such a man will verily die before the Tathāgata has been able to inform him. A holy life, Māluñkyāputta, does not depend upon such dogmas. Whether the world is eternal or not, whether the Perfect One does or does not exist after death, there still remain birth, old age, death, sorrow, lamentation, misery, grief, and despair. Mark well, Māluñkyāputta, what that is which I have explained, and what that is which I have left unexplained. And what have I left unexplained? Whether the world is eternal or not; whether body and soul are identical or are not identical; whether the Perfect One, after death, is or is not; these have I left unexplained. And why have I left them unexplained? Because, Māluñkyāputta, it is useless for you to know these things, because they have nothing to do with true piety; because they do not lead to not-returning, to passionlessness, to cessation, to quietude, to sublime wisdom, to Nibbāna. And what, Māluñkyāputta, have I explained? I have explained Sorrow, the Arising of Sorrow, the Removing of Sorrow, and the Way that leads to the Removing of Sorrow; these have I explained, and why? Because it is profitable for you to know these things; because it belongs to true piety; because it leads to not-returning, to passionlessness, to cessation, to quietude, to sublime wisdom, to Nibbāna."

So far the Buddha. And we, if we have really perceived life to be pain, what other better or more pressing business can we have to attend to than the removal of this pain? Why cumber ourselves with hypotheses? Of what use to ask the Buddha about matters with which he has nothing to do? With one thing, and with one thing only, does the Buddha concern himself, with sorrow and the uprooting of sorrow. What becomes of the earth when the sun disappears? Perhaps this, perhaps that; who knows? What becomes of the elements when the *I*-sun disappears? Perhaps this, perhaps that; who knows? What night is without day, death without life, elements without *I*—this does not concern us. Silent, dark, unsounded, the jaws of eternity gape, ready to swallow us up, as the snake swallows the fascinated, struggling bird. But whoso has learnt of the Tathāgata—he stands unshaken upon his rock, calm and unmoved. He perceives: "All that was to do is done. This world is no more." Neither finitude nor infinitude any more charms or allures him.

XIX

A BRIEF SURVEY OF THE HISTORICAL DEVELOPMENT OF BUDDHISM

THE higher the altitude at which anything stands, the deeper it can sink. This law is verified by all religious movements, but by none more than Buddhism. Whoever brings the Buddha and his crystalline teaching into comparison with modern Buddhism and Tibetan Lamas and Chinese Bonzes, as representatives of the same, will agree without further argument. The lands in which to-day the old spiritual glory is most fully maintained are Ceylon and Burma.

Meanwhile there exist distinctions between these two lands, well-marked distinctions, moreover. To Ceylon must be conceded greater erudition in its individual monks, and a closer relation in language and blood with the motherland of Buddhism. Pāli, the sacred language, in all probability the speech of the Buddha and of his earlier disciples, is taught and spoken in its pure form only in Ceylon; and Sinhalese, like Pāli, belongs to that great Indo-Germanic group of languages which, besides other offshoots, includes Sanskrit, Greek, Latin, and the tongues of modern Europe. It is thus perhaps not altogether idle to point out that the Buddha is related to us both by language and by race. The thoughts that were the product of his mind, and the other great thoughts to which India has given birth, are Indo-Germanic common property, for there is perhaps nothing that is more specific to the Aryan stock than its philosophising. To speak frankly, we have up till now despised turning toward our heritage on the Ganges, simply because we have failed to comprehend its great value.

More than this: the culture and the population of Ceylon—not the aboriginal population indeed, but the higher castes—came from the classic region of Northern India, from the plain of the Ganges. Burma, on the contrary, along with its people, stands outside the Aryan race. Its inhabitants are classed with the great Mongolian stock, and the Burmese tongue, like the Chinese, is not in a position to render unchanged the rich, sonorous Pāli syllables. On the other hand, there stands to Burma's credit the unquestionably greater piety of its people as a whole.

Ceylon, Burma, and Siam together represent what is called Southern Buddhism, having Pāli as the sacred language. Against these three Nepal, Tibet, China, Japan, and Mongolia make up the body of what is called Northern Buddhism. These latter, still further estranged from the pure Teaching than the Southern countries, have made Sanskrit their sacred language. The relationship beween Sanskrit and Pāli is somewhat like that which exists between Latin and Italian, at least so far as the structure of the language is concerned.

It is unquestionably one of the most astonishing facts of world-history that a Teaching which, as its basic doctrine, demands that life be regarded as sorrow has been able to secure such extensive acceptance by the minds of men. Sooth to say it is here very easy to fall a prey to exaggeration. Following the maxim: "Quote figures," it can readily be shown that of all religions Buddhism is the one which can call its own the greatest number of adherents. But this is exactly the consideration that weighs less with this religion than with any other. In conformity with its whole character, Buddhism is extraordinarily well adapted to amalgamate itself with other religions, and this it has done most completely in China and Japan. The enormous number of Buddhists reckoned by our statisticians arises from the fact that they count both these countries as purely Buddhist. But this is decidedly not in accordance with the facts. With as good a reason we might regard China as purely Confucian, and Japan as purely Shinto. But indeed the whole question has another significance than that which at first we might be inclined to attribute to it. More than any other religion, Buddhism, a despiser of all mere externality, consists in an inner change in men, and demands no official "conversion." In such a sense we are justified in saying that not only Eastern and Southern Asia but perhaps the whole continent has adopted the teaching of the Buddha. Not unfitly has Buddhism been called the teacher of Asia; for there can scarcely be any doubt that with its gentle precepts it has effected a slow but thorough transformation in the character of the Asiatic peoples, especially in the character of the peoples of Central Asia. Only in Ceylon, Burma, and Siam is it the sole religion of the country, existing besides in Tibet in the degenerate form of Lamaism.

As already mentioned, Pāli was the tongue of the people at the time of the Buddha; it was the language of Magadha, the kingdom within whose borders he more particularly taught. With respect to language also, the Buddha was an innovator. Up to his time, Sanskrit had been the exclusive vehicle of religion and philosophy, but with kindly look the Buddha recognised that a popular religion ought to be preached in the popular speech. To this point he held tenaciously against the attacks of the erudite among his disciples. He himself laid down the rule: "The word of the Master shall be taught in the language of the Master." Consequently, at the council held soon after his death at Rājagriha (Pāli: Rājagaha, the modern Rajgir), the canon was fixed in Pāli. Pāli became the official language of Buddhism. To be sure, this fixation did not take place in writing, but in that fashion which in India has always been looked upon as most reliable, namely, by being committed to memory by the faithful. In India there has always been an aversion to entrusting religious writings to the pen. Only under the influence of Hellenism did this prejudice pass away, and it passed away first of all in progressive, enlightened Buddhism. But the outward characteristics of these sacred writings, especially of the Sutta Piṭaka, clearly show that they were designed to live in the memory. The frequent and lengthy repetitions with which they abound have no other purpose than the making more easy their retention by the mind of the hearer.

Imagine that Christianity — the teaching of

Jesus of Nazareth—had remained fettered fast in the bonds of the Hebro-Syriac dialect; already its doom had been spoken. Only when the expansive force, developed and accumulated in the womb of the nation, overflowed the narrow bounds of that same nation, and so on into the broad stream of Grecian life, which at that time flooded the whole world of culture—only then, when the Greek language was adopted as its vehicle, did the possibility arise of the little Jewish sect becoming a world-religion.

Now at the time of the Buddha there was in India no language in existence which played the part that Greek played at the time of Christ. Sanskrit indeed extended as far as Aryan culture extended, but it was the language only of the learned; it was out of touch with the body of the people. "Canst thou speak Greek?" the Roman Governor asked Paul the Jew. Under parallel circumstances the question: "Can you speak Sanskrit?" would never have been put in India. On the other hand, Pāli was the language that was sanctioned by the Buddha. And thus it happened that in rigid, perhaps mistakenly rigid, adherence to the words of the Founder of the religion, the dialect of Magadha, a kingdom which indeed was among the powerful in India at that day, but of no particular significance in the Indian world, was, as its official language, forced upon a religion that was destined to provide spiritual nourishment to more than half of Asia.

But let us pass from the outward to the inner aspect of the matter.

Perhaps no religion in the world has afforded

as little scope for ambition as has the Buddhist religion. Looking at the splendid heads of the pupils in the monastery schools of Ceylon, at those faces in which Roman virtue seems only to sleep, the uninitiated cannot understand the process by which these pupils are transformed into the quiet, decorous monks to whom our Bible phrase so fitly applies: "Having food and raiment, let us be therewith content." And yet this metamorphosis has been taking place for centuries and centuries with an almost startling uniformity. Such a result comes about only by the mutual interaction of the teaching of Gautama and the Indian nature.

One easily understands that a teaching which ultimates in a voluntary exit from life, from the circle of sorrow; in a noble, but entirely unparalleled act of renunciation of all;—that such a teaching leaves but little room for ambition—for self-actuated activity. All energy is consumed in the business of the individual *I*—a business which, as we have seen, ultimates in the perceiving of the *I* as only an apparent-*I*, as an illusion. "Above all, save thyself! Use the flying moment of life! Look not to the right: look not to the left! Make haste, make haste! Already, unfortunate one, thy hair is on fire!" Thus rings the warning, and frightens even him who wishes to resist it, so that he is amazed and gives up every thought of activity to sink back into the soft lap of meditation. "So lives he as if his head were surrounded by burning flames, striving only towards one goal: the realm of the imperishable."

Perhaps it is owing to the well-known passivity

of its outward-going tendencies—a passivity involved in its mode of conception—that Buddhism has been more shielded from the earthquake shocks of revolutionary ideas than other religions. Perhaps it is owing to this also that the course of thought in the system has so much of the clear and the mathematical about it. Because it begins with the present and with the facts of the present—therefore is it that so little room is left for mere hypothesis. Already from the earliest times, while the Buddha himself was still teaching, cases of heresy are reported, the most serious being that of his own cousin Devadatta. Besides this, a number of other cases are cited in the Suttas, in which the heretical views of various members of the Order are put a stop to; but here the appeal is always to the understanding; a series of questions are put, derived in strictly logical sequence from the Four Holy Truths, in order to convince the wandering sheep of the falsity of his conclusions, and bring him back to the right path. This is precisely the surpassing excellence of Buddhism—that it always deals with the facts of the understanding and never with dogmas or credos. Every form of fanaticism is thus deprived of its point.

It is worthy of note that the Buddhism of Ceylon, since the time of Mahinda, the Buddhist apostle to the island,—that is to say, since about two hundred and fifty years before Christ,—has remained true to the essentials of the religion. It is true that in the course of the centuries a great number of different sects have arisen, but the distinctions between them have, for the most part, rested upon trivial externalities. At bottom they all strive from a common starting-point towards the same goal.

Now Buddhism, especially Sinhalese Buddhism, has been exposed to a great danger, in that for hundreds of years—indeed, more than ten hundred years—it has been exposed to the influence of Shiva-worshipping, South Indian Malabar. But here precisely is found the best testimony to the unshakeable basis upon which this noble religious teaching rests, that it has always been possible to purify it again from all foreign admixture, and to re-embody it in its pristine purity, just as out of the saline solution the salt-crystal can always be crystallised anew in its former identical shape and purity.

Greater still than the external danger from the quarter of Malabar was the inner danger which threatened the faith from those "chiefest of Buddhist Kings," the Sinhalese monarchs themselves. Up till the time of the great Dutthagamini, in the middle of the second century before Christ, the position of the kings towards the monks was regulated strictly in accordance with the meaning of the injunctions given by the founder of the religion. The monks received from the kings, the same as from private people, only in greater abundance, food, clothing, and shelter. They went, as it is said in the Great Chronicle of Ceylon, "to the King's table." After Dutthagamini, during the period of decay and general confusion, this support, which presupposed a safe and peaceful state of the country, could not always be continued. The kings, often destitute of money, but anxious to be of service to the religion, and to share in the merit of almsgiving, handed over great tracts of land to the Order, and thus turned the heads of the monasteries into great landholders. It is true that the individual monk after, as before, had to remain without private means, yet the introduction of a luxurious manner of life, wholly contrary to the pure doctrine, was unavoidable.

Hence, it was only natural that Buddhism in the neighbourhood of the kings and their residences should have reached its lowest level. Kandy, for example, the last residence of a Sinhalese monarch, even to-day has not quite recovered from the moral and spiritual degradation of its religious brotherhood, for which perhaps is to blame the fact that through its possessing the holy tooth relic it has become the chief place of pilgrimage for Ceylon, and indeed the whole Buddhist world. At the present moment the monasteries along the south coast of Ceylon may be considered those that represent the teaching of the Buddha in its best and purest form, because they have never been so much exposed to the lowering influence of the kings and their presents as the monasteries of Central Ceylon.

The most far-reaching—indeed, perhaps the only far-reaching—movement within the pale of Buddhism was beyond doubt that which led to its division into Northern and Southern Buddhism. It is characteristic of the entire inner life of this religion that this division also—so far as we can ascertain—was brought about in a gradual and entirely pacific manner. Since, under Kanishka, the king of the Yueitschi, the canon for the northern countries was fixed in Sanskrit at the Council held at Kashmir about a hundred years after Christ, this division into North and South must already have been an accomplished fact.

In Northern Buddhism, in the Mahāyāna (Greater Vehicle), two doctrines run alongside one another; the one, original, the word of the Buddha; the other, a parasitic growth upon it, which, through its external trappings of Tantras and Mantras, can easily be recognised as a disguised form of Saivism. It acts no longer with the key-word "knowledge," but instead with the key-word "love." And in utter perversion of thought it has constructed a heaven into which, as into some place of boundless bliss, the pious are received by Amitābha, the Dhyāni-Buddha. And yet it is only speaking the truth to say that the Mahāyāna has conquered the greater part of Asia, because by its invention of this heaven it has conformed itself more to the sentiment of human beings than does pure Buddhism with its marble-like coldness, which speaks of heaven only that it may express its pity and contempt for it.

Now let us cast a glance at the manner and fashion in which Buddhism obtained sway and again fell into decay in Asiatic lands.

In Ceylon and Farther India it found the nature worship of the aborigines flourishing in full bloom. In Ceylon, however, a Brahminical influx from Northern India had already taken place at a previous period, but the times before the apostle Mahinda and his contemporary, King Tissa, are not sufficiently well known to historical research for us to be able to say anything very precise about their religious condition. The story of Ceylon, from the standpoint of history and religion both, only begins with the introduction of Buddhism into the island—about two hundred and fifty years before Christ. The Dhamma of the Buddha came to Farther India, to Burma, with the learned Buddhaghosha in the fifth century after Christ. In both countries it appears to have found swift and easy entry, and to have secured a dominant position.

Needless to say, its position in its motherland, India, was entirely different. Brahmanism already in the Buddha's time had become consolidated into that bony framework which up to the present day still serves as the support of the body of the Indian peoples. Owing to the deeply religious nature of the people, it was inevitable that here there should arise a life-and-death struggle between the two religions.

A slight outward sign sometimes permits one to see right into the heart of a matter, and such a sign we find in the inclination of Buddhism towards propaganda, and the impossibility of such propaganda for Brahmanism. In this seemingly purely external characteristic we have condensed, as it were, the radically different modes of the two religions.

We might almost say that with its stern and gloomy exclusiveness Brahmanism possesses something of the nature of Judaism. It is the caste idea that here makes propaganda impossible, in our sense of the word. Here the word "convert" is deprived of all significance. A Sudra, for example, can as little be converted into a Brahmin as a negro can be washed white. Brahmanism can only exist naturally where caste dominates, and the latter only where the Aryan peoples hold sway. That process, so much loved to-day, of sending religions far over sea to other peoples, the transformation of religion into an article of export, was then quite impossible. The religion was the nation. Caste, so to speak, was religion applied. Propaganda, in our sense of the word, is only conceivable after the destruction of the caste idea.

This caste-bondage the Buddha indeed broke through—completely so far as theory was concerned, but in practice naturally only so far as it was possible for him; that is, within the limits of his own Order. During his lifetime these limits may not have been very great, and freedom from the restrictions of caste, within this limited area, except perhaps to a few far-seeing ones among the Brahmins, may have been more an object of curiosity than of apprehension. But as the little flame, upon which we for so long have quietly looked, by a sudden change in the direction of the wind, may suddenly become an all-threatening blaze, so, in consequence of the favouring of Buddhism by Asoka, this so far purely academic question became a thing in which the very life and constitution of the people of India were involved. By his removal of the restrictions of caste the Buddha had planted in Jambudvīpa (India) a little seed-grain which long, long after his death was destined to develop into a high tree, in the shadow whereof all might rest and flourish,—all except Brahmanism, all except priestly mischief-making, all except exclusiveness and secrecy. Hence the Buddha says in the Tevijja Sutta of the Digha Nikāya: "The three-fold wisdom of these Veda-learned Brahmins may be called a waterless waste; its three-fold wisdom may be called a pathless jungle; its three-fold wisdom is death and corruption."

The entire Indian nationality stands and falls with the system of caste. To the Indian mind this present existence is nothing but the product of previous existences, as also it contains the seed of the existences that are to follow. Since every effect is conditioned by the specific nature of its cause, good deeds produce good results—that is, *in summa*—a favourable birth, and evil deeds bring an unfavourable birth. The consequence is, that one with whom things go badly here below is looked upon as one who must now expiate openly the sins which perhaps he committed in secret in a former existence. In the law-book of Manu it is expressly said: "The unfaithful wife will after her death—that is to say, in rebirth—be afflicted with ailments like consumption and elephantiasis." Worse still than disease is it to be born into a lower caste. According to the Indian idea punishment or reward sets in with the moment of birth. He who is born to low estate is so born that he may meet the consequences of previous sinning; he who is born to high estate is so born in order that he may reap the fruit of his previous good deeds. The Brahmin is not a Brahmin by chance; the Sudra is not a Sudra by chance, but only by reason of a divine and all-powerful justice. Caste is a divine institution. The castes are the four great volumes of the book of life in which divinity inscribes its judgments. Against the sentence, as above instanced, there is no appeal whatever.

Therefore is it that the mixing of the castes

is the most hideous of all crimes. The Brahmin must always remain Brahmin, because he has been placed here by deity to beget Brahmins. The Brahmin woman must always remain a Brahmin woman, because she has been placed here in order that she may bring forth Brahmins from her sacred womb. Caste is nothing but a means whereby is made visible to human eyes the might of divine justice. It is the medium whereby is conveyed to human ears the language of deity. That great moment in the career of the Christian, that great moment when the sheep are divided from the goats, has been transferred by the Indian mind to this present existence.

The institution of caste is the stage upon whose boards this great drama is played before the eyes of all the world. Let men say what they will about the low level of Indian morality, it is certainly, so far as outward signs go, far superior to the Christian variety. That tendency of the human mind to accept unquestioningly something unseen is, in the Indian system of morality, allowed very much less scope. The question of retribution after death, which our intellectualist rabble answer with a shrug of the shoulders, expressive of indifference or derision, has for the Indian mind found a solution of unsurpassable clearness. Each sees in himself, as well as in others, this retribution after death; this present existence is retribution. As the angel of the Apocalypse stands with one foot upon the land and the other upon the sea, so does Indian morality stand with one foot in the "Here" and the other in the "Beyond." The threads run alongside of and through one another. The "Beyond" works itself out in the "Here." So closely do these two intertwine that the thinker is impelled to fuse them together in that great Unity that lies beyond time and space, and is the goal of Indian as of all philosophy.

The abolition of caste was the most daring blow the Buddha ventured to deliver against the time-honoured beliefs of his countrymen; beliefs that had only grown stronger with the lapse of the centuries. It was much more daring than his expressed contempt for asceticism, or his studied neglect of Sanskrit, and it was principally in the reaction against this particular attack that Buddhism perished from the peninsula.

It is customary to represent Buddhism as an offshoot of Brahmanism—as, to a certain extent, a continuation, a spiritualisation of the same; but the connection between them is one that is purely external. Everything in the world must have some foundation upon which it stands, and the Buddha took his stand upon Brahmanism only as a man with an axe takes his stand upon the tree on which he is at work. As regards its inner nature, Buddhism is as utterly opposed to Brahmanism, even to the most spiritualised form of the same, Vedanta, as day is to night, though these latter also arise the one out of the other. It stands as strenuously opposed to Brahmanism as it does, for example, to Christianity or to Islam, out of which two it might equally as well have sprung. For the Brahminical teaching, "All is God" and "All is *I*," like a mystical undercurrent, runs through the entire mass of the world's religions, and, opposed to all of them alike, stands Buddhism with its "All is not-*I*."

Its only affinity with the basis from which it proceeds is that series of watchwords which it carries with it, as the newly hatched chicken carries with it the fragments of the shell from which it has just extricated itself.

In point of fact the Buddha's activity was in the highest degree iconoclastic. We clearly comprehend that when we hear from the lips of a Brahmin the reproach: "A kernel-hewer is this ascetic Gautama, say I; and why do I say so? Because he acts as such against our institutions." In India, at least, amalgamation between Buddhism and Brahmanism was impossible. The Buddha always remained free from fanaticism, and never showed any satisfaction in forcible trials of strength. But, with his reforming activity, one point, of necessity, led to another. In the mathematical plan according to which his system is built up, deductions must be drawn irrespective of where they may lead to, or else the whole structure collapses. The idea of God was abolished, and with it caste also inevitably had to go, for caste depends upon favour with God. If there is no God in particular, then there is no God whose favour is to be sought. It is not he who stands high by birth, but he who stands high morally, that is the true Brahmin, according to the Buddha's way of thinking. In a beautiful passage in the Sutta Nipāta it is said: "Him alone I call a Brahmin who, like water on the lotus-leaf, does not cling to sense-delights. Him alone I call a Brahmin, who is gentle among the fierce, peaceable among the arrogant, among the greedy free from greed. Him alone I call a Brahmin who slips away from lust, anger, pride, and envy as the sesamum-seed from the point of the needle." And in another passage from the Dhammapada it is said: "Whoso knows peace of mind; whoso is quiet, subdued, keeps himself under restraint, is chaste and has ceased to quarrel with any other being, he in truth is a Brahmin, a Samaṅa, a Bhikkhu." After such a fashion does the Buddha deal with the idea of caste, of a Brahmin, and of all the other ideas adopted from Brahmanism. He takes them over, only that they may be dissolved in his superior knowledge, his superior morality.

There was another point in connection with the removal of caste which equally set Buddhism in the most direct opposition to Brahmanism. In this latter a man, after he had gone through his period of apprenticeship under the Brahmins, was obliged to take up household life and found a family. Only when he had looked upon his children's children might he leave his home and retire into the jungle. Only grey old age might devote itself wholly to those thoughts which, free from all earthly considerations, consumed to ashes the gods, together with their sacrifices, Vedas and actions alike, in one mysterious flame. Youth and manhood stood under the terrorising rule of the Indian Gods and of their priests. The Upanishads were closed against them as secret doctrine. Upon this transition from faith to knowledge there lay something not unlike a State ban; it was, so to speak, patented. And with good reason; for the Upanishads, this particular system of knowledge, contained thoughts which, if popularised, would have swept away the entire social system of India.

In the teaching of the Buddha there was nothing in the least resembling a secret. Sorrow was there, and the way to deliverance from sorrow was laid plain and clear before the eyes of all men. The Buddha himself said: "With respect to the truth, the Buddha has nothing like the closed hand of the teacher, who keeps something concealed." Why then remain on the tedious path of Brahmanism? Why languish so long in the chains of sorrow, when a single backward step, a letting go, a single thought, sets one at liberty, free from fear, at peace for ever. In me lies heaven; in me lies hell. What have I to do with the priest and his rules and regulations? Thus the Buddha opened the way to the highest good not only for every caste, but—within certain natural restrictions—for every period of life; the one as well as the other being a death-blow to the Brahmanistic organisation.

The struggle between Brahmanism and Buddhism was perhaps the greatest religious war the world has ever seen. In privacy as well as in public it was waged for over a thousand years. It was not a religious war in the sense that one of the combatants wished to force upon the other its own religious views, but a religious war in the sense that upon the existence of the religion depended also the existence of its representatives.

Through the unstinted support of the kings, weary of the Brahmin yoke, Buddhism quickly achieved an apparent victory. Already, under Asoka, about three hundred years before Christ, it had practically become the religion of India, and the beginning of the second century after Christ saw it, under the patronage of foreign kings like Kanishka, in the zenith of its power. Already, under Asoka, Buddhist propaganda began to overflow the confines of India northwards to Kashmir, Kabul, and so on into Central Asia, but especially southwards into Ceylon. In the latter case Asoka's own son, Mahinda, was made the bearer of the gospel, and Asoka's own daughter, Saṅghamittā, brought over a twig of the sacred Bodhi-tree from Uruvelā as a rare present to King Tissa. This identical tree is still alive to-day in Anurādhapūra, and, with its two thousand one hundred and fifty years or thereabouts, must be the oldest historical tree in the world.

In more than one respect Buddhism may be called a royal religion ; and it has always blossomed most luxuriously in the sunshine of great dynasties. On that account the centuries that followed Kanishka were unfavourable to its progress because that giant kingdom fell away. In strict fact we are not warranted in picturing the act of the adoption of Buddhism on the part of the kings as something of a solemn, official nature, as a definite turning from Brahmanism to Buddhism. The Indian has never been friendly to such acts of faith as have made epochs in Christendom and Islam. Something symmetrical, foreseeing, balance-adjusting is characteristic of the Indian mind. The state recognition of Buddhism on the part of the Indian kings was nothing but a preference for it before Brahmanism. The latter was not uprooted, but only removed from the place of honour ; relegated to the background.

Not only through changes in the political situation of India, but also, and more than anything else, from the internal weakness in Buddhism which resulted from the division into Mahāyāna and Hīnayāna (Northern and Southern Buddhism), did Brahmanism gain new vigour. Always tolerated alongside of Buddhism, and growing ever stronger in the form of Saivism, it finally regained its lost supremacy over India, accompanied by the most frightful bloodshed, if we may believe report. This reversion was accomplished somewhere between the eighth and tenth centuries of our era, and we are confronted by the remarkable fact that the Hindu people, for whom, more than for any other people, life has always meant sorrow, has had taken from it again the religion of sorrow.

Side by side with its internal foe there now grew up for Buddhism an external foe in the shape of Mohammedanism. The countries to the north-west of India, especially Balkh, were strongholds of the true faith. In the middle of the seventh century the teaching of the Buddha here was exchanged for the Koran. At the beginning of the eighth century Sindh followed suit. Farther and farther eastwards Islam pushed itself, until, under the Mongolian Emperors, it became the dominant religion. About the twelfth century of the Christian era Magadha, the central citadel of Buddhism, was captured. The fact is that Brahmanism has defied the ravaging hand of the centuries, whilst Buddhism to-day has wholly disappeared from the Indian continent, like some exotic plant that withers so soon as it is deprived of its accustomed care.

In Java also the teachings of the Buddha had to give way before Islam. Towards the end of the fourteenth century the first Mohammedan apostle appeared, and already, at the end of the fifteenth century, fell with Modjopahit the last and most illustrious of the Buddhist kingdoms of Java. As everywhere, so also here, passive, fanaticism-free Buddhism appears to have quickly given way before Islam.

Quite otherwise than in India was the state of affairs in China and Japan. Here also Buddhism came into contact with old religions, or rather religion-philosophies, but, altogether different from the Indian peoples, the natives of these countries are distinguished for what may be called religious light-heartedness. Hence it was possible for Buddhism to make itself at home and grow up alongside the teaching of Kong-fu-tse in China, and the Shinto religion in Japan; though, it must be confessed, at the cost of its pristine purity. About the fourth century of the Christian era it became the State religion of China.

In strict fact, however, it cannot be said of either of these religions that it is the predominant one; none the less a distinction seems to have been made in China, so that the upper classes adhered to the sober, clear philosophy of Kong-fu-tse, whilst the great mass of the people chose a corrupted form of Buddhism, with its promises of bliss in paradise. In Japan, Shinto is the State religion, yet some of the Buddhist sects are held in high esteem, and, to judge by the number and the splendour of the Buddhist temples scattered about the country, the great mass of the people here also seems to adhere to Buddhism.

Come we now to the principal question of all.

How will Buddhism withstand the onset of

Christianity, which latter religion is preparing to carry out still further the rôle that Islam played in former years. Everything seems to indicate that Northern Buddhism, which, like Christianity, can manipulate with the key-words "Love" and "Heavenly Bliss," will prove itself best able to stand against it, if only for the reason that it has for its supporters peoples who have not been trained so thoroughly in exact science in Christian Mission Schools as have the Sinhalese.

Pure Southern Buddhism, on the other hand, which, like a mighty glacier, is beautiful to the sight but icy to the touch, by the complete passivity of its religious constitution, is without defence against fanaticism, and in this onslaught is as an unarmed man exposed to the attack of a mail-clad warrior.

Lately in Colombo signs of a reaction against Christianity are becoming visible, but this, characteristically enough, does not originate with the priesthood, but with a few zealous, educated, and well-to-do laymen. I was in Colombo in 1900, in the month of Visākha, the birth month of the Buddha, corresponding roughly to our May, according to the Sinhalese calendar, and I had an opportunity of being present at a celebration which was simply an imitation of Christian methods, and in its essence quite foreign to Buddhism. A certain number of boys and girls were gathered together in the grounds of Ânanda College to undergo a public examination in the principles of their religion in the presence of a crowd of grown-up people. At its close presents in the shape of books were handed to the best scholars. The intention was to use ambition in the service of religion. This is quite un-Buddhistic, and only happens in imitation of the Christian Church, which for long has made successful use of this principle in its missionary activities. Members of the Buddhist priesthood naturally were not present.

The most noteworthy feature of this affair was the participation of girls in it, who in former times were entirely neglected as regards religious instruction. Let us hope that the Buddhism of Ceylon has seized the significance of the woman question in all its bearings. Perhaps there is no other question whose solution is more pressing and of more consequence to its continuance in the future than this.

A sort of literary campaign against Christianity also seems to be developing in Colombo. This too from linguistic considerations, is the work of the laity, for only the laity know English. Of the entire monk population of the island, at the present moment, there is not a single one who is a master of the English language, and only one of the pandits (lay teachers of the language and the religion) speaks English fluently enough to be able to communicate his ideas to Occidentals without the help of an interpreter.

Here it ought to be said that it is a good thing that this is so, since a Buddhism that allowed itself to enter into disputation with other religions would no longer be Buddhism. This noble passivity is of the very essence of the religion. Buddhism can as little consist with contention and fanaticism as snow with heat. In its purest form it is finally nothing but the truth of the universally valid laws of nature extended into the realm of morals; poured into the mould of religious observance. Truth, however, is not disseminated by strife and contention, but only by its own excellence. In this sense it may be said that the essence of a religion comes near to truth just to the degree that its propaganda has been a peaceful one; and here surely no one can withhold his admiration for Buddhism, which has made its peaceful way through the storms of the Mongolian steppes, and which, more than needs be asked of any religion, by its moral and philosophical features is better fitted than any other to regulate in peaceful fashion the various relationships of men with one another. Hence the Buddha never triumphed over his opponents by war or strife, but—according to the Suttas, the historic memorials of his teaching—by logical demonstration and, according to legend, by displays of miraculous power. With good right he was able to say to his disciples: "I do not strive with the world, but the world strives with me. A teacher of the truth does not strive with any one whatsoever in all the world."

However passive and lacking in understanding of the dangers of the present day the Buddhist priesthood till now may have shown itself, it has not been able wholly to escape one Western influence: that of modern science, and principally of that science which has made Buddhism its special subject. To what an extent this latter science has grown amongst us during the last ten years is well known. Especially in English an extraordinarily comprehensive literature has sprung up concerning Buddhism. Many European savants visit easily-accessible Ceylon in order to pursue their studies in the monastery libraries of the island, more especially in those of Colombo and Kalutara. Thus, modern views and modern conceptions, in consequence of this contact, are beginning to creep into the cells of Buddhist Vihāras, and the traveller is astonished by some of the monks he meets with making clear to him obscure points in the teachings of the Buddha by means of illustrations drawn from physics and chemistry. Not much, it is true, has as yet been done in this direction; still, a beginning has been made.

Outwardly also the influence of our savants has made itself felt. In the monastery libraries, which formerly consisted solely of known palm-leaf manuscripts, a whole host of European books are now displayed, most of them being presentation copies from the authors themselves.

The most powerful effect produced, however, is this—that the zeal of our savants has roused the native savants, not to combat with them, but to similarly directed effort. The focus of this movement also is to be found in Colombo. At its head stands Sri Sumaṅgala Thera, the venerable head-priest of Maligakanda, the principal monastery in the town. In spite of his great age and continual ill-health, he is strenuously active and in the front rank as a teacher. He and his helper, the young monk Nyāṇissara, are accounted the principal authorities in Buddhist Ceylon at the present time. It appears as if at Colombo a college of professors were in process of formation.

And not only in Colombo but along the whole south-west coast, the classic Sinhalese country, an active life is beginning to dominate. In Kalutara, situated about half-way between Colombo and Point de Galle, lives Subhūti Thera, of all the native savants the one best known in Europe. In Paiyagala, somewhat south of Kalutara, the ex-monk Vagisvara teaches—a man who has made his own, not only the English tongue, but also modern thought at its best. Galle also, Matara, and many other places all have their noticeable features.

Remains to be mentioned the Mahā-Bodhi Society, a society which has set itself the task of winning back the ground lost on the Indian mainland. The headquarters of the Society are in Calcutta, and its leader is Mr. Dharmapāla, who has shown great activity in travelling and lecturing.

But on the whole it must be confessed that Christianity is always gaining fresh ground. When, at the beginning of the sixteenth century, the Portuguese ruled in Ceylon, the stream of religion, and with it the stream of culture, which up till then had always flowed from East to West, began its backward flow, and, doing so, initiated one of the most wonderful movements recorded in world-history—the desire of a daughter to teach her old experienced mother. In plain language, Christian missionary effort began in India.

With the fanaticism native to the Portuguese nation, battle was given on the spot to the indigenous religion, and at the first onslaught Christianity, preached by that hero of the faith, Francis Xavier, appeared to gain a swift victory. During the period of Dutch supremacy what was gained was again lost to a large extent, owing to all other considerations being sacrificed to that of the money-bag. Now, however, under

English rule, Christianity appears to be spreading slowly but surely. None the less, we need not cherish any illusions on the subject. Western religion of itself has made no breach in the religious edifice of the East. Christendom, as represented by missionaries and missions, is producing little effect, but Christianity as the bearer of Western culture is at work in an indirect but highly destructive manner. Here it is not a matter of the overthrow of the religion, not a repetition of the frightful, monstrous examples of Mexico and Peru—of the creation of a pile of ruins with the sole object of being able to plant the banner of the faith upon the highest possible pedestal. The stabbing flame that then shot forth from the bosom of Christianity has ceased. Not Christianity but the West is now at work upon the East. It is not that Buddhism will be destroyed, but the elements out of which it till now has constantly renewed itself will be so transformed in their inner nature, through the shopkeeper-culture of the West and the total change of views that of necessity will accompany it, that they will lose the power of any longer discharging the function they have up to now fulfilled. It might well happen that from this cause the teaching of the Buddha may expire in Ceylon, exactly like a lamp whereof the oil is spent. Yet, looked at beneath the surface, the victory of the West over the East becomes only an apparent victory. In a silent undercurrent, India, the world-source of religion, sends to our fast-living, almost dried-up continent, ever new waves of fresh religious feeling, and this is the passive mission of Buddhism and Vedanta.

Somewhat as in Ceylon is the state of affairs in

Burma, only constantly modified by the difference in the character of the people. The passive, meditative tendency peculiar to the Aryan Indian is quite lacking in the Burman's nature. Merry, light-hearted, given before all things to fun and frolic, this race presents the picture of an activity that is all their own. It is the naïve activity of the child which this happy people have retained even till now—a phenomenon of the greatest rarity in the life of individuals as well as of nations.

This activity finds itself reflected even in the ways of the monks. Not content with the peace of the cloister life, which so easily degenerates into laziness, they have of their own free will made themselves the educators of the people—at least of the male portion thereof. Almost every Burmese village, down to the very poorest, has its monastery; and along with it its monastery school, in which the village boys are instructed in the elements of reading, writing, and arithmetic, as well as in the teachings of the Buddha. Thus it comes about that a person who cannot read and write is much more rare in Burma than in our own civilised state. Hence also into no people has Buddhism been more deeply instilled than into this people. Burma is the Buddhist land *par excellence*, and in unperverted Burma all risings-up and lyings-down, individual as well as collective, are regulated by the religion. Every expression of the life of the people is carried out with continual regard to this religion. But here there is no anxious courting of divinity; here reigns a spontaneity, a joyfulness, a child-likeness which makes the religious life of Burma a phenomenon distinct from all others of its kind.

In the depths of his heart the Burman of the old school is convinced that in no way can he apply his temporal goods to better, I might indeed say to more profitable, use than to works of a religious character. Firm as a rock he holds to the teaching of the cycle of rebirths, and the lavish giver expects repayment with enormous interest in his next life for the good deeds he has done in this. To the unperverted Burman it is a thing incomprehensible the foolishness of Europeans who make no other use of money but to heap up more, or to pamper this wretched, perishable body. Hence, naturally, the whole of Burma abounds with the pious erections of its sons and daughters. Quite unexampled is the pomp that reigns in such religious centres as Rangoon, Mandalay, and old Pegu. Shwe Dagon, the golden pagoda of Rangoon, has not its like for splendour in the world, and many a Burman joyfully starves himself his life long in order to be able to erect a new praying-hall upon its sacred platform.

A peculiar light is thrown upon the relations existing between this people and their religion by the fact that every Burmese boy, from the highest in the land down to the beggar, must, during part of his life, enter a monastery as a monk and keep a monk's vows. The length of time during which he may stay entirely depends upon his own—which practically means his parents'—wish. Many remain only a few days in the monastery; many stay for a whole month; while others again, who think they have found their ideal in this life of peace and meditation, make the monastic state their life-long choice—a state which is the highest and most honourable that can be bestowed in Burma upon any one.

Hence the religious Brotherhood of Burma has a particular impress upon it which essentially distinguishes it from the monkhood of Ceylon. Nowhere can the relations between the laity and the priesthood be so intimate as in a land where every man, from the king down to the poorest peasant, some time or other during his life must have been a monk. Nowhere else, following upon this, can the forsaking of the monk-life be such a matter of everyday occurrence as in Burma; and yet in spite of this nowhere does the monastic order stand at such a high moral level as in this same Burma. This very motion, this continuous circular flow from lay life to monk life and *vice versa* prevents stagnation and corruption. The Burmese priesthood does not stand for a special code of monkish morality; it represents morality in its wholeness and entirety. This precious treasure lies in the custody of the monkhood, and every Burman by entering the cloister makes himself one more custodian of the same. However brief may be his stay, while it lasts he has to keep the rules to their fullest extent. If the senses begin to revolt—well, we are all weak men, and one may lay the Yellow Robe aside any day one chooses. But woe to him who, while in this sacred office, breaks any of the precepts; and especially the chiefest of them, that of chastity. The heaviest life-long punishment of shame and ignominy is the consequence. Hence the monk in Burma enjoys like honour with the image of the Buddha and the pagoda. But it is not the man who is the object of veneration; he is worthy of veneration only so far and so long as he represents morality. The Law of the Buddha is nothing but the highest morality, and therefore the Dhamma, the holy, all-powerful Law, is crystallised and personified in the monk. The Law, symbolically, is adored in the person of the monk. With this meaning the Buddha says: "This is the discipleship of the Exalted One, which is worthy of offerings and gifts, presents and salutations, for it is the holiest state in the world."

We can now quite understand why the value of a monk is rated entirely according to the number of years which he has spent in cloister life. Whoever has lived the greatest number of years in the holy state of monkhood, has practised abstemiousness and meditation for the greatest length of time—he is most worthy of honour. Great intelligence, wide learning, notable gifts of preaching—even these and their like do not count for so much in the eyes of the people. The country does not ask for famous monks, but for those who, without pretension, quietly and unweariedly, travel the path of renunciation towards Nibbāna. Thus the moral standard of the Burmese priesthood, like an electric spark passing quickly from person to person, has moved down the centuries in an apparently continuous flash—a phenomenon whose glory, even at this late day, seems scarcely to have paled a jot.

Nevertheless, the dangers which threaten Buddhism in Burma are perhaps greater than in any other Buddhist country. The edifice of the monkhood still exists as before at its full height, but it is beginning to totter all through because the basis upon which it has hitherto rested is beginning to give way. Here also it is not missionary effort but modern culture that is shaking the supporting beams.

In the cloister schools the boys learn nothing but reading, writing, and arithmetic, the fundamental conceptions of the Buddhist religion, and natural science as it is found in gross and in detail in the Tipiṭaka, the Buddhist canon. That this latter does not meet the demands of our money-grubbing times is clear without further argument. The Burman, mentally alive and awake, and with wants increased by an uninterrupted contact with Western culture, is already beginning to withdraw his sons from the cloister schools and to send them to the public schools, in which are being taught the English language and natural science in its modern form; and also—the Christian religion. The young Burman is indeed in this way being qualified for Government service, but he is losing his Faith, for the cloister is the only place where religious instruction is provided, and the—only too often—brief time spent there is naturally not sufficient for any lasting impression to be left behind.

It is really astonishing how much the state of affairs here has changed in a very short space of time. In former years it was considered a disgrace to enter the service of the State, because conflict with the religion was in this service unavoidable. To-day, Government service is the goal of the desire of all. Hence the cloister schools are deserted, whilst the English schools are overcrowded. Such is the state of affairs in Rangoon, and such also is the case at Mandalay and other large towns. Only in the country districts is the system of cloister schools still in force. In his heart of hearts the Burman well knows what he has gained and what he has lost by this exchange. Most true are the words an intelligent native addressed to an Englishman: "In your schools we learn how to make money; in ours we learn how to be happy and contented."

The reaction against this ever-growing state of affairs is weaker in Burma than in Ceylon. The only instance of which I am aware is the Empress Victoria Buddhist School in Rangoon, which has been called into existence by the zeal of a few of the laity, especially of a Mrs. Hla Oung; and it is supported out of private means. There is a school for boys and one for girls, the latter in particular seeming to prosper well. So far as I know, this is the only Buddhist school in Burma in which instruction is given according to modern methods. As I went through the schoolrooms with Mrs. Oung, she said, pointing to the bright figures of the girls: "These girls will in the future keep their husbands to the Faith."

Nowhere perhaps is the helplessness of the Buddhist church, its lack of reactive force and activity, more clearly apparent than in Burma. But, sooth to say, a certain sublime passivity has always been characteristic of Buddhism; a readiness to tolerate foreign ingredients within itself without, by a species of spiritual suppuration-process, ejecting them from its system. But still we cannot help but be astonished when we see how the fundamentals are weakening to-day, and yet no hand in the religious brotherhood is put forth to support or help.[1] And yet it would be easier to do this in Burma than elsewhere. Here we have to do with a religiously disposed and therefore spiritually susceptible people, who would adopt and carry through any recommendation made by their spiritual leaders. Other religions also are noteworthy for their inability to change with the times, but they are shielded by the armour of fanaticism. But fanaticism Buddhism has always held in contempt; and can still afford to hold in contempt, for it is the only religion that does not stand *a priori* in contradiction to the authentic results of human progress. Without doing any violence to its essential teaching, it might easily bring itself into accord with modern science; infinitely more easily could it do so than the religions that are founded upon revelations. Yet this is precisely what the monkhood does not understand; and so, unresistingly, they permit the youth of the country to be stolen from them, and with them, the future.

[1] Since these words were written, several of the more enlightened among the Burmese monks have bestirred themselves and are now inciting the laity to found schools on modern lines in which their children will receive instruction in the Faith of their fathers. (Translator's Note.)

XX

THE WORLD-MISSION OF BUDDHISM

The attempt has been made, from the forced retreat of Buddhism before other religions, to draw the conclusion that it has passed the period of its zenith and is now in a state of slow but steady decay. Indeed the attempt has been made to prove that Buddhism has attained its commanding position, not through its own merits, but from favouring circumstances, royal favour more especially, and that wherever it was deprived of the help of circumstance, especially wherever it met with a serious resistance, it always has been worsted.

That Buddhism flourished best upon the Indian mainland in the sunshine of royal favour cannot for a moment be denied, but in truth the favour bestowed upon it was simply the legitimate guerdon of its own inherent excellence. Never perhaps to any religious Order have such magnificent gifts been made as to this, but they were given it precisely because it asked so little. No other Order, perhaps, has mixed so little in the affairs of the great as has this.

Just as little can it be denied that in a bout of fisticuffs it has always come off second-best. But, sooth to say, this very defeat has been the direct result of its own excellence; for there is an excellence that defends itself by combat, and there is an excellence that defends itself by yielding; an excellence that reveals itself in activity and an excellence that reveals itself in passivity.

All that we call virtue or excellence within the field of our modern culture is founded upon activity of some kind. Of that excellence which is founded upon "not-doing" we have little or no comprehension. We find it difficult to make a distinction in our minds between "not-doing" and "nothing-doing," and yet "not-doing" is often the most difficult of deeds!

The teaching of "not-doing" is no blossom that required the air of India for its particular unfolding. The wonderful blessing "not-doing" was taught in its purest form by Lao-tse in shopkeeping China, and it runs like a scarlet thread through the thought of all the great Christian Mystics. These three, Buddhism, Taoism, and Christian Mysticism, with Vedanta as a fourth, are like travellers who have met at a cross-road; each comes from his own particular direction, and each proceeds in his own particular direction, but in the doctrine of "not-doing" they all meet together. This is their point of intersection. The doctrine of "not-doing" is the spiritual undercurrent of the world.

"Thence it comes," says Lao-tse, "that the perfect man lets not-doing be his labour"; and, "He lets his instructions consist of silence"; "He pursues not-doing and there is nothing that is not well done." "Cease from striving and ye shall be free from care."

As like as these aphorisms sound to the teachings

of the Buddha, as *unlike* are the goals aimed at by Taoism and Buddhism. In this, the highest product of Chinese Philosophy, there is no intention of teaching how a man may take his departure from the world like one who is weary and satiate of it all; instead, it is meant to teach how, according to nature, one may rule the world by non-resistance, by subjection, without desiring it, without even knowing that one rules. And the further a man proceeds along this path of retreat towards the Tao, the primal root of all created—the more do those differences disappear according to which we worldlings are accustomed to pass our judgments. So young grass, the younger it is, becomes the liker wheat, and still more so is it with spawn and sperm. But the perfect man, the saint, he steals away, ascending to those regions, to mortal sense wrapt in darkness, in which wisdom and foolishness, knowledge and ignorance, moral goodness and badness, dwell undifferentiated in the same sheath. This is the condition in which *ignorando cognoscitur*, "knowing without cognising," obtains; that condition in which all is "vague and confused, deep and obscure" like the Tao itself. In this sense Lao-tse was well entitled to say of himself: "I am like the new-born child that has not yet smiled upon its mother," and, "Ordinary men all have abilities; I alone am circumscribed."

> So seems he dumb and dull of wit:
> To world and worldling, foolish all,

runs a Buddhist monk's song. But in spite of this external likeness, the essence of the two teachings is yet, as said, completely different. Whilst the

Buddha looks at the world through a microscope and, converging all the rays of his thought, leads to one point, Lao-tse dissolves all, stepping back to the primal source of all created, to the primordial seed of all being, to that formlessness that is above all form, that incapacity that is above all capacity, that emotionlessness which is superior to all emotions. He identifies himself with the Tao,[1] which, itself unmoved, gives rise to the most important movements; itself formless, gives rise to the fulness of all forms; itself without qualities, gives rise to qualities in their completeness with an ever-youthful fulness of creative power. Opposed to the absolute renunciation of Buddhism, we have here only a special refinement of potentialised creation.

Leaving this to one side, the fact remains that Buddhism has been dyed through and through in the vat of the doctrine of not-doing. The Buddha characteristically says: "Others shall seize with both hands, and relinquish with difficulty; we, however, shall not seize with both hands and shall relinquish with ease." That act which leads to the abrogation of all action—that is the greatest act of all in Buddhism. No ending is to be found in forward-striving, in forward struggle, though one should strive and struggle for ever; but, one step to the rearwards, letting-go, "not-doing," may well lead to that goal which the Buddha preached as the highest and best.

From all this it is clear that a religion which takes its stand upon such fundamentals is scarcely in a position to support its adherent in worldly strife. It is lacking in every weapon required

[1] Corresponding to the Primal Force, the Absolute, Brahman (Neuter).

for such a conflict. The mere taking-up of such weapons would lead to the nullification of that very teaching in defence whereof they were adopted; the mere intention to give battle would itself be self-defeat. All fanaticism is absent, for where there is true comprehension, there fanaticism cannot exist. There is also absent that outward, official representation which all other religions possess in their priesthood; that corporate body which, out of mere regard for its own existence, must be zealous on behalf of the God it represents. It is the privileged, authorised representative of fanaticism. The Order of the Buddha, however, consists only of monks. Priests—that is to say, people who make a profession of acting as intermediaries between God and man—there naturally cannot be in Buddhism, since God is absent from the system.

We have just said that where there is true comprehension, there can be no fanaticism. Otherwise expressed, this means that fanaticism can only exist where it is a question of creeds and dogmas, of the unknowable. In the Buddha's system there is nothing of this kind. Smoothly his clear thought glides through this world of sorrow, and nowhere comes into contact with an opposing unknown. As an electric current in the absence of resistance produces no glow of light, so Buddhism gives rise to no fiery glow of fanaticism. All resistance is founded upon difference; in Buddhist thought, however, all difference is dissolved in the thought of *not-I*; the distinctions, "I" and "Thou," "soul" and "body," "God" and "world," have all ceased to be.

Non-faith, by destroying all possible foundation for fanaticism, is the principal cause why this system has always been worsted in open combat. Non-faith, moreover, is the fruit—the dangerous fruit—of comprehension. Whoso measures things by the world's standards, whoso hankers after the laurels that the world has to bestow, will do well not to seek this comprehension which the Buddha enjoins, for it sweeps away everything: that which is worthy of being striven for together with the striver therefor.

Where then is to be found the proper domain of this remarkable system of renunciation? Brooding, sorrow-stricken India, the natural field for such a doctrine, under the earthquake shocks of the centuries, has cast the Dhamma out again. The inhabitants of Ceylon, Burma, and Siam are light-hearted folk, for whom the leading tenet of the system: "All life is Sorrow" can scarcely have sense or meaning. In Central and Eastern Asia the doctrine is held only in that corrupted form which is the result of conformity to human requirements. And so once more we have to inquire where is to be found the proper domain of this teaching.

When the Buddha, under the Bodhi-tree at Uruvelā, arrived at full comprehension, his first thought was: Will the world understand me? He rightly saw that his Teaching was no Teaching for the great mass of men. It is not every one who can see sorrow in the natural changes of the body; in the growth of lusty youth as in the dignity of venerable old age. And yet these most natural of all events, just because they are the most unavoidable, are also the greatest of evils. "If it were not for three things that are in the world, O disciples, the Perfect One would never have appeared in the world. Which three things are these? They are birth, old age, and death." In order to escape the most universal of all the laws of nature, Gautama left his home and took to the ascetic life. The doctrine delivered by him has, in fact, value only for those who seek to triumph over transiency because they feel transiency to be sorrow. To escape from transiency, however, means to escape from life. Hence, whoso desires life, the teaching of the Buddha is not for him; nay more, it is repugnant to him.

So there are only a few for whom this doctrine is suited?

Yes, at any one time it is suited only to a few; one after another, however, in succession, it is for all; for the happy as for the unhappy. For, according to the Buddhist view, to every man, even to him who now is most greedy for life, a time at last must come when he will exclaim: "Alas! what sorrow is this life!"

But perhaps, even at one time, the number of those for whom life is the same as sorrow is greater than we are wont to think. The material prepared for the Teaching is there; all that is lacking is acquaintance with the teaching. In the Buddha's sense of the word, one in sorrow is ultimately one who is dissatisfied; one who is searching, one whose thought-activity, to a certain extent, is directed towards other ends, the which is the case with the great bulk of mankind; in a word, one in sorrow is one upon whom has never been bestowed the wonderful gift of faith. Truly, faith is nature's most precious gift. Woe to that poor man into whose lap it is not thrown at birth; no diligence, no striving whatsoever, can earn it. Faith cannot be learnt. Only where there is faith is there God. Each conditions the other mutually, like eye and object seen; without an eye there were no visible world; without a world no seeing eye. Where faith is absent, God is absent. Where there is no faith—there, there is no God.

Now all human bliss depends upon the appeasing of a desire. How deceitful, however,—how mingled with pain all desire is,—this each man of woman born speedily learns. Hence each would certainly renounce all, only that there awaits him in the background that uncreate, true blessedness which consists in his desire after God. Let everything go to wrack and ruin, this, the One, the Great, the Precious, still is mine. And the more he thus imbibes blessedness as from some inexhaustible reservoir, in deeper and ever deeper draughts, the more all mere side-streams are neglected.

Whoso, however, is without either faith or God—for him this inexhaustible source of blessedness does not exist. He may live for long and long without ever knowing of such a thing. But at last it may come to him, flashing upon him like lightning in a dark night, and, terrified, he will exclaim: "What these have, I am without. How shall I too attain to that blessed certitude? Where for me is that place of surety, on which I may fix mine eyes when all around me totters and reels?" But for him it lies not in desiring, in affirming; for affirming is only blessedness where God is affirmed. For such as have no God-belief there is only one way, only one certainty—renunciation, denial. This is the great kingly way—the way of the noble—to which the Buddha directs his fellow-men.

And here we find that the aim, the mission, the domain of Buddhism is nothing limited to this or that time, this or that people;—I hold that the idea "Buddhist people" or "Buddhist kingdom" is a contradiction in itself;—but everywhere where faith is lacking and the unfortunate one seeks after that blessedness, that certainty which lies beyond this changeful scene, there the Buddha quietly comes forward and says: "Come! I will teach thee. Here is needed no faith; here thou needst only have a willingness to be taught; here is needed only earnestness and self-control; here thou shalt meet only that which can be taught and can be learned. Wherefore, despair not! Here mayst thou also, without faith as thou art, yet come to increase, to ripeness, to blessedness, to unshakable certainty!"

With evident partiality, the Buddha calls his teaching that for the sake of which "scions of noble families" leave home, and kindred, and take to the homeless life. In one verse it is said:

> The noble Teaching never older grows.
> The noble always learn it from the noble.

This word "noble" is not to be understood as giving the disciples of the Buddha a title to think themselves superior because they have perceived the absence of God—because they say to the world as to the God dwelling therein: "I need you not." They are not superior; they are only different because their natural disposition is different. Noble, however, are all such as push from them the labour and burden of the day, under whose crushing weight the lives of most men are passed, and who ask themselves the question: "How stands it with me?" For most certainly there is nothing noble about him who merely works and works from budding youth to withered old age, let the goal of his effort be what it may. Self-recollectedness—that is the only true genuine human dignity; and those who consummate this, they are the noble; they are the Aryas; they are the true Brahmanas. That this attention to the within leads one man into the arms of deity, and another to the perception that there is no God,—this has naught to do with nobility or vulgarity, and was never so understood by the Buddha; for he would have been obliged to deny the possibility of God had he declared the unbelieving to be nobler than the believing.

The Buddha divided the entire world into two halves, one believing and the other unbelieving. The unbelieving half, however, is the Buddha's domain; in it holds good the word: "All life is sorrow." For this is the very crown of sorrow that one should seek God, the greatest bliss of all—and should not find! And this is the final reason why transiency is one with sorrow—because in it there is no room for God.

Buddhism stands in opposition to all other religions without distinction, in that these are only differently moulded forms of belief; it alone is unbelief, given habitation and a name. One may confidently place Buddhism and religion over against one another and say, "Everywhere, where the teachings of a man's religion—be that religion whatsoever it may—find no echo in his breast (and like should answer to like), there the Buddha steps in to preserve the poor unfortunate against despair or frivolity. Once the incapacity for belief is perceived, the search for some sort of indemnification begins. In that search the vision is captured by transiency, and with the perception of transiency life becomes sorrow. From this moment, however, the teaching of the Buddha ceases to be unnatural and becomes instead the *summum bonum*. From this moment onward, the spool of life revolves in the reverse direction, unrolling the thread, until at last it has emptied itself. All other religions with their God-beliefs are only so many modes of instruction in the art of keeping the play of life going on for ever. Buddhism alone instructs how to bring the play to an end.

The longing after union with God is nothing but the desire for life, in its most refined form. This desire, like every other form of the desire for life, leads us from one existence to another—keeps us indefinitely in life. The longing for eternal life is indeed itself eternal life. Behind the longing stands nothing but the longing. As the magnet attracts the iron-filing, so do all the religions, through the longing after God, attract the individual and maintain him in eternal life. The God-idea is nothing but the universe's instinct of self-preservation. What the *I*-idea is in the preservation of the individual, that the God-idea is in the preservation of the universe. As, however, sooner or later, there comes to the magnet a moment when its strength declines and some particles fall down, so also, in the domain of religion, for this or that individual there comes a time when union with God ceases to be the goal of his longing, and life is affirmed no more. In reflection the mind that had clung to these, relaxes its grasp, lets go, and a most frightful fall into infidelity and despair were the certain result, if under all these religion-magnets the Buddha had not stretched out the firm, strong safety-net of his doctrine. He thus stands opposed to them all, and is yet the compensation for them all, and this is his mission in the world.

As life-affirmation can assume endless forms, but the denial of life is only one, so the multiplicity of religions stands in contrast to the singleness of Buddhism. In their deeper aspect, these after all may only be two phases of one great universal. As any two complementary colours have split themselves up out of one common, neutral colour, so behind Buddhism and religion may lie some common, undivided unity. This were that Orcus which gives and takes simultaneously, at one and the same time; which in destroying, creates, and in creating, destroys. This is that eternally inexplicable miracle before which every one, the Buddha as well, is stricken silent. Every attempt to put it into words, however, means to speak about God.

At bottom there is a secret interaction between life-affirmation and life-denial. One is conditioned by the other, as the "yes" by the "no"; the "no" by the "yes." And the question, "When every individual has understood life and has denied it, what then?" of itself perishes. The more it is denied, the stronger does life pulsate. The Orcus must receive, that he may be able to give. But thou—let not the Orcus-circle thee distress! Let others brood o'er that, if so they choose. One thing thou possessest: the unshakable certainty that never again shalt thou be whirled about in the maelstrom of rebirth. Wherefore do thou rejoice! Thou art saved!

It may quite well be maintained that Buddhism, in spite of the two and a half thousand years of its existence, has not yet taken possession of its own true field of activity. Only when it has overstepped the circle of the culture of Farther Asia, only when it lies over the whole earth, and like some noble fragrance envelops every man so soon as he mounts above the cramped and dusty atmosphere of the plains—only then shall it have fulfilled its true mission. Only then shall that proud word of the Buddha's hold good which he spoke to his disciples: "Somewhat as in the last month of the rainy season, in the autumn, after the scattering and dispersion of the water-laden clouds, the sun rises in the heavens, and with its rays chases away all vapours from the air, and beams and shines; so also, O monks, does this our manner of living appear, which brings present as well as future weal, and with its rays drives away the verbosities of common ascetics and priests, and beams and shines."

If it is permissible to speak of a world-religion at all, it is certainly Buddhism that must first be considered in that connection. For a religion which, as the representative of the pure light of knowledge, without admixture of the shadows of faith, stands in no sort of contradiction to the facts of the understanding and yet maintains in its adherents the highest, natural morality—that surely is entitled to be called the true world-religion.

Printed by R. & R. CLARK, LIMITED, *Edinburgh*.

By H. FIELDING HALL.

Extra Crown 8vo. 7s. 6d. net.

THE SOUL OF A PEOPLE

ACADEMY.—"An exceedingly interesting book. . . . We wish we had space to quote the abundant, instructive, and fascinating information contained in this charming book."

MORNING POST.—"The book sets one thinking; every chapter is instructive, and Mr. Fielding has assumed the right attitude in endeavouring to see things from within rather than from without, and has entered as far, perhaps, as it is possible for an outsider to enter into the soul of the people."

GUARDIAN.—"A very fascinating book. . . . Without a dull page from start to finish."

STANDARD.—"One of the most striking books which we have encountered."

PALL MALL GAZETTE.—"It is a prose poem, and a fine one too; because it is the picture of a world that must stir all the poetic feeling and sympathy of a man. . . . The book is full of striking matter."

LITERARY WORLD.—"In this book there is something fresh and new. It is a study of Burmese national character, illustrated by stories which throw light on it. It is written from first-hand knowledge by one who has been a part of the scenes he describes, and the author, by his true sympathy with the Burmese people, and by the perfectly simple and unaffected style of his narration, always carries conviction and not seldom touches the heart."

8vo. 10s. net.

A PEOPLE AT SCHOOL

ACADEMY.—"How intimate is Mr. Fielding Hall's knowledge of Burmese customs, and how actual is his sympathy with Burmese thought, every one knows well who has read that very fascinating book, *The Soul of a People*. The present volume has the same wisdom and charm; but the matter is treated from another point of view."

MACMILLAN AND CO., LTD., LONDON.